The Appropriation of Shakespeare:

Post-Renaissance Reconstructions of the Works and the Myth

Edited by
Jean I. Marsden

HARVESTER
WHEATSHEAF

New York   London   Toronto   Sydney   Tokyo   Singapore

First published 1991 by
Harvester Wheatsheaf,
66 Wood Lane End, Hemel Hempstead,
Hertfordshire, HP2 4RG
A division of
Simon & Schuster International Group

Typeset in 10/12pt Goudy
by Witwell Ltd, Southport.

Printed in Great Britain by BPCC Wheatons Ltd, Exeter

British Library Cataloguing in Publication Data

The appropriation of Shakespeare:
Post-Renaissance reconstructions of the works and the myth.
I. Marsden, Jean I.
822.3

ISBN 0-7450-0927-1
ISBN 0-7450-0926-3

1 2 3 4 5 95 94 93 92 91

Contents

List of figures

Introduction

When Ben Jonson said of Shakespeare that 'he was not of an age but for all time,' he could not have realised the double implications of his words. While Jonson's lines were written in praise of Shakespeare's timeless appeal, they can also be seen to describe an ongoing process of literary and cultural appropriation in which each new generation attempts to redefine Shakespeare's genius in contemporary terms, projecting its desires and anxieties onto his work. It is this attempt to make over Shakespeare in our own image which is the primary focus of this collection of essays. Our object is not to study Shakespeare's text, but to examine instead the ways in which post-Renaissance generations have imprinted their own ideology on the plays and on the mythological construct of Shakespeare.

Appropriating Shakespeare

'To appropriate: to take possession of for one's own; to take to one's self.'[1] Associated with abduction, adoption and theft, appropriation's central tenet is the desire for possession. It comprehends both the commandeering of the desired object and the process of making this object one's own, controlling it by possessing it. Appropriation is neither dispassionate nor disinterested; it has connotations of usurpation, of seizure for one's own uses. In the world of literary studies, the process is both necessary and unavoidable. As Hans Robert Jauss writes: 'A literary event can continue to have an effect only if those who come after it still or once again respond to it – if there are readers who again appropriate the past work or authors who want to imitate, outdo or refute it.'[2] This literary appropriation involves a form of usurpation more subtle than physical abduction. It can be as simple as using the figure of Shakespeare in an advertisement or as complex as rewriting a play to support a political agenda. Scrutinised dispassionately, every act of interpretation can be seen as an act of appropriation – making sense of a literary artefact by fitting it into our own parameters. The literary work thus becomes ours; we possess it by reinventing it as surely as if we had secured its physical presence by force.

The essays collected here seek to explore the ways in which our culture, as well as that of generations before us, has 'taken possession' not only of

1

Shakespeare's works but of the author of these works. Laden with the weight of four centuries of cultural accretion, the Shakespeare of twentieth-century popular and academic culture does not necessarily resemble the man who wrote a series of popular plays nearly four hundred years ago. The actual Shakespeare is an ideal subject for mythologising. Little is known of the man, his life, his personality, his faults, and this *tabula rasa* can easily become all things to all people. The appropriation of Shakespeare seems both irresistible and universal, taking a variety of forms from fixing his words upon the page to establishing his political ideology. Edmond Malone, attempting to stabilise Shakespeare's text in his landmark 1790 edition, also represents Shakespeare as reassuringly counter-revolutionary. At the other end of the political spectrum, Hélène Cixous describes Shakespeare as 'neither man nor woman' and because of this androgyny able to transcend binary systems.[3] As the essays in this collection demonstrate, Shakespeare has been seen as both the voice of traditional, conservative values and a spokesman for radical causes.

Through this process Shakespeare evolves into more than a literary figure, becoming established as an icon of western culture. Such idealisation has created The Bard, a near mythic figure who is poet, patriot and cultural artefact all in one. In part this popularity is due to the nature of Shakespeare's works. By writing drama, he produced works which were accessible to a large audience, and the nature of these works was less topical and focused more on what later audiences would call universals than those of his contemporaries. But equally important is the enduring tradition of Shakespeare adulation; once established such hero-worship becomes self-perpetuating.

The potency of Shakespeare's status is perhaps most vividly embodied in the cultural and commercial success of present day Stratford-upon-Avon where catering to worldwide bardolatry has become a highly successful industry.[4] Anyone visiting Stratford today encounters the cultural mecca of the modern tourist. Not only are mementos of Shakespeare displayed for public edification and Shakespeare memorabilia hawked in nearly every shop, but a quasi-religious aura surrounds even the most everyday aspects of the town of Stratford. The half-timbered house where Shakespeare was born is reverently referred to as The Birthplace, and long lines of tourists, most of whom have little actual interest in Shakespearean drama, wait outside this shrine, hoping to see the spot where the Bard first drew breath. This religious quality pervades the town, ennobling even the most mundane objects so that a large cement parking lot becomes The Birthplace Coach Terminal while fast food outlets are sanctified by Tudor charm.

Contemplating Stratford's archetypal nature, Terence Hawkes muses, 'here a river (Nature) joins a canal (Culture) in a setting where one kind of

Englishness (the Royal Shakespeare Theatre) confronts another (a fish-and-chip shop) in the sale of quintessentially English goods.'[5] While the Royal Shakespeare Theatre and the fish-and-chip shop are relatively recent phenomena, the equation of Shakespeare with English culture is not. Even the religiosity is a long standing tradition, stretching back over two centuries to 1769 and Garrick's Shakespeare Jubilee. With its adulation of Shakespeare as the source of universal wisdom, and of Stratford as the source of this fount of truth, the Jubilee established Stratford as the centre of cultural worship. Garrick himself described a visit to Stratford in terms of religious pilgrimage:

> All who have a heart to feel, and a mind to admire the truth of nature and splendour of genius, will rush thither to behold it, as a pilgrim would to the shrine of some loved saint; will deem it holy ground, and dwell with sweet though pensive rapture, on the natal habitation of the poet.[6]

No other literary figure has attained such a prominent position in popular culture; no such hordes swarm outside Milton's birthplace; no industry has arisen around Dante or Goethe. Ironically, perhaps the closest analogue to the culturally inscribed hero-worship which surrounds Shakespeare and Stratford is Graceland, the elaborate Memphis home of Elvis Presley, where thousands come annually to pay homage to The King. It remains to be seen whether the allure of Graceland will, like the venerable tourist industry of Stratford, long outlive its century.

The origins of the glorification of Shakespeare, later dubbed bardolatry by George Bernard Shaw, can be traced back to the First Folio with its portrait of the playwright and host of laudatory verses, of which Jonson's eulogy is the best known. As Graham Holderness and Bryan Loughrey observe in their essay, the First Folio provided purchasers with a carefully constructed picture, both verbal and visual, of a culture hero. Read against the backdrop of our modern canonisation (and commercialisation) of Shakespeare, Jonson's contribution to the myth is rich in ironic overtones. It not only sets the stage for the deification which was to follow in succeeding centuries, but itself predicts that deification as well as contributing to the nascent myth of Shakespeare. In choosing to end his poem with the traditional classical image of apotheosis, Jonson could not have foreseen the multitudinous non-literary forms Shakespeare's actual apotheosis would take, and his vision of poetic immortality is incomplete when compared to the actual fate of Shakespeare and his works.

The appropriation of Shakespeare began in earnest with the reopening of the theatres after the restoration of Charles II. In the succeeding decades, a new generation of playwrights rewrote Shakespeare's plays to please a new audience, adapting them to adjust to the appearance of actresses on the stage and to a changed political climate. At the same time, he was lauded as the English Homer, a representative of English genius and nationalism, although the nature of these attributes varied depending on the political or social views of the speaker. With a few judicious omissions, he could be both a Whiggish spokesman for British liberty and a Tory touting the traditional values of a stable society. The myth of Shakespeare burgeoned in the eighteenth century as he became the hero of English culture, his influence spreading from the stage to other aspects of literary production. Eighteenth-century novelists incorporated allusions to Shakespeare into their works, assuming a knowledge of his works among their increasingly widespread readership. Paralleling this literary assimilation of Shakespeare was a widespread conversational use of the poet's words as a sign of learning. Familiarity with Shakespeare's works thus became a symbol of culture acquisition and a measure of social standing. At the same time the eighteenth century saw the birth of Shakespeare studies, textual analysis of his works coupled with an ever increasing critical apparatus.

Shakespeare as cultural symbol became more firmly embedded in the general consciousness as time went on. The Romantic poets, critics, and novelists extolled him as the ideal poet, unshackled by convention, the antithesis of everything they disliked in their predecessors. Bardolatry flourished, permeating Shakespeare criticism, the stage, and popular culture. The study of Shakespeare's texts became increasingly specialised, and bitter battles were fought over methods of approaching the established Shakespearean canon. This critical attention to detail effectively enshrined Shakespeare's text, and rewriting of the plays ceased, although stage productions continued to reconstruct Shakespearean ideology. This practice thrives in the twentieth century, as seen, for example, in the ultra-patriotic colouring given in Olivier's wartime film of *Henry V*, and in the anti-war overtones of Kenneth Branagh's more recent film of the same play. Today we see Shakespeare's icon on bankcards and hear his words used in advertising, while in the academic community the exegesis of his works has become a full-scale industry.

Appropriation and Shakespeare Studies

The essays in this volume break new ground by considering many of the political and cultural issues raised above. Traditionally, Shakespeare criticism has studiously removed his works from any historical or political context apart from brief glances at the literary climate of the Renaissance.[7] It is only recently that any consistent attempt has been made to view his works as part of an historical context, yet these works, such as Jonathan Dollimore and Alan Sinfield's collection *Political Shakespeare* or Stephen Greenblatt's *Shakespearean Negotiations*, to name only two, most frequently concentrate on rehistoricising Shakespeare within the political context of the Renaissance. In general, when the focus moves beyond the Renaissance, critics limit themselves to examining twentieth-century uses of the plays. Looking back to the sources of twentieth-century bardolatry has come more slowly. While collections of essays which deal specifically with interpreting and reinterpreting the Shakespearean canon are plentiful, until recently only scattered articles and monographs delved into the topic of reception. In the last few years, publication of books such as Jonathan Bate's *Shakespearean Constitutions* or Gary Taylor's *Reinventing Shakespeare* has begun a process which this collection hopes to continue and expand upon.[8]

The scope of this collection is intended to demonstrate the widespread presence of Shakespeare in the theatre, the novel, and in the ever growing field of literary criticism. By doing so, the essays suggest not only various ways of looking at Shakespeare, but also a wider context, the appropriation throughout history of a cultural symbol. By focusing on the manifestations of 'Shakespeare' rather than on the Shakespearean text our intention is not to 'debunk' Shakespeare nor to deny his genius, but rather to illuminate the ways in which even our own interpretation of his works is culturally conditioned. The term 'appropriation' frequently contains explicitly political implications, and many of the contributors to this collection examine the political content of Shakespeare appropriation as embodied in adaptation of the plays or the use of Shakespeare as political figurehead. Other essays scrutinise the social and literary implications of appropriation by considering how it reflects changing attitudes toward gender or literary property.

No collection examining Shakespeare after the Renaissance currently exists, and it is this void that *The Appropriation of Shakespeare* addresses. The essays have been selected to represent a broad range of historical periods, from the Restoration to the present, and to incorporate a variety of critical approaches. Similarly, the subject matter presents a balance of general and specific: some essays such as Michael Dobson's discussion of *Julius Caesar* and Marjorie Garber's examination of the descendants of Rosalind deal with the treatment of a specific work while others such as the essays by Howard Felperin, Hugh Grady and Margreta de Grazia examine the treatment of Shakespeare within a limited time frame. The essays are arranged according to subject matter in roughly chronological order, beginning with the years immediately following the reopening of the theatres in 1660 and concluding with the present.

The first three essays consider the significance of the changes made to

Shakespeare's plays as they were staged in the Restoration and eighteenth century. In 'Accents yet unknown: Canonisation and the Claiming of *Julius Caesar*,' Michael Dobson confronts the question of political appropriation directly, examining the adaptation of *Julius Caesar* by rival political groups throughout the eighteenth century. He finds that Caesar appears alternately as suffering martyr and repressive tyrant while Brutus becomes both regicide and Whig hero supporting British liberty. Dobson suggests that these 'political accents' ultimately conspire to canonise not a political cause but Shakespeare the author, abstracted from his text.

Nancy Klein Maguire focuses more directly on a single period of political upheaval in 'Nahum Tate's *King Lear*: "the king's blest restoration",' concentrating on the turmoil which surrounded the writing of Nahum Tate's notorious adaptation of *King Lear*. Using a more traditionally historical methodology, Maguire delineates the sources of this turmoil as well as the ways in which Tate adapts Shakespeare to support his own political agenda. Yet, while royalist propaganda dominates the play, Maguire finds a note of subversion which suggests that Tate deliberately aimed his text at a bi-partisan audience.

In 'Rewritten Women: Shakespearean Heroines in the Restoration,' Jean Marsden addresses the social rather than political implications of adaptation. Playwrights revised Shakespeare's female characters in order to adapt them to a changed social climate where passive virtue was the ideal of feminine behaviour. She finds that, as a result, adaptations of Shakespeare's plays simultaneously elevate women into icons of virtue and victimise them, a practice which culminates in the insertion of non-Shakespearean scenes of attempted rape.

As the popularity of Shakespeare expanded beyond theatre walls, the representation of Shakespeare in print rather than performance became a crucial issue. In 'Shakespeare in Quotation Marks,' Margreta de Grazia examines the specific grammatical device of quotation, charting the changing use of quotation marks from the late Renaissance to the later eighteenth century in order to determine changing views of authorship and property. Focusing on books of quotations, de Grazia finds that while in the seventeenth century quoted passages serve as *sententiae* to be lifted at will by the reader, by the end of the eighteenth century they come to represent the voice of the author, a shift she attributes to the growing perception of literature as property.

The next two essays examine Shakespeare's influence on the nineteenth-century novel, concentrating on the intersection of fiction and the theatre. Nicola Watson scrutinises the historicisation of Shakespeare and its political ends. In 'Kemble, Scott, and the Mantle of the Bard' she examines the use of Shakespeare and history to support the counter-revolutionary force of Tory nationalism in the early nineteenth century. Beginning with Kemble's attempt to authenticate his Shakespeare revivals by the use of period costumes, Watson centres her essay on another rehistoricisation of Shakespeare: as ultra-patriot in the novels of Sir Walter Scott where his text and his imagined presence serve to support the conservative cause.

Where Watson concentrates on the connection between actual productions and the romantic novel, John Glavin probes novelistic representations of fictional productions. In 'Caught in the Act: Or, the Prosing of Juliet,' Glavin explores the representation of Juliet, in particular the actress playing Juliet, in nineteenth-century prose. Oscar Wilde's *The Portrait of Dorian Gray*, Mrs Humphry Ward's *Miss Bretherton*, Henry James' *The Tragic Muse* and Louisa May Alcott's story 'A Double Tragedy' all portray a woman who like Juliet 'suffers not with the men who adore her, but for them,' a development Glavin links to the complex voyeurism of the nineteenth-century novel. Only outside the world of fiction, in Kierkegaard's factual account of Johanne Luise Heiberg, does the actress triumph in the role.

Two essays use nineteenth-century criticism as a means of contemplating modern critical trends. Hugh Grady examines a specific movement and its ramifications while Howard Felperin's more speculative essay views the broad sweep of historical criticism and its political undercurrents. In 'Disintegration and its Reverberations,' Grady focuses on the work of the New Shakspere Society, a group of mid-Victorian scholars founded by F. J. Furnivall, who sought to bring scientific objectivity to the study of Shakespeare through the use of versification analysis. This intrusion of science into the sacred realm of poetry excited violent objections, and the New Shakspere Society itself eventually disintegrated. Today Grady sees analogues of the disintegrationists' methodology in both the recent Oxford edition of Shakespeare's works and in post-modern approaches to Shakespeare.

In 'Bardolatry Then and Now,' Howard Felperin examines the broader currents of criticism throughout the nineteenth century. Critical approaches to Shakespeare took a variety of forms, from the essentially conservative historicism of the 'anti-Stratfordians' to the search for universals of liberal humanists such as Dowden or Coleridge. Democratic subjectivity contended with growing professionalism in Shakespeare studies in attempting to fill the gaps, to gain access to the mysterious author of Shakespeare's works. Viewing these movements within the context of current Shakespeare studies, Felperin discerns an 'uncanny' resonance and suggests that 'we have not so much escaped or transcended the institutionalised circularities of our precursors as extended and enlarged them.'

In 'The Transvestite's Progress: Rosalind the Yeshiva Boy,' Marjorie Garber traces the descendants of Rosalind, fictional women who dress as men and disturb the erotic equilibrium. She examines these ambiguous characters in two novels, Théophile Gautier's *Mademoiselle de Maupin* and Angela Carter's *The Passion of New Eve*; in I. B. Singer's short story 'Yentl the Yeshiva Boy'; and in Barbra Streisand's film version of the Singer story. In each case, it is the cross-dressed woman, the Ganymede, who becomes the locus of both male and female desire, whether as a student in the yeshiva or an actor/actress playing Rosalind/Ganymede. Garber argues that these appropriations of Ganymede reflect our own questions regarding the interplay between constructed and essential gender identity.

Dympna Callaghan chronicles the work of a single iconoclastic director in 'Buzz Goodbody: Directing for Change.' Working with the Royal Shakespeare Company in the late 1960s and early 1970s, Goodbody deliberately rejected both conventional modes of producing Shakespeare and the elitist culture which such modes embodied. Her feminism and political commitment shaped her interpretation of the plays, sometimes radically, and these new directions, Callaghan argues, made Shakespeare accessible to audiences excluded from more traditional interpretations.

In the penultimate essay, Graham Holderness and Bryan Loughrey shift from contemplating the fate of the Shakespearean text to tracing the development of the Shakespearean image. In 'Shakespearean Features,' they discuss the ways in which Shakespeare's face, those features over which artists, historians and scholars have speculated for centuries, has become as much a part of his cultural identity as his literary works. Ironically, the man whose features appear on bankcards and currency as a symbol of authenticity and value is also the only major author 'whose responsibility for the cultural productions attributed to him has been consistently and systematically questioned.'

Surveying the eighteenth, nineteenth and twentieth centuries, in '*Cymbeline*'s Other Endings,' Ann Thompson concludes the volume by charting the critical and theatrical fate of the ending of one of Shakespeare's less familiar works. Disparaged for centuries, this convoluted conclusion has been rehabilitated in recent years by critics, and revived on the stage. Thompson examines the precarious stage history of the final act, concluding with an assessment of new historicist and psychoanalytic approaches as one more revision of a much revised text.

The essays in this collection present a host of very different appropriations of Shakespeare, many contradictory. They present a view of Shakespeare embedded not only in his own culture but in ours, forcing us to consider both the impact we have on the plays and the impact they have on us. The two issues cannot be separated, for what we think of as 'Shakespeare' is to a disturbing degree culturally determined. One impulse when faced with this plethora of conflicting images may be to ask where the real Shakespeare lies. But is this question answerable or even relevant? In the end, this approach takes us beyond Shakespeare studies and of necessity introduces broader issues of cultural studies. While these essays deal only with the fate of one writer, the patterns they trace are not limited to Shakespeare. These patterns suggest that our vision of our most revered literary figure is largely defined by causes outside the text, causes which determine even which literary qualities we value most. The extra-literary nature of these determinants calls into question the cult of the author, not just of Shakespeare, but of any and all authors. Examined more closely, veneration of an author has as much to do with his or her potential as a cultural hero who can be appropriated to serve our non-literary needs as with literary 'greatness'. Thus the existence of a culturally defined 'Shakespeare' illustrates our need for myths as well as the way we use these myths once they are established.

Just as we cannot separate ourselves and our perceptions from our own culture, the cultural component of any artistic work cannot be separated from the work itself. A literary work 'is not a monument that mono-logically reveals its timeless essence'[9]: much of its permanence lies in its ability to influence and be influenced. It is at this juncture of literature and culture that studies of reception function. In tracing the ongoing mutation of Shakespeare, the essays in this collection suggest the multiple forms appropriation can take, as each generation seeks to possess and ultimately to usurp the literary holdings of a previous generation. The status we bestow upon an author as hero, saint or saviour can in turn authorise our own literary, political and commercial enterprises. The result is a ceaseless and reciprocal interplay of sacred and profane. Our own canonisation of Shakespeare as both schoolroom text and cultural icon constitutes a final irony as literary consumption becomes an act of devotion.

Notes

1. As defined in *The Oxford English Dictionary* (Second Edition), prepared by J. A. Simpson and E. S. C. Weiner (Oxford: Clarendon Press, 1989).
2. Hans Robert Jauss, 'Literary History as a Challenge to Literary Theory,' in *Towards an Aesthetic of Reception*, trans. Timothy Bahti (Minneapolis: University of Minnesota University Press, 1982), p. 22.
3. Hélène Cixous, 'Sorties: Out and Out: Attacks/Ways Out/Forays' in *The Newly Born Woman*, trans. Betsy Wing (Minneapolis: University of Minnesota Press, 1986), p. 122.
4. For a more detailed analysis of the history of Stratford as shrine see Graham Holderness' essay 'Bardolatry: or, The Cultural Materialist's Guide to

Stratford-upon-Avon' in *The Shakespeare Myth*, ed. G. Holderness (Manchester: University of Manchester Press, 1988), pp. 2–15.

5. Terence Hawkes, *That Shakespeherian Rag: Essays on a Critical Process* (London: Methuen, 1986), p. 1.

6. David Garrick, quoted in F. E. Halliday, *The Cult of Shakespeare* (London: Gerald Duckworth and Co., Ltd., 1957), pp. 67–8.

7. In the eighteenth century, for example, the 'barbarism' of the Renaissance was used to excuse Shakespeare's fondness for 'low' forms of humour such as puns and ribaldry.

8. Several contributors to this collection have recently published works on Shakespeare reception. See for example: Margreta de Grazia, *Shakespeare Verbatim: The Reproduction of Authenticity and the 1790 Apparatus* (Oxford: Clarendon Press, 1991); Michael Dobson, *Authorising Shakespeare: Adaptation and Canonization, 1660–1769* (Oxford: Oxford University Press, forthcoming); Hugh Grady, *The Modernist Shakespeare: Critical Texts in a Material World* (Oxford: Clarendon Press, 1991); Graham Holderness, (ed.) *The Shakespeare Myth* (Manchester: Manchester University Press, 1988).

9. Hans Robert Jauss, *op. cit.*, p. 21.

1 Accents Yet Unknown: Canonisation and the Cla Julius Caesar

Michael Dobson

> How many ages hence
> Shall this our lofty scene be acted over,
> In states unborn and accents yet unknown![1]

From our own historical perspective, Cassius' words over the corpse of Caesar inevitably sound like an ironic prophecy not merely of the existence of this play but of the extraordinary status it has come to enjoy over the four centuries since its première. By the late eighteenth century this was already a scene considered worthy of being 'acted over' not just 'in' the English 'state' but as an integral part of it: Francis Gentleman, introducing Bell's acting edition of *Julius Caesar* in 1773, hoped that it might become part of the national constitution:

> *We wish . . . our senators, as a body, were to bespeak it annually; that each would get most of it by heart; that it should be occasionally performed at both universities, and at every public seminary, of any consequence; so would the author receive distinguished, well-earned honour; and the public reap, we doubt not, essential service.*[2]

To Gentleman, clearly, *Julius Caesar* is a play equally instructive and appropriate to all imaginable shades of political opinion, a text on the value of which Parliament should agree 'as a body,' and he similarly assumes that the benefits which his scheme will produce – state ratification of its author's national status, and a 'Shakespearean' enhancement of public life in general – are ones which all his readers, no matter what their allegiances, would seek. The continuing promotion of this particular Set Text as one of the most prestigious components of a supposedly common national culture (both within the repertoire of a State-funded Royal Shakespeare Company and within the British education system as a whole) has long ago brought Gentleman's wishes so close to fulfilment it today his proposal may sound comparatively unsurprising; however, despite its remarkable persistence, the attitude which it registers would have been enthusiastically contested as recently as sixty years earlier, when one of 'our senators', John Sheffield, Earl of Mulgrave, expressed his own views on Shakespeare, public affairs and *Julius Caesar* by completely rewriting the entire play.

In this paper I shall be looking at a whole series of different appropriations of *Julius Caesar* carried out between the 1670s and the 1740s to consider exactly how it was that this play achieved its status as a classic, and to explore the connections between this process and the contemporary installation of Shakespeare as England's National Poet. I shall be examining three pieces of evidence in particular: firstly the altered acting text of *Julius Caesar* published in 1719, parts of which date from as early as the 1670s; secondly the two-part adaptation of the play mentioned above, begun by John Sheffield, Earl of Mulgrave, in the early 1700s and first published, posthumously, in 1723; and lastly a body of allusions to *Julius Caesar* drawn from the early discourse of Bardolatry, in particular those associated with the first 'scholarly' editions of the Complete Works (Rowe's of 1709 and Pope's of 1723-5) and with the first national monument to Shakespeare, the statue by Scheemakers erected in Westminster Abbey in 1741. I hope to suggest how the conflicting revisions of this play occasioned by the constitutional upheavals which transformed the English state between the Exclusion Crisis and the fall of Walpole, revisions which endow the play with political 'accents' certainly 'unknown' to its first audiences, ultimately conspired together not to bury *Julius Caesar* but to canonise it, helping to confer a ghostly immortality on Shakespeare in the process.

*   *   *   *   *

Interest in making explicitly political use of Shakespeare's tragedies and histories in the theatre of the Restoration and early eighteenth century came in three principal waves. The first occurred in the early 1660s, as the newly reopened theatres experimented with their inherited stock of pre-Commonwealth plays, often slanting them towards the celebration of the restored monarchy, as in the prologue to an early revival of *Richard III*, which presents the play as a satirical portrait of Cromwell,[3] or the more famous case of Sir William Davenant's heavily adapted *Macbeth*.[4] The second came with the Exclusion Crisis of 1679-82, as a number of playwrights sought to defend the ailing Carolean regime by adding more anxiously Royalist adaptations (notably Dryden's *Troilus and Cressida; or, Truth Found Too Late* and Nahum Tate's *The History of King Richard the*

Second, The History of King Lear and The Ingratitude of a Common-Wealth: Or, the Fall of Caius Martius Coriolanus) to the number of Shakespearean tragedies already established in the repertory.[5] The last followed in the wake of the Jacobite uprising of 1715, when a less homogenous group of adaptations, to which Sheffield's treatment of *Julius Caesar* belongs, variously, and sometimes simultaneously, asserted British liberty and offered guarded laments for the passing of Stuart autocracy. *Richard II* and *Coriolanus,* for example, deployed in emphatically pro-Richard and pro-Coriolanus versions by Tate four decades earlier, reappeared in contrasting keys in 1720 as Lewis Theobald's wistful *The Tragedy of King Richard II* and John Dennis' less ambivalent *The Invader of his Country: or, The Fatal Resentment.*[6] *Julius Caesar,* perhaps unsurprisingly given its comparatively sympathetic depiction of an assassination easily read as regicide, plays no very conspicuous role in the first two of these movements, but the early eighteenth century would find it both firmly established in the repertory and the subject of earnestly contesting interpretations.

The most widespread of these, which might be called the unambiguously pro-Brutus reading, can be discerned in theatrical treatments of the play as early as the 1670s. The first London revival of *Julius Caesar* after the Restoration (which did not take place until the mid-1660s, despite the play's presence in the repertory of the pre-Commonwealth King's Company),[7] admittedly, supplies it with a prologue which praises neither Brutus nor Caesar, preferring simply to stress its (quasi-royal) author's lack of a conscious design:

> Such Artless beauty lies in *Shakespears* wit,
> 'Twas well in spight of him what ere he writ . . .
> Thus like the drunken Tinker, in his Play,
> He grew a Prince, and never knew which way.[8]

However, by the eve of the Exclusion Crisis one anonymous writer at least was prepared to enlist the play on the side of the conspirators, producing what it is tempting to read as the sole potentially anti-royalist Restoration adaptation of Shakespeare. The copy of the Third Folio used as a promptbook at the Smock Alley theatre in Dublin preserves a fragment of *Julius Caesar,* including the close of an added speech for the dying Brutus:

> poor slavish rome, farwell: Ceasear now be still
> I Kild not thee wth half so good a will
>
> > > > *Dyes.*[9]

These lines correspond exactly with the close of the same speech as reproduced in the acting edition published in 1719, where they immediately follow Brutus' self-stabbing, carried out without the assistance of Strato. Since a Smock Alley cast-list for *Julius Caesar* probably contemporary with this fragment, dating from around 1676, similarly omits Strato, it seems very likely that this Dublin text provided the source for the whole of the defiantly libertarian gesture with which the 1719 Brutus concludes his part:

> *Brut*. . . . Scorning to view his Country's Misery,
>   Thus *Brutus* always strikes for Liberty.
> [Stabs himself]
>   Poor slavish *Rome* farewel, Caesar now be still.
>   I kill'd not thee with half so Good a will.[10]

These alterations, suggestively, were not adopted in London for the time being: meanwhile *Julius Caesar* was laid aside completely during the troubles of 1679–82, left alone, understandably, by managers and playwrights in search of potential Royalist propaganda.[11] The sole exception to this trend is Thomas Otway, whose *Venice Preserv'd* (1682), the most enduringly successful play of the crisis, offers what might be regarded as a domestic variant on Portia, Brutus and Cassius in its claustrophobic central triangle of Belvidera, Jaffeir and Pierre. However, even this determinedly Tory play, with its desperate insistence on the value of a feminised private realm threatened by a corrupt Senate and a corrupt rebellion alike, shares certain features with the emerging pro-conspiracy reading of *Julius Caesar* (Jaffeir, for all his vacillations, dies, like the Dublin Brutus, as a defiantly self-slain revolutionary), and it too would be cited in support of some distinctly non-Tory versions of British liberty in the decades after James II's exile.

Julius Caesar returned to the London repertory in a conservatively abridged text during the mid-1680s.[12] Suggestively, this text seems to have been conflated with the earlier Dublin alterations soon after the Glorious Revolution, producing the heavily accented version of the play, published in 1719, which remained the basis of all London productions from the 1690s to the close of the eighteenth century. The role of Brutus was until 1707 in the hands of Thomas Betterton, the leading tragic actor of the period, and the 1719 text of the play makes it perfectly clear that he was by now being played without reservation as the play's hero, a noble, resolute exemplar of freedom-loving patriotism. Not only are lines depicting him as anything less than perfectly rational excised (his troubled soliloquy over the sleeping Lucius after joining the conspiracy, 2.1, 228–32, for example), but his undaunted opposition to Caesar is emphasised by a series of additions, culminating in the unrepentant dying speech quoted above, and including a splendid rant after the appearance of Caesar's spirit on the eve of Philippi – 'Sure they have raised some Devil to their aid, And think to frighten *Brutus* with a shade. But ere night closes this fatal Day, I'll send more Ghosts this visit to repay' – and an entirely new dialogue with Caesar's spirit, who in this version reappears at

Philippi, only to find that even the prospect of defeat cannot alter Brutus' political convictions:

> Ghost. Cassius, my three and thirty wounds are now reveng'd.
> Brut. What art thou, why com'st thou.
> Ghost. To keep my word and meet thee in Philippi fields.
> Brut. Well, I will see thee then.
> Ghost. Next, ungrateful Brutus, do I call.
> Brut. Ungrateful, Caesar, that wou'd Rome enthral.[13]

This Brutus, needless to say, is a perfect Whig hero, the creation of an implied Shakespeare far removed from the Stuart loyalist invoked by Dryden, Tate and their colleagues. The new, Whiggish Shakespeare, indeed, appeared in person, as it were, in the prologue to a revival of *Julius Caesar* in 1707 to make his political views clear:

> The Ghost of Shakespeare rises to trumpets and flutes,
>   playing alternately.
> Hail, my lov'd Britons! how I'm pleas'd to see
> The great assertors of fair Liberty,
> Assembl'd here upon this solemn day,
> To see this Roman and this English play!
> This tragedy in great Eliza's reign,
> Was writ, when Philip plagu'd both land and main,
> To subjugate the western world to Spain.
> Then I brought mighty Julius on the stage,
> Then Britain heard my godlike Roman's rage,
> And came in crouds, with rapture came, to see,
> The world from its proud tyrant freed by me.
> Rome he enslav'd, for which he died once there;
> But for his introducing slav'ry here,
> Ten times I sacrifice him ev'ry year.
> My noble scenes Eliza's soul inspir'd,
> And Britain with a just disdain was fir'd,
> That we who scorn'd great Caesar here should reign,
> Should take an universal king from Spain.[14]

This reading of *Julius Caesar* as firmly on the side of Brutus and British liberty, Shakespeare's clearest expression of the spirit of Magna Carta and the Bill of Rights, is one which soon became an orthodoxy. It is clearly a premise of the most famous of all Whig plays, Addison's *Cato* (1713), for example, and it was enthusiastically promulgated, first within the theatre and then beyond it, over the ensuing decades. Charles Johnson, offering a conspectus of Shakespeare's greatest hits in the prologue to his adaptation of *As You Like It*, *Love in a Forest*, in 1723, characteristically presents Brutus as a laudable parricide, sacrificing family feeling to *amor patriae*:

> See the Dictator by the Patriot slain,
> And the world's mighty Victor bleed again;
> His ROMANS Speak and Act like ROMANS all,

We hear them Thunder in the Capitol:
Quick *Cassius* raves, and *Brutus*, sternly good,
Pierces the Father's in the Tyrant's Blood.[15]

Seen thus as depicting praiseworthy resistance to a tyrannous Great Man, the play was inevitably seized upon in the 1730s by 'Patriot' writers opposed to Walpole's ministry, in particular by those who criticised Walpole's pacific attitude to the Spanish: an article published in the *Craftsman* in 1739, 'EXTRACTS *from several Political Plays, with* OBSERVATIONS,' uses *Julius Caesar* as a means of claiming Shakespeare as an ally:

> Nor was our *publick-spirited Bard* less assiduous in applauding that Love for *universal Liberty*, which our Nation then shew'd, by assisting the *United Provinces*, in their brave Struggle to throw off the bloody Shackles of *Philip*, King of *Spain*, and erect themselves into *one independent Republick*. How greatly *Shakespear* admir'd, how zealously he propagated the noble Principles, on which *these injured People* acted, when they drew their Swords against *that Tyrant*, with invincible Resolution, either to free themselves, or die, may be seen by the elevated Sentiments, he hath put into the mouths of *Brutus* and *Cassius*, throughout his admirable Tragedy of *Julius Caesar*.[16]

Alongside *Julius Caesar*, the same article celebrates Rowe's *Tamerlane* for its praise of William of Orange and scorn of the French, Addison's *Cato* for its criticism of Queen Anne's last Tory ministry and Otway's *Venice Preserv'd*, cited, ironically enough, as a critique of Charles II's persecution of Shaftesbury. Brutus' status as hero is now beyond question, the retrospective claiming of Shakespeare as a father of English liberty complete. It would, indeed, be a *Julius Caesar* still accented in this direction which Francis Gentleman would hope to see nationally adopted in the 1770s, as the approbatory note he supplies to Brutus' altered death scene makes clear:

> *Bru.* Scorning to view his country's wrongs,
> Thus Brutus *always strikes for liberty.*
> Poor slavish Rome, *farewel.*†
>
> † The *italick* lines are not *Shakespeare's*, but properly added.[17]

*   *   *   *   *

The evidence I have presented so far might appear to confirm what is becoming a familiar view of Shakespeare's canonicity, one which stresses the ease with which his works are assimilated to whatever ideology happens to be dominant at any given historical moment. *Julius Caesar*, the argument would run, was unanimously co-opted, in the aftermath of the Glorious Revolution, as a founding text of the Enlightenment, completely in harmony with new, constitutionalist definitions of the public sphere, and its author was accordingly elevated to the national pantheon as a reward for services rendered to the ruling hegemony.[18] This view would, in this case at least, be an oversimplification. The rationalist, Whiggish appropriation of both *Julius Caesar* and Shakespeare that I have outlined actually encountered considerable resistance, the most sustained example of which was first advertised in the pages of the very edition which confirmed Shakespeare's approach to fully canonical status. Charles Gildon, discussing *Julius Caesar* in the seventh volume he appended to Rowe's epoch-making *The Works of Mr. William Shakespeare* of 1709, takes the opportunity of praising a forthcoming alternative, aristocratic version of the play, which he clearly feels will be an improvement:

> I know that a noble Man of great Judgment in the *Drama* is and has been for some time altering this Play, in which I believe *Shakespeare* will have a better Fate than in most of those which have been alter'd . . . the principle Character, *Caesar*, that is left so little touch'd by *Shakespeare*, will merit his Regard . . .[19]

The noble Man in question was John Sheffield, Earl of Mulgrave and Duke of Buckingham, whose two plays derived from *Julius Caesar*, *The Tragedy of Julius Caesar, altered*, which revises Shakespeare's first three acts, and *The Tragedy of Marcus Brutus*, Shakespeare's Acts 4 and 5, do indeed bestow considerable regard on Caesar.[20] Given Sheffield's own experiences of political conspiracy – his career was devastated by the Glorious Revolution and its aftermath: in 1688 he had just been made James II's Lord Chamberlain, and was suspected of Jacobite sympathies for the rest of his life, losing a seat on the Privy Council in 1696 for refusing to declare William of Orange 'rightful and lawful king'[21] – it is perhaps only appropriate that his version of the play should be noticeably more hostile towards Brutus than the contemporary acting text it sought to replace. Begun during an enforced lull in his waning career as a statesman, during the Whig ascendancy of 1705–10, and probably completed around 1716, after his final dismissal from public office at the accession of George I,[22] *The Tragedy of Julius Caesar, altered* and *The Tragedy of Marcus Brutus* mark the culmination of a long engagement with the play's subject matter. Some years earlier Sheffield had begun work on a biography of Julius Caesar, the surviving fragment of which concentrates on his exploits as a lover,[23] and he had already completed an *Ode on Brutus*,[24] which sets out to refute, point by point, Abraham Cowley's more enthusiastic poem on the same subject. By the early 1700s, apparently, any writer who wished to dramatise either figure needed to take issue with Shakespeare's *Julius Caesar*.[25]

Sheffield's adaptation does just this, not only inverting the post-1688 appropriation of *Julius Caesar* by siding with Caesar instead of with

Brutus, resembling in this respect certain contemporary Tory and Jacobite pamphlets, which attempt similar strategies with the plot of *Cato*,[26] but rejecting the original play's entire delineation of political life. It can be seen, in particular, to interrogate the Whig account of the body politic through its completely recast dramatisation of the relation of the body to politics, a relation which in Sheffield's plays is radically re-sexualised. A telling instance is provided by his rewriting of the crucial orchard scene between Brutus and Portia, Shakespeare's II, i, in which Portia begs her husband to confide in her:

> I grant I am a woman, but withal
> A woman that Lord Brutus took to wife.
> I grant I am a woman, but withal
> A woman well reputed, Cato's daughter.
> Think you I am no stronger than my sex,
> Being so fathered and so husbanded?
> Tell me your counsels; I will not disclose 'em.
> I have made strong proof of my constancy,
> Giving myself a voluntary wound
> Here in the thigh.[27]

In Shakespeare's text this gesture, following so closely on Portia's assertion of her impeccable patriarchal credentials, seems clearly analogous to Lady Macbeth's imagined unsexing of herself before entering into conspiracy with her husband; Portia disfigures her sexual body in order to join the conspirators as an honorary man.[28] In *Julius Caesar*, apparently, as in the writings of Whig theorists such as Locke, the political realm is emphatically gendered male:[29] Portia's sole female counterpart, Calpurnia, participates in public life on condition of sterility, featuring in the Lupercal scenes only because of her infertility, and she is later firmly identified with the domestic when Caesar overrules her advice to stay at home. Sheffield's adaptation, however, deals quite differently with female sexuality and its bearing on politics, refusing to privilege the homosocial over the conjugal, as the prologue to *The Tragedy of Marcus Brutus* suggests:

> *Some Criticks judge, ev'n love itself too mean*
> *A care to mix in such a lofty Scene,*
> *And with those ancient Bards of Greece believe*
> *Friendship has greater charms to please or grieve:*
> *But our more am'rous Poet, finding love*
> *Amidst all other cares still shines above;*
> *Lets not the best of Romans end their lives*
> *Without just softness for the kindest Wives.*[30]

Compared to Shakespeare's bloodless idealist, Sheffield's Brutus seems remarkably uxorious,[31] willing on little persuasion to share his political secrets as a relatively unexceptional part of his physical intimacy with his wife; and consequently in Sheffield's version of the orchard scene Portia's self-wounding, diminished to a token gesture, seems entirely redundant:

> *Brut.* O my soft heart! my Resolution's arm'd
> Against all dangers, nay, against my friend;
> Yet firm to all things else, it yields to love;
> > [*Takes her in his arms*
> It yields to *Portia* . . .
> *Port.* But tell me all.
> *Brut.* Then know that they who came to me this night . . .
> But why should I go on to thee, my *Portia*,
> In any language but in that of love? . . .
> *Port.* But you were just about to let me know.
> *Brut.* Know what? know things that will but trouble thee? . . .
> Oh, press not thus to bear a part in that,
> Which with its weight will crush thy tender mind.
> *Port.* I grant I am a woman, but am *Cato*'s daughter.
> My heart is tender, but to *Brutus* only.
> Think you 'tis nothing, to have such a Father,
> And such a Husband?
> *Brut.* Well then, hear it all.
> *Port.* Hold, dearest *Brutus*!
> I dare not hear it yet; I'll try this first.
> > [*She stabs herself in the Arm.*
>
> *Brut.* Hold, what d'ye mean?
> *Port.* To try my fortitude . . .[32]

Portia's promised immediate initiation into the plot sounds noticeably more physical in Sheffield's version than in Shakespeare's; not so much a painstaking lesson in Latin grammar – '*Brutus* All my engagements I will construe to thee,/All the charactery of my sad brows./Leave me with haste'[33] – as a consummation:

> *Brut.* Oh, wonder of thy sex!
> Gods! make me worthy of this matchless woman.
> Haste, haste, and let thy wound be quickly dress'd.
> Within I'll tell thee all,
> And in thy bosom pour my very soul.[34]

Rather than celebrating Brutus as a stoic, Sheffield's two plays castigate and punish him throughout for the folly of placing an abstract ideal of liberty above his flesh-and-blood obligations to Portia and Caesar. As the last couplet of *The Tragedy of Marcus Brutus*, pronounced by Dolabella over Brutus' body, summarises, 'Yet the just Gods a righteous judgment send / He lov'd his Country; but he kill'd his Friend.'[35] The news of Portia's death, delayed until the battle of Philippi, provides the climax of his punishment – in Sheffield's version it does not reach him until after the suicide of Cassius; and his death scene utterly reverses that of the contemporary acting text of *Julius Caesar*, offering a remorseful Brutus who instead of defying Caesar's ghost dies apologising to it:

> ye Pow'ers immortal know
> With what a heavy heart and troubled mind,
> I help'd my Country by so harsh a means:
> But I most gladly make thee this amends
> [*Caesar's ghost appears and vainshes* [sic]
> Oh Caesar, Caesar! Therefore rest appeas'd;
> I did not kill thee half so willingly.
>   [*Kills himself.*[36]

The most importantly modified character in Sheffield's two plays, however, as Gildon's puff promises, is Caesar himself. Restored to potency in *Julius Caesar*, *altered* by the abolition of all reference to his deafness and his childlessness, he is presented in the play's prologue, with ghastly relish, as the acceptable face of Tarquin:

> *For who can wish a scene more justly fam'd,*
> *When Rome and mighty Julius are but nam'd?*
> *That State of Heroes, who the world had brav'd!*
> *That wondrous man, who such a State inslav'd!*
> *Yet loth he was to take so rough a way,*
> *And after govern'd with so mild a sway,*
> *At distance now of sev'nteen hundred years,*
> *Methinks a lovely ravisher appears;*
> *Whom, though forbid by virtue to excuse,*
> *A Nymph might pardon, and could scarce refuse.*[37]

To use the term that most obviously suggests itself in this context, the whole thrust of Sheffield's adaptation is to present Caesar in a more virile and more favourable light than does Shakespeare. Sheffield's 'ravishing' Caesar in fact seems to embody a nostalgic ideal of the sexily authoritarian Stuart monarchy, his rhetoric often strikingly similar to that associated with the benign father-kings of Restoration tragedy. This is especially noticeable in the scene, actually staged in Sheffield's version, of his near-coronation at the hands of Mark Antony, during which he makes paternalistic asides about the Roman populace which Sheffield's mob scenes carefully endorse:

> Their reason lost, they rave for liberty,
> Like lunatics, confin'd for their own good,
> Strive for a fatal freedom to be ruin'd . . .
> I'll guard them from themselves, their own worst foes,
> And will have pow'r to do whate'er I please;
> Yet bear my thunder in a gentle hand.
> Like Jove, I'll sit above, but 'tis to show
> My love and care of all the world below.[38]

Provided with a kingly Caesar and an erring, repentant Brutus, Shakespeare's play is thus belatedly rescued for the cause of Divine Right, or at least, in that even this mightiest of eighteenth-century Caesars is killed, is appropriated to provide an elegy for it. In this respect *Julius Caesar, altered* and *The Tragedy of Marcus Brutus* may seem merely anachronistic, the Royalist adaptation of *Julius Caesar* Tate never wrote, but they were still sufficiently current in 1729, eight years after Sheffield's death, to have been put into rehearsal at Drury Lane;[39] and they are not the only early eighteenth-century rewritings of Shakespeare suffused with nostalgia for the Stuarts – as witness Lewis Theobald's *The Tragedy of King Richard II* (1720)[40] and that honorary Shakespeare adaptation of the following generation, William Havard's *King Charles the First: An Historical Tragedy, Written in Imitation of Shakespear* (1737). At the very least the existence of Sheffield's plays, and the enthusiasm for them shown by Gildon and, more signally, Alexander Pope, who assisted with their composition, contributing two choruses to *The Tragedy of Marcus Brutus*, demonstrate that the Whig ideology to which *Julius Caesar* was elsewhere being assimilated had its discontents, whose views likewise could be promoted by 'improving' modifications to Shakespeare's text. Perhaps more significantly, this pro-Caesar reading of the play also plays an important part in the canonisation of both *Julius Caesar* and Shakespeare during the 1720s and 1730s, albeit surviving, as I shall show, only as a ghost.

*   *   *   *   *

One of the most striking and paradoxical results of the contending political appropriations of Shakespeare carried out between the Restoration and the 1740s was that in topically and contingently rewriting his plays, Shakespeare's adaptors helped to promote them to a status 'above' politics, cumulatively seeming to demonstrate the transcendent value of the texts to which they laid their ideologically specific claims. This process of canonisation had two corollaries: the first was a trend away from adaptations of Shakespeare's plays which present them in the light of contemporary politics (Sheffield's was the last such revision of *Julius Caesar*) towards alternative forms of appropriation which present contemporary politics in the light of Shakespeare's plays. (A good example of this is the first known political cartoon to deploy a Shakespearean allusion, significantly to *Julius Caesar*: George Bickham's *The Stature of a Great Man or the English Colossus*, 1740, shows Walpole as a bloated Colossus of Rhodes/Caesar with a caption identifying his Opposition foe William Pulteney as a potential Brutus.)[41] The second was an increasing tendency, particularly marked in the new discourse of emergent Bardolatry to abstract Shakespeare from his works and to elevate him to a position above or outside the mere plays he had written. The appropriation of Shakespeare's specific texts gives place to the appropriation of 'Shakespeare' as an idea, and in this process too *Julius Caesar* continues to play a major role.

Jonathan Bate has recently argued in *Shakespearean Constitutions* that 'Shakespeare's "classic" status is a function of both his infinite appropriability. . .and his occasional intractability,'[42] and although the (Bardolatrously) hyperbolic first part of this statement might perhaps be modified – texts surely become classics not because they are innately susceptible to appropriation, but because they actually get appropriated – its stress on the potential resistance of Shakespeare's plays to wholesale repossession is salutary. In the case of *Julius Caesar, altered* and *The Tragedy of Marcus Brutus*, for example, Sheffield's fallible, misguided Brutus may inadvertently prove more rather than less sympathetic than his kingly Caesar, retaining the status conferred on him by the very structure of Shakespeare's original. For Shakespeare's early panegyrists, in similar fashion, the regal Caesar tends to return to prominence unbidden, even for the most determinedly pro-Brutus of Shakespeare's early canonisers, albeit as a figure not for the father-king but for the father-author who arguably came to usurp some of the monarch's residual mystique in the culture of Augustan England. George Sewell, for example, issuing his own revised version of Gildon's added volume of poems and commentary in 1725, this time as a supplement to Pope's edition, shares Gildon's low opinion of Shakespeare's Caesar, but the terms in which he expresses it prove equally to apply to the Bard: of Caesar he declares that:

> if any one were to form an Idea of him from what SHAKESPEARE makes him speak he would make but an indifferent Figure for the *Foremost of Mankind.*[43]

The text of Shakespeare's play, for Sewell, offers only a disfigured version of Caesar's 'idea'; but in a precisely parallel way the texts which embody the Shakespearean *oeuvre* may offer only a disfigured version of Shakespeare's 'idea' too, as Sewell explains elsewhere in terms which strongly suggest an unconscious equation of the immortal Bard with the immortal Caesar. According to Sewell, all previous editions of Shakespeare have reproduced him only as a defaced ghost: discussing their printing errors, he claims that:

> A fine Writer thus treated looks like *Deiphobus* among the Shades, so maim'd by his pretended Friend that the good *Aeneas* hardly knew him again.[44]

However, at the hands of Pope, Shakespeare's corrupt, fallible text will at last be fully and satisfactorily dealt with once and for all; after all:

> When a Genius of similar Fire and Fancy, temper'd with a learned Patience, sits down to consider what SHAKESPEARE would *Think*, as well as what he could *Write*, we may then expect to see his Works answer our Idea of the Man.[45]

Shakespeare's Caesar does not live up to our Idea of Caesar; but then Shakespeare's Shakespeare has hitherto not lived up to our Idea of Shakespeare. Pope's edition, notorious for the unkind cuts it makes to Shakespeare's plays (relegating 'spurious' passages to footnotes, silently correcting metrical 'errors', and so on), is cast by Sewell in the role of Brutus, conferring immortality on Shakespeare by releasing the Idea only latent in his hitherto imperfect textual corpus, just as the play's assassins, inadvertently, release the invulnerable Idea or ghost of Caesar from its bathetic mortal body.

The same irresistible impulse to abstract the figure of Shakespeare the Author from his texts in the image of Caesar's ghost is visible more signally in the work of the committee established in the late 1730s to erect a monument to Shakespeare in Westminster Abbey, who fittingly initiated this definitive act of canonisation by commissioning a benefit performance of *Julius Caesar* at Drury Lane, 28 April 1738.[46] In the prologue and epilogue to this performance, written by Benjamin Martyn and Noel Porter respectively,[47] the pro-Brutus reading of the play can be discerned collaborating inadvertently with the pro-Caesar in the production of Bardolatry as we still know it. Martyn's prologue explicitly favours the pro-Brutus, libertarian view of the play:

> While Brutus bleeds for liberty and Rome,
> Let Britons crowd to deck his Poet's tomb.

The following couplet, however, unconsciously identifies Shakespeare with Caesar, imaginatively completing the coronation begun at the Lupercal, conferring on him the posthumous 'monarch's voice' envisioned by Mark Antony:

> To future times recorded let it stand,
> This head was lawrel'd by the public hand.

Porter's epilogue, likewise, follows a resoundingly Whiggish paean to the conspirators – 'When Portia weeps, all gentle breasts must mourn,/When Brutus arms, all gen'rous bosoms burn./When Rome's firm Patriots on the stage were shewn,/With pride we trace the Patriots of our own;/From bondage sav'd when that bold state we see,/We glow to think that Britain is as free/' – by casting the audience as Mark Antony after the murder, invoking Caesar's spirit in the 'O pardon me, thou bleeding piece of earth' soliloquy:

With grief you saw a bard neglected lie,
Whom tow'ring genius living rais'd so high.
With grief you saw your Shakespeare's slighted state,
And call'd forth merit from the grave of fate.[48]

Finally, this identification of the newly-canonised Bard with the ghost of Caesar is brought resoundingly to consciousness in the prologue written by Lewis Theobald (along with Pope, a member of the committee) for the project's second and last benefit performance, the revival of *Hamlet*[49] played at Covent Garden in the following year:

> Immortal *Shakespear*! we thy claim admit;
> For, like thy *Caesar*, *thou art mighty yet*!
> *Thy spirit walks abroad*; and at our hands
> The honorary tomb, thy right, demands.[50]

Whether *Julius Caesar* was claimed as symbol of the past glories of the English monarchy or the past flowering of English liberty, tinged with Jacobite nostalgia or Whig, Shakespeare's concomitant promotion to the status of Author – immortal, disembodied spirit of his texts – was carried out in large part in the image of the most successfully dis-embodied spirit in *Julius Caesar*. The appropriability of Brutus to Whig ideology may have provided one important rationale for the early eighteenth-century's canonisation of the play and its author, but it is the intractable ghost of Caesar which nonetheless dictates it structure, here visibly providing the blueprint for the sublimation of Shakespeare from the body of his works, a trend which already threatens to remove the Bard from the theatre itself: Theobald's prologue closes with an anxious request to his audience that they should keep returning to Drury Lane, if only to revisit the mortal literary residue of the Author whose ascension they are celebrating: 'Then think, this Pile his honour'd Bones contains, / And frequent Visit – here – the lov'd Remains'. Ironically, the period's rewritings of *Julius Caesar*, despite sharing only a dissatisfaction with the Caesar bequeathed by the Folios, added up to confer, in Gentleman's words, 'distinguished, well-earned honour' on a Bard seemingly self-cast as his own Caesar's ghost. As Porter memorably told the audience of the 1738 benefit:

> Let others boast they smile on living worth;
> You give a buried bard a brighter birth.

As I hope I have shown, the 1719 acting text, Sheffield's adaptation and Pope's edition, whatever their particular accents, all served, too, as midwives to this birth, albeit by Caesarean section.

Notes

1. *Julius Caesar*, III, i, 112–14. All references to Shakespeare are from *The Complete Oxford Shakespeare*, ed. Stanley Wells and Gary Taylor (Oxford: Oxford University Press, 1986), unless stated otherwise.
2. [Francis Gentleman, ed.], *Bell's Edition of Shakespeare's Plays . . . With Notes Critical and Illustrative; By the Authors of the Dramatic Censor* (9 vols, London: 1773–4), V, 'Julius Caesar,' p. 3. Gentleman's hopes for the promotion of this play among senators and at prominent public schools had in fact been anticipated as early as 1728, when the Haymarket Theatre presented the first recorded school production of a Shakespeare play, offering a *Julius Caesar* 'By the young Noblemen of the Westminster School' (*Daily Journal*, 17 February 1728).
3. Preserved in B., A., comp., *Covent Garden Drollery* (London, 1672), p. 11.
4. See Christopher Spencer, *Davenant's Macbeth from the Yale Manuscript* (New Haven: Yale University Press, 1961).
5. On this group of adaptations, see especially Nancy Klein Maguire's essay elsewhere in this volume.
6. On this group of adaptations, see George C. Branam, *Eighteenth-Century Adaptations of Shakespearean Tragedy* (Berkeley: University of California Press, 1956), who rather misleadingly implies that they are all emphatically anti-Jacobite (pp. 62–3).
7. See the lists of plays acted at Court in 1636 and 1638, which apart from their inclusion of *Julius Caesar* correspond very closely to the repertory mounted by the old King's Company's survivors at the Red Bull immediately after the Restoration: Joseph Quincy Adams, ed., *The Dramatic Records of Sir Henry Herbert, Master of the Revels, 1623–73* (New Haven: Yale University Press, 1917), pp. 75, 76, 82.
8. B., A., *op. cit.*, p. 7. For the date of the first revival of *Julius Caesar* after the Restoration (probably some time between May 1663 and June 1665), see John Downes, *Roscius Anglicanus* (London, 1708), p. 8.
9. See R. C. Bald, 'Shakespeare on the Stage in Restoration Dublin,' *PMLA*, LVI (June 1941), pp. 369–78. On all the Restoration and eighteenth-century acting texts of this play, see especially John Ripley, *Julius Caesar on stage in England and America, 1599–1973* (Cambridge: Cambridge University Press, 1980), pp. 24–34, to which I am heavily indebted throughout this discussion.
10. William Davenant and John Dryden, attr. adaptors, *The Tragedy of Julius Caesar . . . as it is now acted . . .* (Dublin, 1719), act V. Reproduced on microfiche in Michael Dobson, ed., *Adaptations and Acting Versions of Shakespeare, 1660–1980*, unit 22 of the *Shakespeariana* collection (Ann Arbor: University Microfilms International, 1990). On this version of the play, see Ripley, *op. cit.*, pp. 25; 29; William Van Lennep, 'The Smock Alley Players of Dublin,' *A Journal of English Literary History*, XIII (September 1946), pp. 216–22.
11. The sole suggestion that the play might have been revived at any time over this period is provided by W. W. Greg, whose *A Bibliography of the English Printed Drama to the Restoration* (4 vols, London: Bibliographical Society, 1939–59) records a copy of the 1684 edition of *Julius Caesar* in which the cast list has been dated '1681' in manuscript (vol. III, pp. 1268–9). It seems unlikely that such a revival took place in 1681. However, given that the cast supplied in the 1684 edition is for a United Company production, the union of the Duke's and King's Companies not having occurred until late 1682, it

seems improbable that the King's Company would or even could have mounted the play in 1681. The King's Company, who until the union of the companies held the sole rights to act *Julius Caesar*, were undergoing a terminal crisis at the time, caused partly by the refusal of their older actors either to perform their stock roles regularly or to relinquish them to younger players. Major Mohun, their Cassius, seems to have become particularly unreliable at this time, perhaps because his avowed Catholicism was attracting hostile audience responses.

12. See the 'Players' Quartos' of 1684–91: Henrietta C. Bartlett, 'Quarto Editions of *Julius Caesar*,' *The Library*, 3rd series, IV (1913), pp. 129–30.
13. J. Ripley, *op. cit.*, pp. 28–9.
14. John Dennis, 'Prologue to the Subscribers for *Julius Caesar*,' in *A Collection and Selection of English Prologues and Epilogues* (4 vols, London, 1779), III, pp. 1–2.
15. Charles Johnson, *Love in a Forest* (London, 1723), 'Prologue.'
16. 'Caleb d'Anvers' [Nicholas Amhurst], ed., *The Craftsman*, no. 668 (April 1739).
17. [Francis Gentleman, ed.], *op. cit.*, vol. V, 'Julius Caesar', pp. 74–5.
18. The liveliest version to date of this account is offered by Gary Taylor in *Reinventing Shakespeare* (London: Hogarth Press, 1990).
19. [Charles Gildon, ed.], *The Works of Mr. William Shakespeare. Volume the Seventh* (London, '1709' [1710]).
20. On the composition of Sheffield's adaptation, see also Dennis Fletcher, 'Three Authors in Search of a Character: Julius Caesar as Seen by Buckingham, Conti and Voltaire,' in *Mélanges à la memoire de Franco Simone: France et Italie dans la culture européenne*, vol. 2 (Geneva: Slatkine, 1981), pp. 439–53.
21. *DNB*, 'Sheffield, John, third Earl of Mulgrave, 1648–1721.'
22. Alexander Pope assisted Sheffield with the composition of at least the second play, to which he contributed two choruses; these, probably added after the completion of the play, were certainly written by 1717, when they appeared in his *Works*.
23. John Sheffield, *The Works of His Grace John Duke of Buckingham, In Verse and Prose. A new Edition, with several Additions, and without any Castrations* (2 vols, London, 1726), vol. II, pp. 157–62. (The subtitle to this edition, prepared, like its predecessor, by Pope, refers to Sheffield's personal memoir of 1688, 'Some Account of the Revolution,' and his satire on, among other things, William of Orange's homosexuality, 'A Feast of the Gods,' excised by the censor from the 1723 edition for their Jacobite tendency).
24. *ibid*, vol. I, pp. 79–91.
25. Shakespeare's play seems to have become the 'canonical' account of the death of Caesar, certainly by the mid-century, as is suggested by John Home's poem *The Fate of Caesar* (1758), a dream-vision account of the assassination which follows what by the 1750s seems to have become the mandatory route to its subject and which concludes by adopting what seems to have become the mandatory position. The poem approaches its topic via *Julius Caesar*:

> As pensive on my bed I lay,
> And mus'd the midnight hours away,
> My bosom glowing with those fires,
> Which Shakespear's magick page inspires . . .

and concludes by endorsing Brutus:

The victim fell, the tyrant dy'd,
And freedom, freedom, loud was cry'd:
Impatient there I join'd the scream,
And waking found 'twas all a dream.
London Magazine 27 (1758), pp. 421-2.

26. See, for example, the anonymous pamphlet *Mr. Addison Turn'd Tory* (London, 1713), which claims that Cato's virtues are Tory and Caesar's vices Whig, or the more seditious *Cato's Ghost* (London, 1716; attributed by the British Library to William Meeston), which applies Addison's Caesar as a portrait of Cromwell, and Cato as a figure for the wronged and righteous Stuarts. The printer Charles Hornby was whipped for publishing this poem in July 1716: see *The Historical Register*, 1716, pp. 356-7.

27. *Julius Caesar*, II, i, 291-300.

28. This is hardly a new interpretation of this moment; one Victorian burlesque of the play, *Julius Caesar Travestie* (1871), renders this speech as:
    Sir, I'm a most strong-minded, plucky *she*-male,
    Braver, I think, than many a blustering *he* male.
    See Stanley Wells, ed., *Nineteenth-Century Shakespeare Burlesques* (4 vols, London: Diploma Press, 1978), vol. IV p. 20.

29. On Whig contractualism and gender, see especially Carole Pateman, *The Sexual Contract* (Stanford: Stanford University Press, 1988).

30. Sheffield, *op. cit.*, vol. I, pp. 187-8.

31. Cf. Genest's scandalised response to this scene of the adaptation:
    Act 2d. Brutus' Soliloquy and the scene with the
    Conspirators are altered for the worse – that between
    Brutus and Portia is turned into a contemptible love
    dialogue – Brutus in love!!!
        John Genest, *Some Account of the English
        Stage, from the Restoration in 1660 to 1830* (10
        vols, Bath, 1832), vol. III, p. 89.

32. Sheffield, *op. cit.*, vol. I, pp. 146-7. The 1719 acting edition of *Julius Caesar* similarly emends Portia's wound from the thigh to the arm, but only in the interests of Augustan modesty; the emphasis on Portia's proving that she can overcome her physicality remains intact.

33. *Julius Caesar*, II, i, 306-8.

34. J. Sheffield, *op. cit.*, vol. I, p. 147.

35. *ibid.*, p. 255.

36. *ibid.*, p. 214.

37. *ibid.*, p. 115.

38. *ibid.*, p. 124.

39. The production never took place: as *The Companion to the Play-House* records, the adaptation:
    . . . was intended . . . to have been represented in the Year 1729, for which Purpose the Choruses were all set to Music by the great *Bononcini*, but *English* voices being not sufficiently numerous, the *Italians* were applied to, who imagining they might make their own Price, demanded more for their nightly Performance than the Receipts of the House could amount to at the usual Rates; on which Account the Design was laid aside.
        The Companion to the Play-House (2 vols, London,
        1764), vol. I, F2r.

40. The anxiety with which Theobald's prologue to this play strenuously attempts
    to deflect potential accusations of Jacobitism is especially telling:
    . . . Our Author labours in a humbler Strain,
    But hopes to soothe you with a pleasing Pain;
    To move your Hearts, and force your Eyes to flow
    With Tears drawn from an ENGLISH *Monarch's Woe.*
    Justly his Pen's mistaken Task he'll own,
    If you can see a Prince, without a Groan,
    Forc'd by his Subjects to renounce his Throne.
    If recent Times more fresh Examples bring,
    How we can murther, *or depose a King,*
    Fearful of Censure, and offended Law,
    The Muse presumes no Parallels to draw;
    Nor aims to make the sullen, factious Stage
    Bellow with Anti-Revolution Rage.
    From Richard's Ruin, only, she intends
    To wound your Souls, and make you Richard's Friends *. . .*
    Lewis Theobald, *The Tragedy of King Richard II*
    (London, 1720), 'Prologue'.
41. '. . . The fault, dear P---y, is not in our Stars, But in our Selves, that we are
    Underlings.' British Museum Catalogue 2458; cited in Jonathan Bate, *Shake-
    spearean Constitutions* (Oxford: Oxford University Press, 1989), p. 70.
42. *ibid.*, p. 210.
43. George Sewell, *The Works of Shakespeare, Collated and Corrected* [ed. Alex-
    ander Pope, 6 vols, London, 1723–5], 'Volume Seven,' p. xiii.
44. *ibid*, p. viii. On the figuration of Shakespeare as a ghost, particularly Caesar's,
    see especially Marjorie Garber, *Shakespeare's Ghost Writers: Literature as
    Uncanny Causality* (New York and London: Methuen, 1987).
45. G. Sewell, *ibid.*
46. On this project, see J. Bate, *op. cit.*, p. 27; Morris R. Brownell, *Alexander Pope
    and the Arts of Georgian England* (Oxford: Clarendon Press, 1978), pp. 354–6;
    and David Piper, *The Image of the Poet: British Poets and their Portraits* (Oxford:
    Clarendon Press, 1982), pp. 78–82. Ultimately the monument would identify
    Shakespeare not with Caesar but with Prospero; see Michael Dobson,
    'Remember / First to possess his books: the appropriation of *The Tempest*,
    1700–1800,' *Shakespeare Survey* 43 (1991), pp. 99–107.
47. Printed in [Pierre Bayle, *et al.*], *A General Dictionary . . .* (10 vols, London,
    1734–41), vol. IX, p. 189.
48. Cf. *Julius Caesar*, III, i, 258ff.
49. On *Hamlet* and canonisation, see Michael Dobson, *Authorizing Shakespeare*
    (Oxford: Oxford University Press, forthcoming).
50. *London Daily Post and Advertiser*, 12 April 1739.

2 Nahum Tate's *King Lear*: 'the king's blest restoration'

Nancy Klein Maguire

'Legitimacy / At last has got it'

Nahum Tate's 'improved', and infamous, *The History of King Lear* (1680) kept Shakespeare's *King Lear* from the stage for more than 150 years.[1] Oddly enough, except for a few articles in the 1960s,[2] critics and theatre historians have ignored Tate's *coup de théâtre*. Even the pioneering history/literature scholars of the past five years[3] have more or less bypassed this theatrical marvel. Unless a century and a half of theatregoers can be dismissed as insensitive and ignorant Philistines, Tate's adaptation demands more serious attention.

Tate himself claimed that he found *The History of King Lear* 'well received by my audience.'[4] He understated. Audiences endorsed his adaptation from the 1680s to 1838. Major critics even pronounced *The History of King Lear* superior to Shakespeare's *King Lear* – indeed, Samuel Johnson in 1765 concluded, 'In the present case the publick has decided.'[5] Although poet laureate from 1692 until his death in 1715, Tate was at best a competent poet. With the possible exception of his translation of the psalms, nothing Tate did was as successful as *The History of King Lear*. Why and how did a merely competent playwright capture the *Lear* market for more than a century and a half?

Theatre historians typically list the following structural modifications in Tate's adaptation: the addition of an Edgar–Cordelia love story, increased importance to the love triangle, enlarged female roles, the deletion of the role of the Fool, and the changed ending. Traditionally dismissive of Tate's *Lear*, scholars, not bothering to examine the play very closely, have attributed these changes to the shift in aesthetic standards and to theatrical innovations, such as the use of actresses and elaborate stage sets.[6] Tate himself, however, insisted that he 'attempted the revival of it with alterations' out of 'my zeal for all the remains of Shakespeare.'[7] Nonetheless, in spite of Tate's disclaimer, I suspect that his motives for

29

adapting *Lear* in 1680 were more disingenuous.

In a 1683 'Letter to a Friend,' printed by the Whig stationer, Francis Smith, an anonymous author complains that ' 'Tis a fine Age, when Mercinary Poets shall become Politicians, and their Plays business of State.' He particularly resents that 'the most important Affair of the *Succession* must by the parallel of this impious Libeller be canvas'd upon the Stage.'[8] I would argue that Tate was one of those 'Mercinary Poets' and that he very shrewdly chose to rewrite Shakespeare's previously unadapted *Lear* because, among other reasons, the play could easily and safely comment on the 1678–83 Exclusion Crisis. In terms of Tim Harris's study of propaganda and politics during the reign of Charles II,[9] Tate's *Lear* was part of the Tory counter-propaganda campaign. In short, as John M. Wallace notes, 'The audience in 1681 would have had to have been asleep if it failed to recognize it was watching another anti-Exclusion play.'[10]

I Regicide Revisited

As Wallace and Matthew H. Wikander have already pointed out, the entire spate of Shakespearean adaptations written between 1677 and 1682 responded to the Exclusion Crisis. George W. Whiting and Christopher Spencer clearly read superficially when they exclude *The History of King Lear* from political plays in the eighties.[11] Not only did Tate's neglected and maligned adaptation appear with the emergence of party politics,[12] but it survives as the only Shakespearean adaptation to end happily, in a political 'restoration'. Although various playwrights paralleled the forties with the eighties, only Tate's play, among the adaptations or other plays, uniquely copies Tory party-line propaganda by using restoration, as well as regicide, to attack Exclusion.

The Duke's Company most likely produced Tate's *Lear* in October or December of 1680.[13] To understand the play, we need to understand the wide-ranging and deeply-rooted anxieties galvanised by the disquieting prospect of yet another monarchical crisis. Titus Oates' exposure of the Popish Plot in September of 1678 brought, in Harris's words, 'a new and terrifying immediacy to the problem of the catholic succession.'[14] Two months later, the idea of excluding the catholic Duke of York from the throne first appeared. In November of 1680, the House of Commons approved the second bill aimed at excluding James, and not until March of the next year did Charles II effectively destroy Parliamentary Exclusion by dissolving the Oxford Parliament. Even though both Whigs and Tories, carefully reconsidering their options, balked at the prospect of repeating

1640–60, a non-Parliamentary Exclusion movement persisted until the summer of 1683. During the unsettling five-year crisis, Whigs and Tories evoked the political and emotional trauma of mid-century for ideological support, consciously stirring up 'the whole battery of public memories and anxieties'[15] already dredged up by the Popish Plot.

Even non-theatrical Englishmen saw, or imagined, blatant parallels to mid-century. The Whigs, for instance, emphasised the historical repetition. Reprinting worrisome civil-war tracts in their bulky pamphlet literature, they advocated Exclusion as a means of again defeating popery and arbitrary government. As eagerly as the Parliamentarians had searched for precedents to execute Charles I,[16] the Whigs outlined the legal and historical precedents to exclude the Duke of York. Yet, they portrayed themselves as loyal defenders of the crown and claimed to fight against the king in order to preserve the king, thus imitating the manoeuvring of Parliament in the earlier crisis. Obviously, there *were* parallels. Jonathan Scott, in fact, plainly states that 'the crisis the government endured from 1678–83 was largely a repeat screening of the crisis of the reign of Charles I.'[17] Like his father, for instance, Charles II failed to control Parliament. Both Stuarts irritated their Protestant subjects by favoring Catholics: Charles II, in fact, crazed a nation hysterically afraid of popery by his impolitic preference for his 'whore of Babylon', the Duchess of Portsmouth.

In their counter-propaganda campaign, Tory dramatists, pamphleteers, poets, politicians, and even publishers invoked 'public memories and anxieties' to vilify the Whigs. Applying an extremely negative parallel, the Tories equated them with 'commonwealth's men', descended politically from the regicides and striving 'To make Eighty-one to out-do Forty-eight.' Indeed, Tory poets stressed, 'Think on His *Martyr'd Father*, and beware' and issued the warning, 'Tho their Blest *Father* perisht in their Snare, / The Gods with his *Sons Lives* that *Martyrs* loss Repair.' Another poet explicitly advises Charles II to, 'Consider on't, you're in a woful [*sic*] straight, / Think but on *Forty one*, and *Forty eight*'; indeed, Charles himself told Henry Mildmay, an MP for Essex, that 'he remembred 40 and 41.'[18] The work of the Tory publisher Nathaniel Thompson frequently accuses the Whigs, in Thompson's own words, of again attempting to mount '*Rebels* upon *Thrones* and *Monarchs* upon *Scaffolds*.'[19] Tory publishers reprinted 1649 Royalist propaganda *verbatim*. After nearly a twenty-year hiatus, for example in 1681, Richard Royston reprinted *Eikon Basilike*; according to his printer, Royston 'would not Print it, until he had the King's Leave.'[20] Underscoring the long-term impact of 1649, R. White's frontispiece to John Nalson's 1682 *Impartial Collection of the Great Affairs of State* depicts 'Britannia Mourning the Execution of Charles I.' The 'Mind of the Frontispiece' invites the reader to:

> view that piercing Eye,
> Which saw and winkt at the Conspiracy,
> Till Heaven's Enemies were ripe for doom,
> Then saw the *Martyr*'s Son Return with Triumph Home.

Even in the House of Commons, the Tories flaunted the act of regicide: 'The King's Father was murdered, and you take his Brother from him.'[21]

Tory publicists obsessively emphasised the appalling parallels between regicide and Exclusion. In February, 1681, for instance, a month prior to Charles II's dissolution of the Oxford Parliament, a 'Country-man' advises Charles II to:

> Read o're thy Martyr'd Father's Tragick Story,
> Learn by his Murder, different ways to glory.
> How fatal 'tis, by him is understood,
> To yield to Subjects, when they thirst for Blood,
> And cloak their black designs with Publick Good.[22]

In an anonymous broadside, printed in the same month and entitled 'The Ghost of the late house of Commons, to the New one appointed to meet at Oxford,' the 'Ghost' actually confesses to the 'Legal Murder' of Charles I and complains that 'my small *Jehu* at a Furious Rate, / Was driving *Eighty* back to *Forty Eight*.' 'Jehu', the 'little Guide, / Who every Foard [*sic*] of Villany had try'd,' apparently mocks Anthony Ashley Cooper, the First Earl of Shaftesbury, 'Satan's Vicegerent',[23] and ostensibly the leader of the Whig exclusionists. Summing up Tory disgust, the 'Countryman' groans, 'all this wrought by old known Cheats and Rooks / God! to be twice Cajol'd by Cants and Looks!'[24]

Like other propagandists, playwrights consciously looked for the opportunity to remind their audience of 'the crisis of the reign of Charles I.' Condemning 'that fowl Monster Civil-War' in his 1680 adaptation of *2 and 3 Henry VI*, unequivocally entitled *The Misery of Civil-War*, John Crowne emphatically states: 'this Tragedy a Rod will prove,/To whip us for a Fault, we too much Love,/And have for ages liv'd, call'd Civil Strife.'[25] Crowne's fellow playwright Nahum Tate had particular reason to remember the 'fowl Monster': when his father, 'Faithful Teate', informed on the Irish rebels in 1641, they plundered and burnt the family home and injured his wife and children, three children dying of injuries. Tate's frequent allusions to the act of regicide suggest his absorption in the resurrected Caroline crisis; indeed, his allusions in *Lear* to 'the King's inhumane Wrongs' (p. 64) recall the highly emotional Royalist pamphlets of 1649. As late as his 1685 elegy on Charles II, Tate emphasises that the country 'has mourn'd a *Martyr-King* before.'[26]

Perhaps applying the cautionary lesson he learned from the banning of his *Richard II* (disingenuously retitled *The Sicilian Usurper* or perhaps *The Tyrant of Sicily*),[27] Tate explicitly designed his third play as Tory propaganda. In the dedication of *The Ingratitude of a Common-wealth, or the Fall of Caius Martius Coriolanus* (premiered December 1681?), Tate asks, 'Where is the harm of letting the People see what Miseries Common=wealths have been involv'd in, by a blind Compliance with their popular Misleaders.' Putting Exclusion in the context of regicide, Tate mirrors 'the busie *Faction* of our own time' by specifically alluding to 'the sufferings of His late Majesty.' He concludes: 'The Moral therefore of these Scenes being to Recommend Submission and Adherence to Establisht lawful Power, which in a word, is *Loyalty.*'[28] Tate repeats this Tory propaganda the following year. In *The Second Part of Absalom and Achitophel* (1682), Tate emphatically states 'Wo! to that Kingdom where the Monarch Falls.'[29] Blaming the anti-royalists of 1640–60 for the turmoil of Exclusion, he enlists the act of regicide to support the 'Martyred Monarch's' second son, claiming that:

> the *Good Old Cause* that did excite
> Th' Original Rebells Wiles, Revenge and Spight.
> These raise the Plot to have the Scandal thrown
> Upon the bright Successor of the Crown. (II, p. 65).

Like everyone else at the time, Tate felt that by excluding 'the bright Successor of the Crown', the nation would re-enact the 1649 'Scene of Woes', which 'unknowing We renew, / And madly, ev'n those ills we Fear, pursue'. Recalling Tate's family experience of civil war, we should not be surprised that he highlights the 'Bleeding Scars, / And fresh Remembrance of Intestine Wars' (II, p. 82, 83).

II. The Restoration of King Lear

James Black misunderstands either the Restoration audience or Shakespeare's play when he says that '*King Lear* was not a play that recommended itself to Restoration audiences.'[30] Shakespeare's own text, in fact, was available to the Restoration audience both as a separate quarto (1655) and as part of the 1664 folio. The Duke's Company produced Shakespeare's unaltered *Lear* at least twice, in 1664 and 1675, as their prompter John Downes underscores: '*Lear*, being *Acted* exactly as Mr. *Shakespear* Wrote it.'[31] Tate probably chose, in part, to adapt *Lear* because Shakespeare's play resonated with the Restoration audience's experience: the mid-century division of the king's two bodies, for instance, and misplaced succession, the danger of power unwisely delegated, and, of course, civil war. B. Behrens, indeed, claims that Englishmen 'increasingly believed, between 1678 and 1681, that a revolution would in fact take place.'[32] By chosing to adapt a play which depicts war among family members, Tate struck immediately at the horrors of civil war and thus of Exclusion. Dividing along party lines, Shakespeare's *Lear* accommodates the acute division and intense bitterness in England during Exclusion.[33]

Particularly suiting the Tories, Shakespeare's text could be used to defeat the Exclusion platform in various ways: some Monmouth-promoting Whigs, for example, dredged up precedents for elevating bastards to the throne, and Shakespeare dramatises the result of Gloucester's unfortunate desire to 'work the means / To make thee capable' (II, i, 84–5). Shakespeare's *Lear* also exposes the dangers of having a king with only the name of King; the destabilisation of monarchy in Lear's England must have reverberated with the exclusionist challenge to royal authority. Indeed, on 27 April 1679, a shrewd, or perhaps panicky, Charles II had himself proposed that the powers of a Catholic successor be limited,[34] and at the Oxford Parliament, members of the House of Commons repeatedly postulated that 'should the Duke of *York* come to the Crown, he should retain the name only of King.' Under this expedient to Exclusion, 'the next Heir, under the title of Regent, or Protector, should have the Administration of the Government';[35] in the regency alternative to Exclusion, in a sense, James and Mary parallel Lear and his ungrateful daughters. At any rate, after Mary's succession in 1688, pamphleteers capitalised on the similarity; a 1689 lampoon even accuses Mary of being 'worse than cruel lustful Goneril, thou! / She took but what her father did allow; / But thou, more impious, robb'st thy father's brow.'[36] In Shakespeare's England, the division of the kingdom gave rise to anarchy, and during the Exclusion Crisis, the threat to monarchy resulted in 'a state of affairs to which anarchy seemed the next step.'[37]

Even without Tate's alterations, Shakespeare's original text provided the Tories with ready-made character parallels. Even a semi-alert audience, for instance, would have seen the parallel between the staunchly loyal Kent, banished and threatened with death if 'Thy banish'd trunk be found in our dominions' (I, i, 177), and the Duke of York. In adapting Shakespeare, Tate, as Wallace recently pointed out, accentuates the banishment threatening James by having Gloster and Lear banish Edgar, Cordelia, and Kent in the first 175 lines of Tate's text.[38] By adding such disingenuous lines as 'And possibly a king might be my Sire' and 'Thus would I reign could I but mount a Throne' (pp. 39, 86), Tate almost heavy-handedly points the parallel between Edmund and the Duke of Monmouth, Charles II's illegitimate eldest son and the Whigs' most visible and popular candidate for the throne. Tory pamphleteers advise Monmouth, 'strive not to Legitimate your Blood,'[39] and Tate conspicuously omits Edmund's line, 'Now, gods, stand up for bastards!' (I, ii,

22). As Spencer points out, the line 'would seem most impolitic under the circumstances.'[40]

Although Tate equivocates to some degree in *Lear*, more so than in either *Richard II* or *The Ingratitude of a Common-wealth*, he politicises nonetheless. Perhaps James himself appreciated Tate's anti-Exclusion propaganda. At any rate, Tate's adaptation of *King Lear* was produced at Whitehall not only on 9 May 1687, but again on 29 February 1688,[41] less than ten months before James fled London. Reading Tate's play closely reveals subtle alterations which suggest why his *History of King Lear* was even more politically suitable to the post-regicide and pre-Glorious Revolution audience than was Shakespeare's original text.

Tate intensifies the application of Shakespeare's *Lear* to Exclusion by making both structural and rhetorical changes. Certainly commenting on Exclusion, Tate, like other Tory propagandists, frequently does so through manipulating the emotionally powerful memories of 1649. Pointing toward both the past and the present, his *Lear*, in fact, parallels the story of Charles I and his two sons. Indeed, all four quartos of the play substitute 'beheaded' for 'bareheaded' in the storm on the heath scene (III, ii, 60); and in the context of the entire play, Tate's compositors were perhaps not entirely in error. Tate's *Lear* vividly recalls and nearly re-enacts the act of regicide. Tate makes regicide more horrendous by replacing Edmund's 'my writ / Is on the life of Lear and on Cordelia' (V, iii, 246-7) with Goneril's order to 'dispatch your prisoners. / Our empire can have no sure settlement / But in their death. . . . Let me hear they are dead' (p. 82). Fearing that Lear's 'age has charms in it, his title more, / To draw the commons once more to his side' (p. 82), Edmund strategically reinforces Goneril's command; in much the same way, perhaps, as Cromwell pushed through the execution of Charles I.

Reflecting the shifting post-regicide and Exclusionist perception of monarchy, Tate changes Lear's imperious pronouncement that 'Only we shall retain / The name, and all th' addition to a king' (I, i, 135-6) to the diminished edict that 'The name alone of King remain with me' (p. 12). William Lilly had described Charles I as 'a King: yet afterwards it appeared hee had not the power of a *King*, to conclude anything,'[42] and Lear becomes another *King and No King*. Tate continually emphasises the powerless divine right of Lear (and of Charles I and his sons); Tate has Cordelia, for instance, plead with the gods:

> Your image suffers when a monarch bleeds.
> 'Tis your own cause, for that your succors bring,
> Revenge yourselves, and right an injured king. (p. 78)

The 'injured king,' of course, refers both to the Duke of York and Charles II, as well as their father. Supporting the established regime against the encroaching Whigs, Tate underscores Shakespeare's loyalty to hierarchical structures. When Cordelia begs Gloster for 'succor for a father and a king, / An injured father and an injured king,' Gloster responds, 'I have already plotted to restore / My injured master' (p. 42). The 'injured master' again obviously glances at all three Stuart kings. Emphatically dismissing Gloster's suggestion that it was 'the king that wronged thee,' Cordelia responds, 'he did not, could not wrong me,' (p. 42) and Gloster later concludes, 'Well have I sold my eyes, if the event / Prove happy for the injured king' (p. 61).

Tate's characters show much more political awareness than the political innocents in the original text. Gloster, for instance, uses his blindness shrewdly: 'with these bleeding rings / I will present me to the pitying crowd' to 'Enflame 'em to revenge their king and me' (p. 58). Edmund's officer describes the effect:

> old Gloster
> (A moving spectacle) led through their ranks,
> Whose powerful tongue, and more prevailing wrongs,
> Have so enraged their rustic spirits that with
> Th' approaching dawn we must expect their battle. (p. 80)

Echoes of the civil-war years recur, and Tate's militarised Kent commands Lear's troops like a civil-war Royalist, perhaps recalling the loyalty and determination of Prince Rupert, Charles I's sometime favoured and superb general. Shakespeare's tragic aristocrats, Gloucester, Edgar, Kent, Lear, and Cordelia, become the disenfranchised and poverty-stricken Royalist exiles of the 1650s. Imitating the chaos of 1659, Tate's depiction of the government of Goneril and Regan accentuates Shakespeare's division of the king's two bodies. Gloster comments:

> This change in the state sits uneasy. The commons repine aloud at their female tyrants. Already they cry out for the reinstallment of their good old king, whose injuries I fear will inflame 'em into mutiny. (pp. 40-1).

Jones points out that the structure of politics underwent 'constant and major changes' during the Exclusion Crisis,[43] and, in Tate's adaptation, episodic situations in quick succession mimic the political disruptions of 1678-83. By act III, in fact, Tate already hints at and prepares for restoration/succession as an escape from disruptive and Whiggish tyrants.

In Tate's hands, Shakespeare's villains become bolder, more prominent, and more politically astute. Rather than opening with a conversation between Kent and Gloucester, Tate begins with Edmund's famous soliloquy: 'Thou, Nature, art my goddess' (p. 7). Edmund achieves more prominence as a Hobbesian villain. Professing love to both sisters, for example, he concludes, 'Suppose it be the same; why best of all, / And I have then my lesson ready conned' (p. 59). Identifying himself as 'born a libertine, and so I keep me' (p. 85), Edmund even plans to rape Cordelia:

> like the vig'rous Jove I will enjoy
> This Semele in a storm. 'Twill deaf her cries
> Like drums in battle, lest her groans should pierce
> My pitying ear, and make the amorous fight less fierce. (pp. 43–4).

The evil libertine characters carouse at a masque while the virtuous Tory characters endure the storm of Whiggish banishment. Both sisters become more ruthless: Regan tells Edmund that her husband's 'wound grows dangerous – I hope mortal' (p. 59), and Goneril plots to kill her husband as well as her father. The two sisters poison each other and snarl over the remains of Edmund as all three lovers are dying.

Thomas Hobbes's *Leviathan*, republished in 1676, 1678, and 1681, conveniently stresses that 'the want of an Absolute and Arbitrary Legislative Power' is 'one of the causes of the Dissolutions of Commonwealths.'[44] James Black argues that Hobbes specifically influenced Tate's *Lear*,[45] and Tate tellingly amplifies Shakespeare's frightening depiction of a dissolving commonwealth. Perhaps also responding to the fear of civil war, Tate increases the number of lines alluding to rebellion: Cornwall, for instance, sees 'a plot upon our state,' and Regan demands that their forces 'drive this monster of rebellion back' (pp. 55, 60). Even the Whiggish Edmund acknowledges that:

> The riots of these proud imperial sisters
> Already have imposed the galling yoke
> Of taxes and hard impositions on
> The drudging peasants' neck, who bellow out
> Their loud complaints in vain. (pp. 39–40)

An officer reports in act IV that 'The peasants are all up in mutiny, / And only want a chief to lead 'em on / To storm your palace' and 'That now that mutiny which long had crept / Takes wing, and threatens your best powers' (p. 60). Gloster repeats the story of mutiny to Kent, again stressing the need for a 'chief' or an accepted successor: 'Our injured country is at length in arms, / Urged by the king's inhuman wrongs and mine, / And only want a chief to lead 'em on' (p. 64). By ending with civil war rather than war with France, Tate evokes the mid-century trauma, as well as carefully avoiding offence to the pro-France Charles and James.

By reducing the complexity of Shakespeare's vision, and of the complexity of 1649, to two opposing forces which move toward regicide or restoration, Tate mirrors England's instinct toward polarising in 1678–83. Indeed, Jones expressly notes the Whigs' 'readiness to take short cuts, to evade thinking out the fundamental causes of the crisis.'[46] In contrast to the vast amount of divergent political speculation during the civil war, as

Behrens points out, pampheteers only expressed Whig, Tory, and Trimmer opinions during the Exclusion Crisis. Albany suggests the telescoped movement from regicide to restoration when he frees Lear:

> Thou injured majesty,
> The wheel of Fortune now has made her circle,
> And blessings yet stand 'twixt thy grave and thee. (p. 91)

Albany's statement, of course, alludes to both Charles I and Charles II, and by March of 1681, to James. The last-minute Fletcherian rescue of Lear, Kent, and Cordelia must have reminded the audience of the apparently extemporaneous Restoration of Charles II and the anticipated rescue of James. Indeed, Cordelia prays, 'The gods restore you' (p. 77). The word 'restore' recurs frequently in Tate's text, and the adaptation ends in 'the king's blest restoration' as Gloster hails Lear's 'second birth of empire' (p. 93). By making Lear both the 'Martyr-King' and the restored king, Tate reverses the act of regicide. Usurpation is corrected; as Lear himself says, 'Old Lear shall be / A king again' (p. 93). The themes of regicide, Restoration, and Exclusion, of Charles I and his sons, converge in Tate's adaptation as Lear becomes both the Martyr-King of 1649 and the restored Charles II/James II.

Tate, of course, changes the closing lines significantly, and the concluding stanzas in his play and Shakespeare's play are as far apart as the 1649 execution of Charles I and the 1660 Restoration of his sons. The ending moves from Edgar's:

> The weight of this sad time we must obey,
> Speak what we feel, not what we ought to say:
> The oldest hath borne most; we that are young
> Shall never see so much, nor live so long.
> *Exeunt with a dead march.* (V, iii, 324-7)

to these flowery lines to Cordelia (reminiscent of those addressed to Henrietta Maria and Charles I in *Salmacida Spolia*):[47]

> Our drooping country now erects her head,
> Peace spreads her balmy wings, and Plenty blooms.
> Divine Cordelia, all the gods can witness
> How much thy love to empire I prefer!
> Thy bright example shall convince the world
> (Whatever storms of Fortune are decreed)
> That truth and viture [*sic*] shall at last succeed. (p. 95)

The Stuart myth requires 'truth and viture' to succeed 'at last'. According to Stuart mythographers, Charles I paid for the miraculous Restoration of Charles II by suffering martyrdom, and, in Tate's mind, at least, the Martyred Monarch also paid for the succession of his younger son. Edgar assures Cordelia, 'The gods have weighed our sufferings; / W'are past the fire, and now must shine to ages' (p. 90). In masque-like terms, Lear's last lines refer to 'the prosperous reign / Of this celestial pair' (pp. 94–5). Like Henrietta Maria's celebrated virtues, Cordelia's 'bright example shall adorn the scene, / And teach the world perfection' (p. 54). Appropriately, Edmund/Monmouth concedes James's victory: 'Legitimacy / At last has got it' (p. 87).

Although a number of factors, some of which have been discussed by others,[48] contributed to the popularity of Tate's *King Lear*, the topicality of the play does explain its immediate success. I suspect that *Lear* continued to be popular because Tate equivocated sufficiently to permit a somewhat Whiggish reading after 1688. Although accommodating a restored (or resurrected?) Martyr-King, Tate's adaptation leaves us with a sense that 'the king's blest restoration' has not quite put things back together. Although left alive at the end of the play, Lear sinks into a needed retirement instead of retaining the crown. His restoration is not completely unlike that of Charles II or of the succession of his brother. The happy (and Whiggish) agreement to have Cordelia and Edgar rule is, in a sense, elective monarchy rather than divine right, and their joint rule, of course, foreshadows the succession of Mary and William in 1688. Tate certainly catered to his Tory audience, but aspects of his adaptation, as well as his choice of texts featuring irresponsible monarchs, suggest that Tate, as well as members of his audience, hedged his bets.

Notes

I first presented this material in seminars at the 1986 International Shakespeare conference in West Berlin and at the 1988 International Shakespeare conference in Stratford-upon-Avon. A version of the essay was delivered at the 1988 Modern Language Association of America in New Orleans.

1. At least three dozen editions and impressions of Tate's *Lear* were published, and Garrick, Colman, and Kemble used portions of Tate's text in their versions of the play. Playbills in 1743 advertise the play as having 'Restorations from Shakespeare' (Charles Beecher Hogan, *Shakespeare in the Theatre, 1701–1800*, 2 vols. [Oxford: Clarendon Press, 1952], 2, p. 263), and an 1820 edition printed by R. W. Elliston in London claims to be 'Chiefly from N. Tate – with some restorations from the original text'. The tragic ending was not successfully restored until 1834, and the Fool was not restored until 1838.

2. See, for example, Christopher Spencer, 'A Word for Tate's *King Lear*,' *Studies in English Literature* (Spring, 1963), 3, pp. 241–51; W. Moelwyn Merchant, 'Shakespeare "Made Fit",' *Restoration Theatre*, Stratford-upon-Avon Studies, 6 (London: Edward Arnold, 1965), pp. 195–219; James Black's, 'The Influence of Hobbes on Nahum Tate's *King Lear*,' *Studies in English Literature* (1967), 7, pp. 377–85; and 'An Augustan Stage-History: Nahum Tate's *King*

Lear,' Restoration and 18th Century Theatre Research (May, 1967), 6, pp. 36–54.

3. As early as 1982, Katherine Eisaman Maus in 'Arcadia Lost: Politics and Revision in the Restoration Tempest' discussed the political implications of the Dryden/Davenant The Tempest (Renaissance Drama, NS 13, ed. Leonard Barkan [Evanston: Northwestern University Press, 1982], pp. 169–209). The more recent discussions focus on 1677–82. J. Douglas Canfield, for example, considers a few of the adaptations of Nahum Tate and John Crowne in his article 'Royalism's Last Dramatic Stand: English Political Tragedy, 1679–89,' Studies in Philology, 82 (Spring 1985), pp. 234–63. John M. Wallace briefly discusses other adaptations in 'Otway's Caius Marius and the Exclusion Crisis,' Modern Philology, 85 (May, 1988), pp. 363–72, and Timothy J. Viator discusses 'Nahum Tate's Richard II' in Theatre Notebook, 42, no. 3 (1988), pp. 109–117. The most comprehensive discussion of the spate of adaptations produced between 1677 and 1682 is Matthew H. Wikander's 'The Spitted Infant: Scenic Emblem and Exclusionist Politics in Restoration Adaptations of Shakespeare,' Shakespeare Quarterly, 37 (Autumn, 1986), pp. 340–58.

4. Nahum Tate, 'Dedicatory Letter,' The History of King Lear, ed. James Black, Regents Restoration Drama Series, gen. ed. John Loftis (Lincoln: University of Nebraska Press, 1975), p. 2; further references to Tate's adaptation are from this edition. All references to Shakespeare's King Lear are taken from The Riverside Shakespeare, ed. G. Blakemore Evans (Boston: Houghton Mifflin Company, 1974). The Duke's Company staged the adaptation with a strong cast, but there are no extant records of its immediate reception.

5. Samuel Johnson, Selections from Johnson on Shakespeare, ed. Bertrand H. Bronson with Jean M. O'Meara (New Haven: Yale University Press, 1986), p. 240.

6. Primarily concerned with changes in 'the vivid language of spectacle' (p. 355), Wikander's two-page reading of Tate's Lear is the lengthiest discussion since Black's 1975 edition. For a detailed stage history and a study of the influence of the innovations, see James Black, 'An Augustan Stage-History: Nahum Tate's King Lear,' Restoration and 18th Century Theatre Research, (May, 1967), pp. 36–54.

7. N. Tate, 'Dedicatory Letter,' The History of King Lear, p. 1.

8. [Thomas Shadwell], Some Reflections upon the Pretended Parallel in the Play called The Duke of Guise (London: Printed for Francis Smith, 1683), sigs. D3r, B1v.

9. Tim Harris, London Crowds in the Reign of Charles II: Propaganda and Politics from the Restoration until the exclusion crisis, Cambridge Studies in Early Modern British History (Cambridge: Cambridge University Press, 1987), chapters 5 and 6; the fullest account of the Exclusion Crisis is still J. R. Jones's The First Whigs: the Politics of the Exclusion Crisis 1678–1683 (London: Oxford University Press, 1961); for a description of the political manoeuvring of both parties, see Ronald Hutton, Charles the Second: King of England, Scotland, and Ireland (Oxford: Clarendon Press, 1989), chapters 13 and 14.

10. J. M. Wallace, op. cit., pp. 363–4.

11. George W. Whiting argues convincingly that theatre and politics were particularly close in the early eighties, yet his discussion conspicuously misses Tate's Lear; Christopher Spencer claims that 'political considerations had a minimum of direct effect on Tate's first adaptation'; Whiting, 'Political Satire

in London Stage Plays, 1680–83,' *Modern Philology* (August, 1930), 28, pp. 29–43; Spencer, *Nahum Tate* (New York: Twayne Publishers, 1972), p. 68.

12. Harris argues for 'the existence of a fundamental divide along whig/tory lines at the level of the London crowd during the exclusion crisis' (p. 188). See also O. W. Furley, 'The Whig Exclusionists: Pamphlet Literature in the Exclusion Campaign, 1679–81,' *Cambridge Historical Journal* 8 (1957), p. 27, and T. Harris, *op. cit.*, pp. 188 and 223.

13. In 'Dating Play Premières from Publication Data, 1660–1700', *Harvard Library Bulletin*, 22 (October, 1974), p. 390, Judith Milhous and Robert D. Hume accept Black's range of October, 1680 to early January 1681, for the première of *Lear* ('Augustan Stage History,' pp. 36–7). In private correspondence, A. H. Scouten presents a convincing argument for a première in either October or December.

14. T. Harris, *op. cit.*, p. 96.

15. Jonathan Scott, 'Radicalism and Restoration: The Shape of the Stuart Experience,' *The Historical Journal* (1988), 31, p. 460.

16. See O. W. Furley, *op. cit.*, 25–30.

17. Scott, *op. cit.*, p. 459.

18. Anon, 'The Wine Coopers Delight' (London: Printed for H. L., 1681), broadside; 'Collected by N.[athaniel] T.[hompson],' *A Collection of 86 Loyal Poems* (London: Printed by N. T., 1685), sigs. 2B8v, R6r; Thompson, sig. B3v; *Correspondence of the Family of Hatton*, ed. Edward Maunde Thompson, 2 vols. ([Westminster]: Camden Society, 1878), 1, p. 220.

19. Thompson, *op. cit.*, sig. A3v. For further examples of the exploitation of the 'Royal Martyr', see sigs. B6r, M1v, N6r, Q5r, R6r, R6v, R8r, 2B8v.

20. [Thomas Wagstaffe], *A Vindication of K. Charles the Martyr*, 3rd edn (London: R. Wilkin, 1711), sig. X2r.

21. John Nalson, *An Impartial Collection of the Great Affairs of State*, 2 vols. (London: S. Mearne, E. Dring, B. Tooke, T. Sawbridge, and C. Mearney, 1682, 1683), I; Anchitell Grey, *Debates of the House of Commons, From the Year 1667 to the Year 1694*, 10 vols. (London: Printed for D. Henry, R. Cave, and J. Emonson, 1763), 8, sig. Y5r.

22. Anon., *The Country-mans Complaint, and Advice to the King* (London: n.p., 1681), broadside; the Newberry Library's reprint in *Poetry Longwaies*, no. 100, notes in longhand 'February, 1680/81'; the broadside is also reprinted in Thompson, sigs. G8r-v.

23. Anon., *The Ghost of the late House of Commons, To the New one appointed to meet at Oxford* (London: Printed for Benjamin Harris, 1681), broadside; reprinted in Thompson, sigs. C6r-C7r. An anonymous Tory poet alludes to '*Satan*, or his Vicegerent *Shaftsbury*,' Thompson, sig. D1r.

24. 'Countryman's Complaint,' Thompson, sig. G8v.

25. John Crowne, *The Misery of Civil-War. A Tragedy* (London: R. Bentley and M. Magnes, 1680), sigs. [A4r], K4v.

26. N. Tate, 'On the Sacred Memory of our Late Sovereign: With a Congratulation to his Present Majesty' (London: Printed by J. Playford for Henry Playford, 1685), sig. A2v.

27. For a compilation of primary documents relating to the debacle, see Judith Milhous and Robert D. Hume, *A Register of English Theatrical Documents, 1660–1737* (Carbondale: Southern Illinois Press, 1991), pp. 217–18. For the best review of scholarship concerning the production history of Tate's *Richard II*, see T. J. Viator, 'Nahum Tate's *Richard II, op. cit.*, pp. 109–117. A

Folger newsletter refers to the adaptation by the title *Tyrant of Sicily*; see John Harold Wilson, 'Theatre Notes from the Newdigate Newsletters', *Theatre Notebook* (Spring, 1961), 15, p. 80.

28. N. Tate, *The Ingratitude of a Common-wealth: Or, the Fall of Caius Martius Coriolanus* (London: Printed by L. M. for Joseph Hindmarsh, 1682), sigs. A2v, A2r-v, A2v.

29. John Dryden, *The Works of John Dryden*, 20 vols. in progress, eds for vol. II, H. T. Swedenberg, Jr. and Vinton A. Dearing (Berkeley: University of California Press, 1972), 2, p. 83. Tate wrote the major portion of *The Second Part of Absalom and Achitophel*.

30. J. Black, 'Introduction', *The History of King Lear*, *op. cit.*, p. xvi.

31. John Downes, *Roscius Anglicanus, or an Historical Review of the Stage* (London: H. Playford, 1708); Augustan reprint facsimile, introduction by John Loftis (Los Angeles: William Andrews Clark Memorial Library, 1969), p. 33.

32. B. Behrens, 'The Whig Theory of the Constitution in the Reign of Charles II,' *Cambridge Historical Journal*, 7 (1941), p. 43.

33. See J. R. Jones, *op. cit.*, 'the nation was divided with a bitterness and intensity unknown in the eighteenth century,' p. 3.

34. See R. Hutton, *op. cit.*, and J. R. Jones, *op. cit.*, p. 64.

35. Grey, *op. cit.*, sig. X8v.

36. 'The Female Parricide' in *Poems on Affairs of State: Augustan Satirical Verse, 1660–1714*, 7 vols, ed. George deF. Lord (New Haven: Yale University Press, 1963–75), 5, p. 157.

37. B. Behrens, *op. cit.*, p. 53.

38. J. M. Wallace, *op. cit.*, p. 363.

39. Thompson, *op. cit.*, sig. K1r.

40. Spencer, *Nahum Tate op. cit.*, p. 74.

41. See Allardyce Nicoll, *A History of English Drama, 1660–1900*, 6 vols., 4th edn (Cambridge: Cambridge University Press, 1952–59), I, p. 351.

42. William Lilly, *Monarchy or No Monarchy in England* (London: Printed for Humfrey Blunden, 1651), sig. G2v.

43. See J. R. Jones, *op. cit.*, pp. 3–4.

44. Thomas Hobbes, *Leviathan*, ed. A. R. Waller (Cambridge: Cambridge University Press, 1935), p. 522.

45. J. Black, 'The Influence of Hobbes on Nahum Tate's *King Lear*,' *op. cit.*

46. Jones, *op. cit.*, p. 215. Jones further comments that if the Whigs 'evaded the fundamental causes of the crisis, and over-simplified the issues, this very crudity or simplicity of their approach increased its appeal' *op. cit.*, (p. 216).

47. Stephen Orgel and Roy Strong, *Inigo Jones: The Theatre of the Stuart Court*, 2 vols. (Berkeley: University of California Press, 1973), 2, p. 733.

48. See, especially, C. Spencer, 'A Word for Tate's *King Lear*,' *op. cit.*, and Black's 'Introduction' *op. cit.*; one might also wonder whether, as with other plays, the tidy theatrical packaging of Tate's *Lear*, with readymade sets, contributed to its long theatrical life.

3 Rewritten Women: Shakespearean Heroines in the Restoration

Jean I. Marsden

> I come unknown to any of the rest,
> To tell you news; I saw the lady drest;
> The woman plays to-day: mistake me not
> No man in gown, or page in petticoat.[1]

With the reopening of the London theatres in 1660, actresses appeared on the public stage consistently for the first time in English history.[2] The new female presence and new ideals of femininity which typified this female presence created major changes in the drama of the later seventeenth century. While the number of female characters increased, the nature of these roles was constricted, an outgrowth of social as well as theatrical change. Drama devoted new attention to the subjects of family, love and marriage, a development closely linked to the definition of women as inhabitants of the private or domestic sphere[3] and their exclusion from the public world of politics and commerce. Theatrical interest in what could be called the feminine realm found its strongest expression in the pathetic drama, a form which depends for its pathos on the sufferings of women.[4] These developments coincided with widespread adaptation of Shakespeare designed to accommodate his works to the later seventeenth-century theatre repertoire. In the process, Shakespearean women were radically revised to reflect social ideals, thus affecting the portrayal of subject matter, character, and genre in almost every play.

Restoration playwrights were quick to rework Shakespeare's plots in order to take advantage of the new dramatic possibilities the actresses offered. On the most basic level, there was the simple titillation value of seeing women on the stage, and many of the adaptations exploit this voyeuristic impulse by creating breeches roles for their new female characters. In addition to the successful adaptations of *Cymbeline* (1682) and *The Merchant of Venice* (1701) and the later, less popular, adaptations of *As You Like It* and *Twelfth Night*,[5] breeches roles were created for the character of Lady Elinor Butler in *The Misery of Civil War* (1680) and, several decades later, for Harriet in *Henry V* (1723), both deserted mistresses who rush off to war to seek out their unfaithful lovers. While the numerous breeches roles in Shakespeare's original plays allowed boy actors to play more realistic parts, the popularity of these roles in the Restoration and eighteenth century is clearly due to the opportunity they gave of showing off a well-turned feminine ankle.

A less obvious form of titillation developed out of the popularity of pathetic drama in the late seventeenth century. The pathetic plays strive to provoke the sympathy of their audience and depend for their effect on the sufferings of oppressed and helpless virtue. The object of this pathos is almost inevitably a woman. Robert D. Hume has described the pathetic play as 'the one important new mode established in the early [seventeen] eighties,'[6] but the impulse toward pathos appeared on the stage well before the genre of the pathetic play became established. Pathos as a dramatic device appears in almost all forms of drama after the Restoration, consistently absent only in the cynical sex comedies. This widespread introduction of pathos exposes deeper social and philosophical issues, depending as it does on the sufferings of women.

The change in women's roles within society after the Restoration has now become a critical and historical commonplace.[7] While not a simple causal relationship, the changes in women's social role correspond to changes in literary representation, particularly in the drama. Laura Brown has argued for the importance of social attitudes toward women in shaping the development of drama:

> The history of serious drama is closely wedded to the changing position of women in English society. The evolving attitudes toward property marriage, toward women's economic functions, toward the nature and importance of the family, and toward female chastity, which result, in part, in the eighteenth-century bourgeois cult of womanhood, produce a new female prototype that is reflected in the crucial role of the passive virtuous woman in these plays.[8]

But what was the Restoration idea of a virtuous woman? A brief survey of the attitude toward women expressed by contemporary courtesy books provides a useful backdrop for the portrayal of women in the adaptations. The conduct books are a particularly good source because, by their exemplary nature, they define proper female behaviour and thus present an idealised picture of femininity – a function filled also by the virtuous paragons in the adaptations of the late seventeenth and early eighteenth century. Conduct books most frequently describe proper feminine behaviour in terms of studious passivity, stressing the necessary role of 'meekness' in virtuous behaviour. Meekness appeared near the head of any list of a woman's virtues, identified as both a woman's

Christian duty and as a physiological necessity. In *The Ladies Calling* (1673), the most widely read of the courtesy books, Richard Allestree cites meekness as 'particularly enjoin'd to Women,' a virtue which 'even Nature seems to teach, which abhors monstrosities and disproportions, and therefore having allotted to women a more smooth and soft composition of body, infers thereby her intention, that the mind should correspond with it.'[9] In the eyes of Allestree and his contemporaries, passivity was part of a woman's physical as well as emotional nature. To act against its biological imperative could label the woman a 'monstrosity'.

In addition to discussing a woman's physiological nature, courtesy books stress that she inhabits a world which is distinctly different from that of her male contemporaries. As Allestree observes in his 'Preface', the temptations men are subject to are 'out of [women's] road', for while men 'converse in the world,' women do not.[10] A woman's 'world' is of limited compass, comprising her home and family, a constricted setting for which, Allestree adds, she should be grateful as it makes the path to virtue so much smoother. In contrast, men, the stronger and more resilient sex, were suited for 'converse' outside this world. In *The Lady's New-Years Gift* (1688), the Marquis of Halifax explained such differentiation to his daughter as the law of nature:

> You must first lay it down for a Foundation in general, that there is *Inequality* in *Sexes*, and that for the better Oeconomy of the World; the *Men* who were to be the Lawgivers, and the larger share of *Reason* bestowed upon them; by which means your sex is the better prepar'd for the *Compliance* that is necessary for the performance of those *duties* which seem'd to be most properly assign'd to it.[11]

Compliance, a passive virtue like meekness, becomes a necessary part of the female character, and a woman's 'duties', presumably marriage and motherhood, are dependent on this passivity. As Halifax explains, feminine submission is part of God's greater plan; to behave differently would be to go against nature.

The ideal woman could be said to be characterised by 'piety and devotion, meekness, modesty, submission', as in *The Vertuous Wife is the Glory of her Husband* (1667).[12] Paradoxically, these passive virtues are said to constitute her strengths as well as defining her emotive nature. As Allestree reminds his readers, 'the Female Sex, which being of softer mold, is more pliant and yielding to the impressions of pitty.'[13] Such feminine softness makes women particularly sensitive to the two 'most sensible passions', namely 'Fear and Love'.[14] This perception of women, prevalent throughout the later seventeenth and eighteenth centuries, corresponds to alterations made to Shakespeare's plays as, in keeping with the nature of the pathetic play, adaptors add scenes featuring helpless female virtue, ennobled by love and fraught by fear. With the possible exception of Desdemona and Ophelia, both of whom appeared virtually unaltered on the Restoration stage, Shakespeare's women are rarely meek and seldom passive. While many could qualify as monstrosities under Allestree's definition, the same is not true of female characters in the adaptations. Instead, the plays recreate a patriarchal system in which women have no power beyond the masochistic ability to arouse sympathy by their suffering,[15] an ability mirrored in the audience response to pathos. This suffering is rarely caused by the heroine's own wrong-doing; it results instead from her selfless love or from her passive attempts to defend her virtue against malefactors. In effect, virtuous women in these plays, as in pathetic drama, prove their virtue by their ability to suffer, and the adaptations abound with pictures of helpless women, suffering under the oppression of villains. Apart from a few of the female characters in the romantic comedies (rarely performed in the late seventeenth century), women who display impatient or aggressive tendencies are uniformly represented as villainesses such Regan, Goneril and Lady Macbeth.

Because the women of the adaptations inhabit a world different from that of their Shakespearean counterparts, a world in which women have been defined by their emotive qualities, they are excluded from the public world of politics and government. Good women are detached from their political context, leaving adaptors uncertain of how to treat women who are neither apolitical nor passive. Even, or perhaps especially, Shakespeare's strongest and least domestic women are rewritten to fit into this category. Dryden's All for Love (1677), although not strictly an adaptation, provides a succinct expression of the new Shakespearean heroine when Cleopatra, according to Dryden a 'pattern of unlawful love', laments her failure to conform to the feminine ideal and comments wistfully:

> Nature meant me
> A Wife, a silly harmless houshold Dove,
> Fond without art; and kind without deceit;
> But Fortune, that has made a Mistress of me,
> Has thrust me out to the wide World, unfurnish'd
> Of falshood to be happy.[16]

Cleopatra's words set up a dichotomy between the woman happy in her restricted domestic world and the woman who transgresses and moves beyond this realm into 'the wide World'. Cleopatra falls uncomfortably between these two extremes, wanting the 'proper' role, but forced unwillingly into impropriety by 'Fortune'. Her definition echoes the views of women's place expressed by Allestree: by nature good women cannot survive in the outside world – only those furnished with sufficient falseness can be happy. She has sinned because she has stepped outside the household into a realm where, as Allestree emphasised, the path to virtue is not so smooth. Other adaptors adhere to this vision of women, and rewritten characters like D'Urfey's Eugenia or Tate's Virgilia are just the domestic doves Cleopatra would like to be. Dryden's Cleopatra is still a queen, but her disclaimer suggests that, in the Restoration at least, uneasy lies the female head that wears a crown.

Ironically, one of the strongest statements regarding a woman's proper realm comes from the mouth of Lady Macbeth when, maddened by guilt, she faults her husband for listening to her advice:

> You were a Man.
> And by the Charter of your Sex you shou'd
> Have govern'd me, there was more crime in you
> When you obey'd my Councels, then I contracted
> By my giving it.[17]

This explanation negates the power of Shakespeare's Lady Macbeth by recasting her strength as Macbeth's weakness. The passage's legal language ('charter', 'Govern'd', 'crime', 'contracted') emphasises the natural law ('Charter of Sex') which makes it a 'crime' to step outside of approved sexual roles; women should not dabble in the public realm as does Lady Macbeth. Lady Macbeth is further marginalised by the increased focus on Lady Macduff, a harbinger of the passive heroines in the pathetic drama whose suffering brought vicarious pleasure to Restoration and eighteenth-century audiences. While Shakespeare's Lady Macduff appears only once, the thumbnail sketch Shakespeare gives of a wife and mother develops into a picture of wifely devotion, the great love interest of the play. She provides the play with a sympathetic moral voice as D'Avenant exploits the opposition between the Macbeths and the Macduffs, creating parallel scenes between the two couples. Every scene in which Lady Macbeth entices her husband into crime is juxtaposed with one in which Lady Macduff warns hers of ambition's evils and urges him to resist its temptation.

With few exceptions, the women in these plays are governed by love, either marital or maternal, while those women who do not display this feminine attribute are invariably villains, such as Lady Macbeth, the evil sisters in Lear, or Tamara in Titus Andronicus. Such a recasting of feminine nature requires major revisions to Shakespeare's works in general, for, while love is an important element in the romantic comedies and in some tragedies, it does not play a central role in the political plays and the histories. By contrast, in the adaptations a focus on love is no longer restricted by genre. Almost every play focuses on a love story; where no love story is present in the original plays, new plots are created; where a love interest seems understated, adaptors re-emphasise its importance, focusing attention more strongly on the domestic realm, marriage, love, and family. Even the political adaptations with their strong didactic messages move closer to the domestic realm than their Shakespearean originals. Virtuous kings and princes, like the ladies and gentlemen of other plays, are motivated by love above all else. Like the plays which preceded and followed them, they include a non-Shakespearean emphasis on love.[18]

Where love interests could already be said to exist, adaptors generally took one of two paths. Some, like D'Avenant, simply multiplied the number of couples in the plays. Faced with the lacklustre romances of *Measure for Measure*, D'Avenant added Beatrice and Benedict from *Much Ado about Nothing* and created a somewhat unconvincing attachment between Isabel and Angelo for good measure. In his *Macbeth* (1664) he augmented the role of Lady Macduff to provide a loving, domestic counterpart to Lady Macbeth, and, with Dryden's help, scattered couples throughout *The Tempest*; even Ariel has a helpmeet. Few playwrights had D'Avenant's fascination with balance; most chose to augment relationships which were present, if understated, in the original plays. Both Tate and Dennis stress the sentimental in their revisions of *Coriolanus*, and even the ill-fated adaptations of *Richard II* are careful to accentuate the affection between the doomed monarch and his queen.[19]

The emphasis on love necessitates a wholesale revision of most Shakespearean heroines in order to accommodate their new romantic function. Dryden, a consummate adaptor himself, articulated what many other playwrights clearly saw as a weakness in Shakespearean drama: 'Let us applaud his Scenes of Love; but, let us confess that he understood not either greatness or perfect honour in the parts of any of his women.'[20] Shakespeare's women lack what *The Ladies Dictionary* defines as that 'pliant and yielding nature'[21] conducive to self-abnegating love, the quality which provides the fount for female 'greatness' in Restoration pathetic drama. The desire to elevate Shakespeare's earthbound women dovetails with the generally acclaimed heightening effect of love, and, as a result, love becomes the ruling characteristic for virtuous women. It motivates all proper female action, and can only be checked by proper filial duty. To preserve the impression of feminine meekness and modesty, a woman should display initiative only if motivated by love, so that Portia in Gildon's *The Jew of Venice* (1701) explains that she disguised herself as the learned doctor in order to increase Bassanio's love for her. These changes have the cumulative effect of 'elevating' Shakespeare's women by flattening them into one-dimensional icons of virtue who, not surprisingly, share many characteristics with the idealised women described in conduct books. The emphasis on love as a defining characteristic erases many more active qualities and, because love acts as the general cause of female suffering, its prominence stresses the heroines' ability to suffer passively, once again evoking pathos. Moreover, emphasising a woman's role as loving and beloved defines her in relation to a man and de-emphasises her autonomy as well as her political significance. Thus Tate's Cordelia gives up her dowry and the political power it represents to remain true to her heart, and by the same token, D'Urfey's Imogen, significantly rebaptised Eugenia, a name which emphasises her noble birth rather than her link to any British Queen, loses her position as heir to the throne of Britain and, like Tate's Cordelia, sins by loving against her father's wishes rather than by creating a possible political misalliance. These rewritten women are Cleopatra's doves, paragons of a purely domestic realm where home and family are the only honourable concerns.

The most notorious of the superadded love interests appears in Tate's *King Lear*, where Tate creates a long-standing attachment between Cordelia and Edgar, two characters who, as Tate himself notes, never speak to each other in Shakespeare's play. Tate congratulates himself on the discovery of this structural and emotional bonus:

> 'Twas my good Fortune to light on one Expedient to rectifie what was wanting in the Regularity and probability of the Tale, which was to run throught the whole, a *Love* betwixt *Edgar* and *Cordelia*, that never chang'd word with each other in the Original. This renders *Cordelia*'s Indifference and her Father's Passion in the first scene probable. It likewise gives Countenance to *Edgar*'s Disguise, making that a generous Design that was before a poor Shift to save his Life. The Distress of the Story is evidently heightened by it.[22]

Tate's goal, to 'rectifie' a wrong and make what was improbable probable, hinges on the characterization of Cordelia who represents the major source of *King Lear*'s improbability. By furnishing her with a love interest, Tate provides a motive for her seeming lack of filial tenderness which thus becomes more 'probable'; lack of filial duty is unnatural, but romantic love is not. Cordelia's elevation into a pattern of virtuous love brings a corresponding change in Edgar, and the result is more 'distress' or pathos for the audience to savour. Tate here makes explicit not only the link between suffering and dramatic pleasure, but also the role love plays in inducing such suffering.

Revised to fit in with Tate's rubric of probability, Cordelia's comments in the opening scene are motivated entirely by her love for Edgar and her desire to avoid the political marriage sanctioned by her father. Torn by her duty to her father and her selfless love for the noble Edgar, she explains her plight to the audience:

> Now comes my Trial, how am I distrest,
> That must with cold speech tempt the chol'rick King
> Rather to leave me Dowerless, than condemn me
> To loath'd Embraces![23]

What could be seen as the dross of Cordelia's character, her seemingly harsh answer to her father, is refined into an act of maiden purity. Thus Cordelia's character is defined by her affection for her father and for Edgar, and she rarely ventures beyond the limits of these familial and romantic concerns. Unlike her Shakespearean original, she does not appear at the head of an army avenging her father's wrongs. Instead, Edgar leads the army while Cordelia's only weapons are her beauty and her tears. Ironically, in view of the frequent citation in contemporary conduct books of tears as one of the most powerful weapons in a woman's arsenal,[24] Cordelia's tears are unavailing when she is faced with danger: unable to help herself, she must await the assistance of Edgar or her father.

In other plays, adaptors kept the pre-existing love interests, but, through careful cutting and rewriting, made these love interests the central focus of the plays. Adaptors of *Cymbeline* and *Troilus and Cressida*, two plays in which love is only one aspect of a multi-plotted drama, foreground the romantic stories while discarding other characters and subplots which they found irrelevant. In *Troilus and Cressida* (1678), Dryden's energies are directed toward reshaping Shakespeare's portrayal of two flawed lovers into a tragic story of star-crossed love – hence the subtitle 'Truth Found Too Late.' Carrying out this interpretation requires considerable pruning and reshaping: Dryden trims away many of the scenes depicting the Greek camp to focus attention on the story of Troilus and Cressida.[25] His portrayal of virtuous and faithful lovers causes radical alterations to Shakespeare's play. Dryden's Cressida is a virtuous maid who agrees to spend the night with her lover only when Troilus promises to marry her, and whose constancy never wavers. This premise necessitates major changes once Cressida arrives in the Greek camp: while Dryden follows the general outline of Shakespeare's play, he carefully explains the reasons behind the conduct of his characters. A faithful daughter as well as a faithful lover, Dryden's Cressida feigns love to Diomede only as a means to help her father escape back to Troy. As Calchas explains:

> You must dissemble love to *Diomede* still:
> False *Diomede*, bred in *Ulysses* School,
> Can never be deceiv'd,
> But by strong Arts and blandishments of love:
> Put 'em in practice all; seem lost and won,
> And draw him on, and give him line again.
> This *Argus* then may close his hundred eyes
> And leave our flight more easy.[26]

When Cressida asks, 'How can I answer this to love and *Troilus?*' her father replies, 'Why 'tis for him you do it' (IV, ii, 262-3). Dryden's adaptation stresses the fact of Cressida's innocence, the 'truth' which was found too late. This emphasis forces a conclusion rife with the sense of tragic romantic closure which Shakespeare's play so carefully avoids.

Troilus accuses Cressida of infidelity but refuses to listen to her pleas of innocence. To prove her point, she stabs herself, and the play ends in a blood bath. When the 'truth' which has defined Cressida's character is questioned, self-destruction becomes her only means of expressing herself and reinstating her virtue. She is not allowed to exist as a cipher, virtuous but dishonoured. Death removes that ambiguity, allowing her to remain an exemplary pathetic heroine, chaste and silent forever.

By stressing the pathos of the defenceless woman, such alterations better fitted Shakespeare to the dramatic climate of the Restoration and to the eighteenth century. A generation later, an anonymous critic praises both Tate's *Lear* and Hill's *Henry V* for their skilful interpolation of love interests. In a pamphlet letter to Colley Cibber he advises Cibber to follow their example:

> An Instance of improving or heightening a Character we have in *Edgar*, (in *King Lear*) as well as in *Cordelia*, between whom a Love Episode is not ill woven. – Another yet stronger is in *Catherine* (in *Henry* the fifth) whose Character in *Shakespear* is abominably low and obscene – The Improvement of her's has naturally rais'd that of *Harry* – Other Instances might be produced to shew, where *Shakespear* might admit, with great Beauty and Propriety, of strong Alterations, nay Amendments.[27]

Echoing Dryden's sense of the 'lowness' of many Shakespearean heroines, the author advocates love as the great ennobler, thus attesting to the success of the early adaptations. As with Tate's own comments on *Lear*, the author associates a 'heightened' or 'improved' female character with love, once again reiterating the views found in conduct book descriptions of female character.[28] The motif of height, used repeatedly in discussions of Shakespeare's women, suggests a hierarchical conception of drama which corresponds to the role played by women. Laura Brown claims correctly that the 'development of English tragedy is bound to the ideology of the defenseless woman,'[29] but this statement should be expanded to include the pathetic play and its precursors. These 'higher' forms of serious drama depend for their emotional impact on the sufferings of a helpless but virtuous woman, her character 'elevated' by love and self-denial.

Because of the essential connection between the suffering woman and serious drama, the issue of genre becomes key to the fate of Shakespeare's heroines. Shakespearean tragedies and histories were popular throughout the late seventeenth century, but, with the exception of the D'Avenant/Dryden *Tempest*, Shakespeare's comedies were rarely performed before 1700.[30] Restoration theatre depended instead on a variety of different modes of comedy,[31] most notably the so-called Comedy of Manners in which ladies and gentlemen of polite society engage in witty banter and which frequently contains an underlying current of contemporary social satire. Comparing the portrayal of women in drama to those in fiction, Jane Spencer is only partially correct when she describes women in Restoration drama as 'passionate, sexual being[s]' in contrast to 'the innocent, passionless, easily deceived creature gaining ascendancy in [the fiction of] the early eighteenth century.'[32] Those characters which Spencer describes as passionate and sexual are, however, the heroines of Restoration comedies, plays built around the issue of marriage and frequently dependent on marriage to establish a sense of comic closure. Women can be portrayed as more active and outspoken because their power is once again limited to the domestic realm. Despite their wit and passion, they are still to some extent 'harmless houshold Dove[s]'. More common in the tragedies, pathetic plays, and later so-called sentimental comedies are characters who act as exemplary figures, suffering patiently at the hands of a villain, thus not only proving their own innocence by their inability to react aggressively, but also providing concrete evidence of the villainy of their oppressors.[33]

The pathos of passive female virtue appears in its most extreme form in the adaptors' fondness for scenes of attempted rape. While the threat of rape is uncommon in Shakespeare's plays,[34] it appears repeatedly in the adaptations. In *The Injured Princess* (1682), D'Urfey creates a new character, Pisanio's virtuous daughter Clarinda, to share the role of innocent victim with Imogen/Eugenia. In a series of new scenes heavily laden with sensationalist melodrama, the Queen accuses Clarinda of foiling her plans by helping Eugenia escape. Cloten and his drunken companion Jachimo (the Shakespearean Jachimo has been rebaptised Shattillion) promise to provide 'punishment' and prepare to rape her. Pisanio arrives in the nick of time and kills Jachimo just as he is about to carry out his evil designs. Likewise, in Tate's *Lear*, Edmund, not content with Regan and Goneril, compounds his villainy by resolving to kidnap Cordelia:

> Where like the vig'rous *Jove* I will enjoy
> This *Semele* in a Storm, 'twill deaf her Cries
> Like Drums in Battle, lest her Groans shou'd pierce
> My pittying Ear, and make the amorous Fight less fierce.[35]

Fortunately, Edgar appears just in time to save Cordelia, and she is able to beseech him piteously to 'befriend a wretched Virgin' (III, iv, 33). Tate uses the titillation of attempted rape yet again in *The Ingratitude of a Common-Wealth* (1681), his adaptation of *Coriolanus*, where Aufidius plans to 'glut' his last minutes by raping Virgilia (who has come to find her husband), taunting Coriolanus that 'to thy Face I'll Force her . . . And in Revenges Sweets and Loves, Expire'.[36] Once again this evil is thwarted, but tragically, for Virgilia has chosen to die rather than meet a fate worse than death. She explains her suicide in terms of preserving a commodity as rape becomes a theft rather than a violation:

> My Noble *Martius*, 'tis a *Roman* Wound,
> Giv'n by *Virgilia*'s Hand, that rather chose
> To sink this Vessel in a Sea of Blood,
> Than to suffer its chast Treasure, to become
> Th' unhallowed *Pyrates* Prize.[37]

Virgilia here follows the example of Lucrece, another Roman matron, preserving her honour by destroying herself. She acts to protect her virtue, but can do so only in a negative way, sinking the vessel rather than saving it. Dryden's Cressida reacts similarly when her virtue is called into question. For the virtuous women in the adaptations, suicide is an acceptable alternative action. It reaffirms both virtue and femininity while completing the picture of pathetic suffering.

In each case the attempted rape functions to establish moral distinctions. It represents an assault on innocent virtue and provides clear evidence of villainy, making the distance between good and evil characters more obvious. The scenes present an obvious exposition of masculine evil. By being set in opposition to this evil, female virtue, particularly virtue in the form of chastity, is made to appear more absolute. Only pure, virtuous women are the victims of would-be rapists (who are attracted by their very innocence) as the plays suggest that only true chastity can be threatened by rape. Thus, in these scenes, an attempted rape becomes perverse proof that such chastity exists. If the character is not virtuous, rape cannot be a threat. Such chastity, and by extension feminine virtue in general, is a valuable commodity which becomes useless if marred; hence the suicide of characters such as Virgilia and Cressida. Chaste virtue must be destroyed if damaged because it has become a contradiction in terms.[38]

The scenes of near-rape suggest the disturbing implications of passive womanhood and provide a harsh illustration of the ways Shakespeare's women have been rewritten to accommodate a new patriarchal agenda. These scenes problematise the helplessness characteristic of the idealised women found in literature and social documents such as the Restoration conduct books. Perversely, it is a woman's purity that attracts her ravisher, and her passivity that prevents her from repelling his attack. Thus the depiction of women as icons of virtue also leaves them defenceless against the world, seemingly glorifying them while actually camouflaging their ultimate victimisation. Passive rather than active, meek rather than aggressive, these paragons of virtue cannot survive outside their narrowly defined sphere. Simultaneously elevated and exploited, they provide a spectacle of female suffering which underscores the contradictory nature of a world where chastity represents sexuality and pathos becomes a source of pleasure.

Notes

1. 'Prologue' to *Othello*, performed 8 December 1660.
2. Actresses had long since been performing in other parts of Europe. Spain, for example, had never used boy actors to play women's parts while in France actresses had been on the stage throughout the seventeenth century, even appearing occasionally on the English stage, as in 1635 when Queen Henrietta Maria imported a troupe of French actors and actresses.
3. This development has been documented by many feminist historians, beginning with Alice Clark's landmark study *The Working Life of Women in the Seventeenth Century* (1919, rpt. New York: Augustus M. Kelley, 1968). See also Robert D. Hume's discussion of the position of women and its effect on comedy in the later seventeenth century, 'Marital Discord in English Comedy from Dryden to Fielding,' *Modern Philology*, 74 (1977), pp. 248–72. The essay has been reprinted more recently in a collection of Hume's essays, *The Rakish Stage: Studies in English Drama, 1660–1800* (Carbondale, Illinois: Southern Illinois University Press, 1983), pp. 176–213.
4. In her assessment of the new 'myth of passive womanhood', Ellen Pollak notes, 'Concern with the practical responsibilities of females had become markedly less pronounced. The predominant emphasis of popular writings was now on the inculcation of a code of manners which sought to insure self-mastery in women, rather than on the provision of a practical means for acquiring more externally oriented forms of competence.' *The Poetics of Sexual Myth: Gender and Ideology in the Verse of Swift and Pope* (Chicago: University of Chicago Press, 1985), p. 42.
5. *As You Like It* appeared as Charles Johnson's *Love in a Forest* (1723) and *Twelfth Night* as William Burnaby's *Love Betray'd; Or, the Agreeable Disapointment* (1703).
6. Robert D. Hume, *The Development of English Drama in the Late Seventeenth Century* (Oxford: Oxford University Press, 1976), p. 350.
7. Critics and historians have approached the topic from a variety of angles. For two different views see Clark, *The Working Life of Women in the Seventeenth Century* and Lawrence Stone, *The Family, Sex and Marriage in England 1500–1800* (New York: Harper and Row, 1977).
8. Laura Brown, *English Dramatic Form, 1660–1760* (New Haven: Yale University Press, 1981), p. 99. Brown develops this idea in a later article, 'The Defenseless Woman and the Development of English Tragedy,' *Studies in English Literature 1500–1900* vol. 22, no. 3 (Summer 1982), pp. 429–43.
9. Richard Allestree, *The Ladies Calling* (Oxford, 1673), p. 29.
10. R. Allestree, *op. cit.*, 'The Preface'.
11. George Savile, Marquis of Halifax, *The Lady's New-Years Gift: Or, Advice to a Daughter* (London, 1688), p. 26.
12. *The Vertuous Wife is the Glory of her Husband* (1667), p. 9.
13. R. Allestree, *op. cit.*, p. 49.
14. *ibid.*, p. 81.

15. Conduct books stress that a woman's strongest weapons are her passive virtues. When wrongfully accused of adultery, for example, a woman should not defend herself with angry words, but with an additional show of meekness and modesty (see R. Allestree, *op. cit.*, 'Of Wives').

16. John Dryden, *All for Love* in *The Works of John Dryden* (Berkeley: University of California Press, 1984), IV, 1, 91–6.

17. William D'Avenant, *Macbeth* in *Five Restoration Adaptations of Shakespeare*, ed. Christopher Spencer (Urbana: University of Illinois Press, 1965), IV, iv, 54–7.

18. Thomas Otway's *Caius Marius* (1679) is the one exception as Otway sacrifices some of the focus on the love plot to a new emphasis on politics. In arguing that domesticity and politics can coexist I differ from Matthew H. Wikander who downplays this juncture. (See Wikander, 'The Spitted Infant: Scenic Emblem and Exclusionist Politics in Restoration Adaptations of Shakespeare,' *Shakespeare Quarterly*, vol. 37, no. 3, pp. 340–58.)

19. The list of new love interests is long. By my calculations, new or augmented love interests appear in at least nine of the approximately sixteen adaptations of Shakespeare which appeared before 1700.

20. John Dryden, *A Defence of the Epilogue, Or, An Essay on the Dramatic Poetry of the Last Age* (1672) in *Of Dramatic Poesy and Other Critical Essays*, ed. George Watson (London: J. M. Dent and Sons, Ltd., 1962), vol. I, p. 182.

21. *The Ladies Dictionary; Being a General Entertainment for the Fair Sex* (1694), p. 136.

22. Nahum Tate, 'Dedication' to *The History of King Lear* in *Five Restoration Adaptations of Shakespeare*, ed. C. Spencer, *op. cit.*

23. N. Tate, *King Lear*, I, i, 92–6, in C. Spencer (ed.), *op. cit.*

24. 'You have more strength in your *Looks*, then we have in our *Laws*; and more power by your *Tears*, than we have by our *Arguments*' (Halifax, *The Lady's New-Years Gift*, *op. cit.*, p. 28).

25. The Trojans thus become the heroes of the play, in keeping with Dryden's patriotic promise to tell 'how *Trojan* valour did the *Greek* excell' and 'Your great forefathers shall their fame regain.' ('Prologue,' *Troilus and Cressida* in *The Works of John Dryden*, vol. XIII, 1, 38; 39).

26. J. Dryden, *Troilus and Cressida*, *op. cit.*, IV, ii, 254–61.

27. Anon., 'A Letter to *Colley Cibber*, Esq; On His Transformance of *King John*' (London, 1745), p. 12. In contrast to his praise for Tate's *Lear* and Hill's *Henry V*, the author of the pamphlet is unrelentingly critical of Cibber's adaptation.

28. In Shakespeare's *Henry V* Catherine's character appears only in two broadly comic scenes which turn upon bilingual play of language; in Aaron Hill's version she becomes a central figure whose love for Henry V, as the author states, 'improves' her character and thus 'raises' the entire play.

29. L. Brown, 'The Defenseless Woman and the Development of English Tragedy,' *op. cit.*, p. 443.

30. *The London Stage* cites only the following: *The Comedy of Errors* (evidence that it was acted, probably in the 1670s); *The Merry Wives of Windsor* (1660, 1661, 1667, 1675, 1691); *A Midsummer Night's Dream* (1662; later the play was used as the basis for Purcell's opera *The Fairy Queen*, 1692–3); *Twelfth Night* (1661). As these figures indicate, the comedies appeared most frequently shortly after the theatres opened when the repertoire was limited and managers needed ready-made plays. Many of the other comedies were

assigned to companies, but there is no evidence that they were ever acted. The tragedies and histories were performed at least two or three times as often. Although the records for the later seventeenth century in *The London Stage* are not complete, these listings suggest that Shakespearean comedy was not popular at this time.

31. Three essays in Robert D. Hume's *The Rakish Stage, op. cit.*, deal directly with this topic: '"Restoration Comedy" and its Audiences, 1660–1776' (with Arthur Scouten), 'Marital Discord in English Comedy from Dryden to Fielding,' and 'The Multifarious Forms of Eighteenth-Century Comedy.'

32. Jane Spencer, *The Rise of the Woman Moralist* (Oxford: Basil Blackwell Ltd, 1986), p. 58

33. Laura Brown discusses the role of the exemplary female character in *English Dramatic Form: 1660–1760, op. cit.* See especially chapters three, 'Affective Tragedy,' and five, 'Dramatic Moral Action'.

34. Actual rape (as opposed to symbolic rape) is rare in Shakespeare. The only rape which occurs is the rape of Lavinia in *Titus Andronicus*. Two other contemplated rapes are mocked: in *Pericles*, the attempt to ravish Marina by selling her to a brothel backfires ridiculously when, rather than losing her virtue, she manages to convert all potential ravishers, thus destroying the brothel's formerly profitable business; and in *Cymbeline*, Cloten declares his intention to kill Posthumus and rape Imogen in a burst of bravado, a boast he does not put into effect.

35. N. Tate, *King Lear*, II, ii, 122–5, in C. Spencer (ed.), *op. cit.*

36. Nahum Tate, *The Ingratitude of a Commonwealth* (1681), p. 60.

37. *ibid.*, p. 61.

38. My discussion of the function of rape in the adaptations is indebted to Susan Staves and her discussion of attempted rape in the works of Fielding in a paper given at the Houghton Library in February, 1987.

4   Shakespeare in Quotation Marks

Margreta de Grazia

A new longing for writing in Shakespeare's own person emerged in the later eighteenth century. The Shakespearean corpus as defined by the 1623 Folio was a dramatic corpus consisting exclusively of plays in a plurality of voices, none of which could be assuredly identified with Shakespeare. In hope of supplying this lack, Shakespeareans searched for the letters Shakespeare was imagined to have written to friends and family in Stratford during his visits to London.[1] With more consequence, they took an unprecedented interest in Shakespeare's Sonnets, the only work ostensibly written in his own person.[2] At the same time that chests were rifled for letters and sonnets probed for revelations, a new bibliographic format was devised to enable Shakespeare to speak for himself. From the middle of the eighteenth century through the nineteenth and beyond, Shakespeare circulated in volumes of collected quotations. Whether or not references were provided, the format gave the impression that Shakespeare himself was speaking directly through the quotations. This essay will consider this emergent form in the context of what appears to be a new preoccupation with *who spoke what*, with the proper attribution and the accurate reproduction of written materials.

I

Although the most frequently quoted author in English, Shakespeare himself did not use quotation marks to distinguish the words of another from his own. This is not simply because the playtext form in which he primarily wrote admitted no authorial first person; nor is it because in his playtexts speech prefixes and typographical spacing distinguished one person's words from another's. Even in those cases when one character quotes another, quotation marks are not used. When Feste recalls Malvolio's taunt, when Macbeth remembers the witches' prophecy, when Hamlet repeats the Ghost's injunction, no quotation marks appear in the quartos or Folio to signal that the words had been spoken earlier, and by another. Sometimes a colon or comma would function to separate the enunciating speaker from the cited one, but for the purpose of marking grammatical breaks rather than setting off 'lifted' passages. Whether the punctuation, or lack of it, reflects Shakespeare's practice or that of the printing house is mainly irrelevant, for the convention of flagging speech originating elsewhere – in another text, in another speaker – is relatively recent. Only toward the end of the eighteenth century did grammar books make quotation marks mandatory.[3] Only then did novels begin uniformly to bracket off passages in order to distinguish the words of one character from those of another or of the narrator.[4]

In Shakespeare's time, quotation marks were never used to enclose passages. Commas and inverted commas, single and double, were generally placed only at the onset of a passage. They were used interchangeably with the pointing index finger that directed the reader's eye to passages of special note, pointing the reader to a special point. Both signals appeared in the margin rather than within the text itself, the space where aids to the reader were supplied. The word 'quotation' stemmed from *quotation quadrants*, the instruments used to measure the distance between passages printed in the margin.[5] Accordingly, 'quotations' were originally notices in the margin intended to catch the reader's attention. They instructed the reader to look: *to quote* was *to mark* in the double sense of making a mark but also of heeding or minding it, a double sense preserved in the still current locution, 'mark my words.'[6] Quotation marks highlighted remarkable passages, tried and true passages that deserved to be re-marked, marked again after their initial marking in characters. They thus indicated not that a passage originated elsewhere, but rather simply that it was important. (Italicized print served the same function.[7]) These import-ant passages were generally *sententiae* or commonplaces, authoritative statements drawn from the great books of the past, primarily the Bible and the ancient classics.[8] It was not every utterance, therefore, that could qualify for quotation: only important ones uttered by authorities whose words had been validated over the ages, authoritative authors who were invariably dead.[9] Erasmus's *Adagia* (1536), one of the most popular books of the Renaissance, contained well over 4,000 adages from classical authors and authorities. Quotation marks functioned to separate not one writer's words from another's, but *contingent* words (subject to error) from *certain* words (established by authority, confirmed by consensus). The quotation marks surrounding a passage now serve to fence in a passage as property of another; in earlier centuries, however, they served to advertise its appropriability. They now mark off private property; before the eighteenth century, they signalled communal ground or commonplaces. They marked material to be copied by readers in their copy-books or commonplace books, thereby assuring that the common-places would become more common still. By simply perusing the margins of a text, readers might lift material for their own personalised storehouse of wise and therefore widely applicable sayings.

By no means commonplace in the present sense of worn or trite, *sententiae* or commonplaces issued from the commonplace tradition that originated in the *Topics* of Aristotle and Cicero and extended to sixteenth-century England via Boethius, Agricola, and Thomas Wilson, the last of whom translated the Greek *eikonos topoi* and the Latin *locis communis* as commonplaces.[10] The topics were both rhetorical and dialectical classifications in which traditional wisdom was stored. In preparing to make an argument or speech, a writer or speaker could run through the *places* in order to extract proper arguments or tropes. Derived from authority and verified by consensus, they were regarded as valid bases for making both logical and rhetorical statements; they provided the general truths by which to treat particular cases.

In addition to having an established relation to truth, the topics had an affinity to memory. Both were imagined as spatial constructs. The *topoi* or *loci* were represented as literal *places*, as in the following description from the first logic published in England comparing the finding or coming upon (inventing) *places* to coney-catching and fox-hunting:

> For these places be nothyng else but couertes or boroughes, wherein if any one searche diligentlie, he maie fynde game at pleasure. And although perhappes one place fayle him, yet shal he finde a dousen other places, to accomplishe his purpose.[11]

Their spatial dimension made them particularly amenable to the classical art of memory as described in *Ad Herennium* as well as by Cicero and Quintillian, a mnemonic system consisting of a series of places (generally of a building, a theatre, for example) to which the points of a speech or subject were keyed. The places were transported to the compartments of memory.[12] In the realm of the occult, a properly structured and informed memory was thought to impart magical knowledge and power to the bearer on the assumption that its divisions corresponded with the cosmic system itself.[13] In more mundane contexts too, commonplaces were associated with memory; the memory, imagined as a wax tablet, was inscribed with authoritative biblical and humanistic texts. Quotation marks reproduced this long-standing association of commonplaces and memory; they signalled what was memorable or worth commemorating, what deserved to be inscribed, or reinscribed, on those two writing surfaces or tablets: the memory or the commonplace book.[14]

Thus quotation in Shakespeare's time attested to, and confirmed, the special status of a passage; its source was of concern only insofar as it

accounted for its authority. That it originated elsewhere was less important than its possession of superior moral, theological, and philosophical
validity. Quotation marks did not indicate the exclusivity of the locution
but rather its communality: a commonplace belonged everywhere and to
everyone. According to the entries in the OED, it was not until the end of
the eighteenth century, that *commonplace* was used pejoratively to denote
not what was true on the basis of authority and consensus but what was
platitudinous because commonly or vulgarly known. Not until then, too,
did *sententious* take on the sense of pompous rather than pithy, meaningful, and generally applicable.

At the same time that quotation marks moved from the white border of
the page into the text itself, they came to be considered a form of
punctuation rather than a cue to the reader. In Renaissance grammars,
however, they are nowhere mentioned, for punctuation and pointing,
both deriving from *punctum*, distributed four types of small points (.,;:) to
indicate stops or pauses at grammatical divisions; they signalled intervals
during which an orator could take a breath. Ben Jonson follows classical
tradition in describing the purpose of these points, in a sentence itself
meticulously pointed:

> For, whereas our breath is by nature so short, that we cannot continue
> without a stay to speake long together; it was thought necessarie as well for
> the speakers ease, as for the plainer deliverance of the things spoken to
> invent this meanes, whereby men pausing a pretty while, the whole speech
> might never the worse be understood.[15]

Quotation marks in the Renaissance contribute nothing to a passage's
grammatical structure or its mode of delivery, functioning instead to
distinguish a passage as authoritative and therefore noteworthy.[16] By the
end of the eighteenth century, the position and function of quotation
marks has shifted, even reversed itself. Within the text itself rather than
on its periphery, they enclose rather than highlight passages, drawing
attention to words that are imported from elsewhere rather than important words; belonging to one speaker or writer rather than to all. Different
criteria determine what is quotable: anyone can be quoted, not just
authorities. And as we shall see, when quotation marks enter the text
proper to rope off textual pieces, a new guarantee is constituted: not only
that the text has been properly assigned, but that it has been accurately
duplicated.

II

In the second half of the eighteenth century, books of Shakespearean
quotations begin to proliferate, beginning in 1752 with William Dodd's

Beauties of Shakspear, reprinted through the nineteenth century thirty-nine times.[17] The book's extraordinary popularity is generally taken as a sign of Shakespeare's ever-expanding reputation, its publication occurring so near the event that is often taken to mark the beginning of Shakespeare bardolatry, the 1769 Shakespeare Jubilee. While such an explanation accounts for the increase in any form of Shakespearean publication or performance, it does not explain this particular phenomenon. The book's popularity finds a more specific explanation in the same impulse as that underlying the emergence of compulsory quotation marks: the impulse to identify exactly what was said and by whom. In fact, as we shall see, the changes introduced to the compendia's formatting between the first edition and its later eighteenth-century reprints suggest the same shift in what qualifies as quotable material. Dodd's original edition is clearly an extension of the commonplace tradition; the principles governing his selection and organization of quotations derive from the topics or places of rhetoric and logic. When his compilation is reproduced at the end of the century, however, it loses this relation and becomes instead a register of Shakespeare's singular utterances.

Shakespeare was first anthologized in 1600 in two collections of quotations, John Bodenham's *Belvedere, or the Garden of the Muses* and *England's Parnassus* generally attributed to Robert Allot.[18] While collections of select passages had appeared in Latin and Greek, and while collections of select passages from the classics and the Bible had appeared in English, these were the first collections to include contemporary English writers.[19] Both anthologies were designed to offer readers passages by which to enrich and refine their own speech and writing. Each entry offered itself up under a topic alphabetically listed: Abstinence, Adversitie, Affection, Ambition, etc. Under any given 'head' or 'argument' the writer or speaker could cull his material, choosing the appropriate 'most learned, graue, and wittie sentences'. It is easy to see how these publications were put to use within the commonplace tradition. A rhetorician or logician needed simply to turn to the appropriate place and extract suitable arguments or tropes and schemes. The collections facilitated the acquisition of literary and philosophical competence by providing authoritative and tested materials.

The same tradition is evident in 1657 and 1677 when another compendium of quotes was published: *The English Parnassus: or, A Helpe To English Poesie . . . with some General Forms upon all Occasions, Subjects, and Theams, Alphabetically digested.* That the purpose of this publication was to assist readers in their own speaking and writing rather than to preserve the best lines from the best authors is more apparent still. Although the names of 'The Books principally made use of in compiling of this Work' are listed at the beginning of the collection, no names are subscribed to the quotations.[20] Even more surprising, the quotations under any given category are not even distinguished by spacing. One author's words run head on into another's, as Shakespeare's can be seen to do in the following selection from *Sleep*:

> He that knits up the ravell'd sleave of care.
> The death of each dayes life. Sore labours bath,
> Balme of hurt minds. Great natures second course.
> Chief nourisher in lifes feast. Peacefull sleepe,
> All care and anguish doth in Lethe steepe
> When sleep his poppy on the temples sheds . . .[21]

The format is designed not to differentiate one writer's words from another but rather to accommodate the reader's needs by providing an organised storehouse of material, 'for the greater ease and conversion of those that shall be desirous to advance themselves thereby.'

Separating Dodd's collection from the earlier compendia is the neo-classical critical tradition of determining Beauties and Faults, an exercise that required and refined the generally interchangeable faculties of Taste, Judgement, and Reason. Analysis of an author's Beauties and Faults (Excellencies and Blemishes) involved major critical issues, the rivalry between art and nature, for example, or between rules and genius.[22] Dryden was apparently the first to apply the categories to Shakespeare, but the major eighteenth-century editors from Rowe (1709) to Samuel Johnson in 1765 regarded the judging of Beauties and Faults as one of the editor's major duties.[23] Alexander Pope proved the most notorious practitioner of this mode of criticism: in editing Shakespeare's Works (1725), he signalled 'shining passages' with a quotation mark and dropped inferior ones to the bottom of the page. Although his use of the quotation cipher has been considered quite arbitrary, it was perfectly in keeping with sixteenth- and seventeenth-century practices of drawing attention to notable passages. In fact, a good many of Pope's 'shining passages' are *sententiae*. (In *Hamlet*, for example, Polonius's advice to Laertes and Claudius's attempt to pray are applauded.[24]) The majority of the rest also fall readily into the places of the earlier rhetorical and logical tradition, for they tend to be self-contained passages that need not depend on their dramatic context. Warburton (1745) followed Pope's arbitrations and to a lesser degree so did Hanmer (1747). Dodd's collection contains many of the passages these editors highlighted; in fact, Dodd's format suggests that he went through the plays much as Pope had, marking distinguished passages which he then transcribed for publication.

Though Johnson, in editing the Works, avoided Pope's typographic system of evaluating Shakespeare, his judicial comments abound in the final remarks to each of the plays. In his preface, he claims to have exercised only as much judgement as would suffice to instruct the reader himself to become a 'candidate of criticism'.[25] Like Pope, Johnson maintained that Shakespeare's vices matched, even surpassed, his virtues: 'Shakespeare with his excellencies has likewise faults, and faults sufficient to obscure and overwhelm any other merit';[26] it was therefore as necessary to censure as to applaud him. It was particularly in respect to morality that Johnson faulted him: 'his precepts and axioms drop casually from him; he makes no just distribution of good or evil, nor is always careful to shew in the virtuous a disapprobation of the wicked.'[27] It was precisely because Shakespeare afforded, in Pope's words, 'the most numerous as well as the most conspicuous instances, both of Beauties and Faults of all sorts' that he provided the 'fairest and fullest subject for Criticism', the best material for developing and refining Taste.[28] Thus while Johnson proposed 'that from his works may be collected a system of civil and oeconomical prudence,' he warned against extrapolating such a system solely from 'particular passages': 'he that tries to recommend him by select quotations will succeed like the pedant . . . who, when he offered his house to sale, carried a brick in his pocket as a specimen.'[29] Shakespeare could be instructive only in the context of the critic's arbitrations.

Though Dodd entitled his collection the *Beauties of Shakspear* rather than *Beauties and Faults*, he seems to have shared Johnson's belief that enthusiasm for Shakespeare had to be tempered by judicious criticism. In both the 1752 and the revised 1780 editions, Dodd sometimes puts forth negative judgements of Shakespeare, both after each 'Beauty' and in the final remarks to each play. Dodd's efforts, like those of Shakespeare's editors from Rowe to Johnson, must be seen in the light of an expansive cultural project of cultivating the reader's Taste, his and her aesthetic and moral judgement. The *Spectator* and the *Tatler* concerned themselves with the same project; Addison comments that his primary purpose as a critic is to teach the reader to love Beauties and loath Faults.[30] All the major critical treatises of the period featured similar discussions in which quotations from Shakespeare served as prime examples. Edward Bysshe's *The Art of English Poetry* (1702) includes a 'Collection of Beauties'; Charles Gildon's *The Complete Art of Poetry* (1712) features a section entitled 'Shakespeareana: Most beautiful topics, descriptions, and similes . . .'; Lord Kames's *Elements of Criticism* (1762) is extensively illustrated with Shakespearean quotations. Shakespeare is quoted in all these publications – anthologies, editions, periodicals, and critical essays – because, in all of his irregularity, he offers 'the fairest and fullest subject for Criticism', providing the critic with both positive and negative examples of moral probity and literary decorum.

In the same way that the quotations from *Belvedere, England's Parnassus* and *English Parnassus* should be seen as adjuncts to the commonplace tradition that collected and organised all that it was necessary to know, so

Dodd's *Beauties* belongs in the context of the larger project of cultivating stylistic and ethical Judgement. Other collections of Shakespearean quotations followed suit, notably one anonymously prepared and also entitled *The Beauties of Shakspeare* (1784) that aimed at 'inculcating the noblest system of morality.' Mrs. Elizabeth Griffith's *The Morality of Shakespeare's Drama Illustrated* (1775) was another popular collection of quotations, organised like Dodd's by play, act, and scene. Insisting that 'our Author's poetic beauties are undoubtedly so striking as scarcely to require the being particularly pointed out,' Griffith focuses on his moral precepts. Like Dodd, she does not leave Shakespeare to speak for himself: more often than not, morality lies 'couched in Fable' and must be discovered by her commentary: 'I have given his moral instruction in detail.'[31] The occasion enables her to prove what might otherwise pass notice, Shakespeare's 'Ethical merits in a more conspicuous point of view'.[32]

In all three of these publications, the quotations from Shakespeare have a heuristic function, serving to illustrate standards of poetic and moral excellence. Although they lose their relation to the plays at large, they are situated within new critical and philosophical contexts. Yet by the nineteenth century, quotations are collected and reproduced independent of any context. No outside system of good and bad will be evoked; in many cases, the dramatic context will be omitted or abbreviated. Editions of *Beauties of Shakspear* after 1818 drop Dodd's commentary. No commentary prescribes their use in establishing and refining Judgement; unattended, often assigned no dramatic speaker, they give the impression of being Shakespeare's own utterances: his self-expression.

At the same time, Shakespeare quotations are being reproduced in a new format that goes farther still in identifying the quotations with what Shakespeare thought and felt. In 1787, the first Shakespeare concordance is published: Andrew Beckett's, *A Concordance to Shakespeare . . . in which the distinguished and parallel passages in the plays of that justly admired writer are methodologically arranged.* The edition, calling itself 'a topical index' in which 'each group of passages forms a concordantia', draws on earlier layouts. The index of topics derives from editions of *Beauties of Shakspear* (which themselves drew on the places or *topoi* of the earlier compendia) and the parallel passages making up each topic have been collected from notes to editions of Shakespeare from Theobald (1733) up to and including Malone (1790). The publication has a new and different purpose: 'The design of the present publication, is to bring into one view the parallel passages of the poet, so as to form a kind of Concordance to his works.' By offering all that Shakespeare said on a given topic ('Ambition', for example), the concordance appeared to be providing Shakespeare's views on it. The 'concordantia' of passages implied an agreement or at least coherence to these views. There is, no doubt, a relation between this form of reproducing quotations and nineteenth-century criticism that, starting with Goethe (who first read Shakespeare in Dodd's *Beauties*), Schlegel, and Coleridge, considers Shakespeare as a profound thinker and philosopher. The *topoi* that once structured the truths and opinions of logic and rhetoric have now become the topics which organise Shakespeare's consciousness. As if to underscore the shift from discursive commonplaces to unique consciousness, another book of quotations appears in 1812 entitled *Aphorisms from Shakespeare* with the intention 'to present him to our contemplations as a pre-eminently philosophical and moral Poet.'[33]

From this point on, Shakespearean quotations cease to serve as material for garnering seventeenth-century traditional wisdom or cultivating eighteenth-century bourgeois taste. Once reproduced outside of these contexts, they give the illusion that Shakespeare is thinking behind them and speaking through them. Every home could possess a succinct record of what he thought and said on any given topic. Their titles suggest as much: *Shakespeare's Genius* (1821), *The Mind of Shakespeare As Exhibited in his Works* (1876), *The Wisdom of Shakespeare* (1909), *What Shakespeare Said About It* (1935). Jane Austen in 1814 remarked that Shakespeare's 'thoughts and beauties are so spread abroad that one touches them every where . . . His celebrated passages are quoted by every body'; on the other side of the Atlantic, de Tocqueville in 1835 found that 'There is hardly a pioneer's hut which does not contain a few odd volumes of Shakespeare.'[34] Subjects and citizens alike owned volumes of memorable lines, Shakespeare's unique utterances, produced not by the dramatic characters, not by sources, not by theatrical and printing-house practices, not by the motivations of history and language (not by chance, certainly) but by Shakespeare exclusively.

Shakespeare quotations circulated in Romantic poetry and criticism as well as in the popular anthologies and concordances. An important recent study reveals the astonishing frequency with which Shakespearean quotations are woven into the verse and prose of Romantic poets and critics.[35] It relates this phenomenon to the Bloomian problem of how a poet is to come to terms with his poetic forefathers, especially when the ascendancy of originality excludes imitation as a response. The prospect of imitating Shakespeare presented a particular challenge, for how could a writer imitate the poet who was thought himself never to have imitated? Quotation with its variants of allusion and echo is seen to offer the poet release from the Oedipal deadlock with his overbearing poetic forebear, providing him with a means of assimilating Shakespeare into his own discourse that enables him 'to speak words that are both his own and another's.'[36] By repeating Shakespeare's words within his own text, the poet fused his own voice with that of his eminent predecessor. The ideal form of citation, according to this argument, is unconscious allusion because it allows the two texts to mesh inextricably: 'an unconscious allusion shows that the precursor-text has literally penetrated the recesses of the later writer's mind.'

The above discussion of quotation would complicate the possibility of such a happy and reconciliatory synthesis. Once encased in quotation marks, even implied ones, a passage becomes hypostatised. Unlike other forms of reiteration – allusion, echo, paraphrase – a quoted passage must remain true to the original, duplicating it verbatim. Direct quotation of Shakespeare, therefore, prevents the merger of quoting and quoted voices. While imitation allows, indeed requires, that the original be assimilated by the imitation, quotation forbids it. The marks cordoning off the locution signal: *Private Property. No Trespassing.* Once the boundaries are strictly demarcated, appropriations that were once routine become instances of transgression. It is predictable, therefore, that the pervasive use of quotation be attended by recurring charges of plagiarism. Both Coleridge and Byron were hounded by charges of plagiarism, the failure to surround lifted material with legitimising quotes; their writing has recently been described as so honeycombed by plagiarisms as to itself constitute a mode of composition.[37] Wordsworth too worried about omitting quotations marks from the Shakespeare quoted in his verse, despite De Quincey's assurance that such an omission 'carries with it no charge of plagarism.'[38] When quotations appear around Shakespearean lines – whether in compendia or verse – his words cannot slip into those of another. It is no longer possible to have phrases by different authors blending into each other, as they did in the seventeenth-century *England's Parnassus*. Property boundaries are strictly set at the start and exactly preserved in reproduction.

The extent to which Romantic poets incorporated Shakespeare's lines into their own, reveals not only how important Shakespeare's words were to the Romantics, but also how important their own words were to themselves. For the protective brackets around Shakespeare's words also guaranteed the inviolability of their own. The conventions that safeguard the third person cover the first as well: marking the *suum* simultaneously situates the *meum*. So too the words of the subjects in Austen's parlours and the citizens in de Toqueville's huts were sanctioned by their volumes of Shakespeare quotations. The format for both quoting and reproducing Shakespeare inscribed an individual's entitlement to language.

III

'What does it matter who is speaking?' Foucault asks at the end of the essay 'What is an Author?'[39] By the end of the eighteenth century, it appears to have mattered a great deal. A grammatical convention is established which mandates that the words of others be graphically and typographically distinguished. A popular bibliographic format appears which contains what Shakespeare (and only Shakespeare) said on given subjects. Poets and critics can no longer cite or allude to Shakespeare without questioning its propriety and legitimacy.

Yet the question does not seem to have mattered much in the Renaissance judging by the attributions of the compendia surveyed above. *Belvedere* provides what the modern editor deems an 'inaccurate and misleading' preliminary list of writers quoted; some of the authors named are not represented while other authors' names are omitted whose works are quoted.[40] While *England's Parnassus* follows most quotes with a subscription, 68 are unsigned and 130 are wrongly assigned.[41] By the middle of the nineteenth century, however, such inaccuracies have become intolerable, indeed unconscionable. One scholar spent 'not far from fifty years labour' trying to track the *Parnassus* quotations back to their sources'; 'It constantly happens that famous passages belonging to one distinguished poet are attributed to another.'[42] Thus Gaunt's famous encomium to England is assigned to Drayton, while passages from Daniel's *Civil Wars* are credited to Shakespeare. By correcting misattributions, this scholar attempted 'to restore property to its right owner', an effort that involved not only correct attribution but correct transcription: 'Restoring the property as well as the language' (p. xiv). Misquoting, like misattribution, constitutes, in William Blackstone's discussion of literary property, 'an invasion of [the writer's] right of property'.[43] That this scholar was John Payne Collier who ended up fabricating both sources and corrections, bears witness to the futility of his task: how can origins and correct originals be found for *sententiae* or commonplaces that are integral to discourse itself?[44]

Collier was not the last to think it imperative to assign and reproduce the quotations accurately, as is demonstrated by the labours of the twentieth-century editors of both *Englands Parnassus* and *Belvedere*. Like Collier they have assumed that quotations enclose private and stable texts, not considering that at an earlier period they simply flagged public and malleable prescripts. Collier attributed the 'hundreds of . . . absurd mistakes' and 'abundantly strange' misattributions to the irresponsibility of the editors (p. xiii). His twentieth-century successor similarly believed that the inaccurate subscriptions and transcriptions are merely the unfortunate result of unsystematic compiling and careless printing.[45] Yet at a period when quotations were valued for their applicability, the specifics of their origin or of their precise phraseology were hardly matters of urgency. Proper attribution and reproduction are the requirements of ownership. It is only when a passage belongs to a writer that loose quotation or casual attribution constitutes violation.

'Who speaks in this way? . . . We can never know, for the good reason that writing is the destruction of every voice, every origin . . .'[46] From Barthes' vantage, the verbal strands comprising a text are all quotations, uniformly without pedigree, eclectically lifted from the extensive elsewhere of signifying practice: 'The quotations from which a text is constructed are anonymous, irrecoverable, and yet *already read*: they are quotations without quotation marks.'[47] Affixing a quotation to a speaker is motivated by the same impulse as affiliating a work to an author: both work to limit the generativity of language, confining it to the perimeters of a single consciousness (and its complementary unconscious), ordinary or extraordinary. Tying the quotation to its originator, tying the work to its author are modes of denying and curbing discursive possibility. Were the quotation and work to break away from those ties, they would be lost to the infinitely expansive signifying network, Barthes' and Kristeva's 'intertextuality': Such an unloosening would frustrate attempts to fasten words to their begetters, as children are filiated to their fathers: 'the Text can be read without its father's guarantee; the restoration of the intertext abolishes inheritance'.[48]

Quotation takes on new forms in the same decades that the traditional construct of authorship emerges. Both coincide with the gradual formulation of authorial rights. The author comes to have legal rights over his or her work that are fashioned after those protecting private property. Quotation marks are copyright writ small, extending the same kind of claim over smaller units of text.[49] Their presence on the pages we read and write is more than a convention of literacy. It is a ubiquitous reminder that every locution worth repeating is a piece of property with a proprietor. The eye that scans these proprietary marks and the hand that inscribes them, or prompts a machine to do so, are perforce impressed by the determining force of the *meum* and *suum*. This essay has discussed one of the many modes by which the reproduction of Shakespeare since the Enlightenment has endorsed this abiding dispensation.

Notes

1. On the late eighteenth-century desire for writing in Shakespeare's own person, see Margreta de Grazia, *Shakespeare Verbatim: The Reproduction of Authenticity and the 1790 Apparatus* (Oxford, 1991), pp. 152–63.

2. It was not until 1780 that the 1609 Sonnets were given a full textual apparatus and not until 1790 that they were published as part of the corpus itself. See M. de Grazia, *op. cit.*, pp. 152–3; 162.

3. See C. J. Mitchell, 'Quotation Marks, Compositorial Habits, and False Imprints,' *The Library*, 6th ser. (1983), pp. 359–84.

4. See Vivienne Mylne, 'The Punctuation of Dialogue in Eighteenth-Century French and English Fiction,' *The Library*, 6th ser. (1979), pp. 43–61.

5. On the use of 'quotation quadrants', see Joseph Moxon, *Mechanick Exercises on the Whole Art of Printing (1663–4)*, ed. Herbert Davis and Harry Carter (London, 1958), p. 349.

6. Seventeenth-century dictionaries defined *quote* as to 'marke in the margent, to note by the way', Randle Cotgrave, *A Dictionarie of the French and English Tongues* (London, 1611). The verb 'note' contains the same ambiguity as 'mark', signifying both to make a note and to take notice.

7. Then, as now, italic print was a form of highlighting or emphasis. In the Folios and quartos repeated passages that modern editions enclose in quotation marks are sometimes italicised, not to indicate their origin in another speaker or text, but to stress their importance. The same rationale could be applied to the Folio's relatively consistent italicising of letters. For the relation between authorial and authorative emphasis and italics, see Joseph Loewenstein '"Idem:' italics and the Genetics of Authorship', *Journal of Medieval and Renaissance Studies*, 20 (1990), pp. 205–24.

8. See G. K. Hunter, 'The Marking of *Sententiae* in Elizabethan Plays, Poems, and Romances,' *The Library*, 5th ser. (1951), pp. 171–88.

9. As A. J. Minnis has demonstrated, quotations in the Middle Ages were taken exclusively from authorities; indeed the term *auctoritas* referred to a quotation or extract from the writing of an *auctor*. *Medieval Theory of Authorship*, 2nd edn (Philadelphia, 1988), p. 10.

10. For the importance of the *loci communes* in the sixteenth and seventeenth centuries, see Sister Joan Marie Lechner, *Renaissance Concepts of the Commonplaces* (N.Y., 1962), especially Ch. II, pp. 65–152. See also Wilbur Samuel Howell, *Logic and Rhetoric in England, 1500–1700* (Princeton, 1956), pp. 16–18, 24–31.

11. Thomas Wilson, *The Rule of Reason* (1551; facs. rpt. *The English Experience*, Amsterdam, 1970), no. 261, sign. J5v–J5r; also quoted by Howell, *op. cit.*, p. 24.

12. For the recovery and decline of the ancient art of memory, see Mary Carruthers, *The Book of Memory: A Study of Memory in Medieval Culture* (Cambridge, 1990).

13. See Frances Yates, *Giordano Bruno and the Hermetic Tradition* (New York, 1969), esp. pp. 190–201; 325–35.

14. On these two sites of inscription in Hamlet, see Jonathan Goldberg, 'Hamlet's Hand,' *Shakespeare Quarterly*, 39 (1988) no. 3, pp. 311–13.

15. *The English Grammar* in *The Works of Benjamin Jonson*, eds. C. H. Herford, Percy Simpson and Evelyn Simpson, 11 vols (Oxford, 1929–52) vol. VIII, p. 55.

16. They retain this function too when they enclose technical terms, neologisms, jargon, words ironically intended. In each of these cases the quoted text is dissociated from that in which it is quoted.

17. On the popularity of Dodd's anthology, see Jonathan Bate, *Shakespeare and the English Romantic Imagination* (Oxford, 1986), pp. 30; 200 and Gary Taylor,

Reinventing Shakespeare: A Cultural History, from the Restoration to the Present (New York, 1989), pp. 91; 108.

18. *Bodenham's Belvedere, or The Garden of the Muses* (Manchester, 1875), Preface.

19. As the Preface to the former makes clear, although the florilegium format is ancient in origin, 'in imitation of Textus in the Latine,' 'not unlike the Thesaurus Poeticus in Latine,' its application to English is entirely new, 'there having not anything of this kind appeared upon the English stage before.'

20. For a partial list of which quotations in the digest are by Shakespeare, see John Munro, *The Shakespeare Allusion Book: A Collection of Allusions to Shakespeare from 1591–1700*, 2 vols. (London, 1932), vol. 2; 479.

21. *Bodenham's Belvedere, op. cit.*, p. 484.

22. See Brian Vickers' introduction to *Shakespeare: The Critical Heritage 1765–1774*, 6 vols (London and Boston, 1979), pp. 4–5.

23. On evaluation as an editorial duty, see de Grazia, *op. cit.*, pp. 120–1.

24. See John Butt, *Pope's Taste in Shakespeare* (London, 1936).

25. Preface to *The Plays of William Shakespeare* (1765), in *Eighteenth Century Essays on Shakespeare*, ed. D. Nichol Smith (Oxford, 1963), p. 142.

26. *ibid.*, p. 113.

27. *ibid.*, p. 114.

28. *ibid.*, p. 44.

29. Preface, in Nichol Smith, *op. cit.*, p. 107.

30. *The Spectator*, ed. Donald F. Bond (Oxford, 1965), vol. 1, p. 245.

31. *The Morality of Shakespeare's Drama Illustrated* (London, 1775), p. xii.

32. *ibid.*, p. ix.

33. The preface to the anthology is by Capel Lofft, though he credits 'a young Lady' with the idea for the selection and most of its execution, p. xxv.

34. Quoted by G. Taylor, *op. cit.*, pp. 110–11; 197.

35. See J. Bate, *op. cit.*, p. 36.

36. *ibid.*, p. 36.

37. Thomas McFarland, *Coleridge and the Pantheist Tradition* (Oxford, 1969), p. 28, quoted by J. Bate, *op. cit.*, p. 25.

38. See J. Bate, *op. cit.*, pp. 104; 106–7, 180. See also Susan Eilenberg, 'Mortal Pages: Wordsworth and the Reform of Copyright,' ELH, 56, (Summer, 1989), pp. 351–74.

39. *Textual Strategies: Perspectives in Post-Structuralist Criticism*, ed. Josue V. Harari (Ithaca, N.Y., 1979), pp. 141–60.

40. See Appendix D *op. cit.*, pp. 489–518.

41. *Englands Parnassus Compiled by Robert Allot* (1600), ed. Charles Crawford (Oxford, 1913), p. xxv.

42. *Seven English Poetical Miscellanies*, reproduced under the care of J. Payne Collier (London, 1867), p. xvi.

43. *Commentaries on the Laws of England* 4 vols (London, 1766), vol. 2, p. 406.

44. For an account of Collier as scholar and forger, see S. Schoenbaum, *Shakespeare's Lives* (Oxford and N.Y., 1970), pp. 332–61. For his inaccuracies and misascriptions in editing *Englands Parnassus*, see C. Crawford, *op. cit.*, p. 383.

45. See *Englands Parnassus*, C. Crawford, *op. cit.*, pp. xxvi; xxvii. Crawford finds an explanation for *Belvedere's* anomalies in the meddling of a 'poetaster'. See Appendix D in J. Munro, *op. cit.*, pp. 490–1.

46. 'The Death of the Author,' *The Rustle of Language*, trans. Richard Howard (Berkeley and Los Angeles, 1989), p. 49.

47. R. Barthes, 'From Work to Text,' *op. cit.*, p. 60.
48. *ibid.*, p. 61.
49. For a discussion of quotation in the context of eighteenth-century copyright, see M. de Grazia, *op. cit.*, Ch. 5, 'Shakespeare's Entitlement: Literary Property and Discursive Enclosure', pp. 177–221.

5 Kemble, Scott, and the Mantle of the Bard

Nicola J. Watson

There might be said to be a familiar 'Romantic' Shakespeare: unactable, according to Charles Lamb,[1] all but unrepresentable, according to Alderman Boydell,[2] straining towards the impalpable in the paintings of Fuseli,[3] impersonalised in Keats' myth of 'negative capability'. My business here is with a relatively unfamiliar Romantic Shakespeare, one which, so far from shoring up the privatised and (apparently) apolitical Romantic Imagination, is pressed into the emphatically public service of Tory nationalism. Historicised rather than timeless,[4] novelistic rather than poetic,[5] this Shakespeare is in essence the one which modern popular culture continues to cherish, transmitted in a direct line from Kemble and Scott, via the reverential biographies and sentimental novelisations of the Victorians, to the open-top bus tour commentaries that echo perpetually across the roofs of Shakespeare's Birthplace, Anne Hathaway's Cottage, and the rest.

In pursuit of this other Shakespeare, this paper juxtaposes two influential exercises in historical fancy dress carried out in Britain in the wake of the French Revolution: John Philip Kemble's project of authenticating his Shakespeare revivals of the 1820s by the use of meticulously researched period costumes, thereby fostering the promotion of Shakespeare's history plays to the status of actual history; and his biographer, friend and admirer Sir Walter Scott's comparable injection of 'authentic' historical detail, underwritten by the authority of Shakespeare, into the suspect discourse of fiction, in the process of which he would successfully legitimise himself as 'The Shakespeare of novelists'. As I shall show, both Kemble and Scott, like their friend and adviser Edmond Malone, successfully claim Shakespeare for a view of history heavily dependent upon Edmund Burke's *Reflections on the Revolution in France*, a view which imagines an ideal 'organic' State premised upon conserving past institutions, however corrupt, incomprehensible, or incoherent, out of respectful nostalgia for the essentially feudal wisdom of the past; both actor-manager and novelist thus participate enthusiastically in the counter-revolutionary reformulation of English cultural identity carried out at the turn of the nineteenth century. On the stages of the Theatres Royal and in the pages of the Waverley Novels, Shakespeare is mobilised as a national ancestor, father of the British Constitution by virtue of his position as the father of British Literature.

I Antiquarians and Anti-Jacobins

The late eighteenth century's general interest in historicising Shakespeare became thoroughly identified during the 1790s as a reassuringly counter-revolutionary (or 'anti-Jacobin') cultural strategy. This development was reflected in the increasing preoccupation of Shakespeare scholarship with the question of the 'authenticity' of the Shakespearean text.[6] The massive editorial project of Malone,[7] coupled with his attempt to repossess Shakespeare's original cultural context in his *Historical Account of the English Stage*, found its appropriate counterpart in the Ireland forgeries, which capitalised upon, while eventually being exposed by, the contemporary passion for the 'true' Shakespeare, a Shakespeare who could be, as it were, expanded upon and authenticated by an appeal to historical evidence. Malone's edition professed to purge the Shakespearean corpus of corruptions in order to return to the original text, indeed, if possible, to the original intention of the author, by-passing all intervening editions between his own time and the First Folio and Good Quartos; his business in *An Inquiry into the Authenticity of Certain Miscellaneous Papers . . . Attributed to Shakespeare* (1796) is to explode the Ireland forgeries by a similar excavation in textual history. The connection between this drive to preserve the original Shakespeare from adulteration by appealing to antiquarian expertise and contemporary anxieties about the threat posed by the French Revolution to the time-honoured British Constitution is suggested by the manifesto which opens *An Inquiry . . .*:

> [P]roportionate to our respect and veneration for that extraordinary man ought to be our care of his fame, and of those valuable writings that he has left us; and our solicitude to preserve them pure and unpolluted by any modern sophistication or foreign admixture whatsoever.[8]

This political valence is underscored by Malone's sudden departure from a weighty historical analysis of spelling, designed to expose the incompetent pish-tushery of Ireland's fabrication, into immediate hysterical polemic against the French; from quoting extensively from an anti-French passage in Sir John Fortescue's *The Difference between an Absolute and Limited Monarchy*, Malone sweeps into a three-page footnote which suggests that some sort of permanent barrier between England and France should be established as a pre-condition for peace talks, concluding his tirade with a strategic misquotation of John of Gaunt's speech from *Richard II*, effectively prophesying the imminent extinction of the British monarchy unless such appropriate steps be taken.[9] The re-entry of Shakespeare in this context makes it plain that Shakespeare as national poet is being 'authenticated' by Malone in the service of anti-Jacobinism, a political appropriation that is registered by both reviewers and Edmund Burke himself, who commented in a letter to Malone:

> Your admiration of Shakespeare would be ill-sorted indeed, if your taste
> . . . did not lead you to a perfect abhorrence of the French revolution and all
> its works.[10]

If Malone's historical project can be linked with counter-revolutionary ideology, so too may that of Kemble, who was not only given to consulting Malone on textual points, but was also a contributor to the posthumously completed revision of Malone's edition issued in 1821, known as the Boswell–Malone edition.[11] Kemble's well-documented scholarly obsession with the (supposedly) 'genuine' text (running to the possession of a copy of the First Folio) and his risky and idiosyncratic adherence to 'original' and therefore presumably authentic pronunciation[12] found its visual corollary in the full-blown costume extravaganza designed by James Robinson Planché for Kemble's 1823 production of *King John*, in which Kemble's early interest in 'correct' costume culminated. Initiating a long series of equally meticulously researched productions of Shakespeare under the auspices of Charles Kemble – including *1 and 2 Henry IV* (1824), *As You Like It, Hamlet, Othello, The Merchant of Venice* (1825), and *Richard III* (1829) – the Kemble/Planché *King John* successfully 'authorised' a historicised version of Shakespeare, thanks both to Planché's standing as an antiquarian and to Kemble's own position as Shakespearean interpreter to the times; '[n]o man has studied Shakespeare more critically – none more happily conceives him. While England venerates Shakespeare, it must cherish Kemble.'[13]

The play-bill to *King John* makes it quite clear that this project was, like Malone's, founded upon an idea of retrieving Shakespeare from the abuses of the past age by buttressing an 'authentic' text with an impressive array of other archaeological 'indisputable authorities, such as Monuments, Seals, illuminated Manuscripts, painted glass etc.'.[14] As James Boaden pointed out in his *Memoirs of the Life of Kemble*, this enterprise was at once an entrepreneurial gamble and an attempt to 'perfect' a Shakespeare hitherto imperfectly and corruptly realised:

> It struck [Kemble] . . . that a grand and permanent attraction might be given
> to Drury Lane by encreasing the power of Shakespeare. This he proposed to
> effect by a more stately and perfect representation of his plays – to attend to
> all the details as well as the grand features, and by the aids of scenery and
> dress to perfect the dramatic illusion . . .[15]

This heavily researched, more 'perfect representation' is peculiarly
conservative in its preference for the feudal and heraldic (one recalls
Burke's famous lament for the 'age of chivalry', one of the more notorious
passages in *Reflections on the Revolution in France*) over the anarchic
modern. Boaden describes the innovative costuming in terms of an
imposition of proper heraldic discipline onto the hitherto haphazard
practices of the theatre:

> Upon the London stage, nearly everything, as to correctness, was to be
> done. The ancient kings of England, or Scotland, or Denmark, wore the
> court-dress of our own times as to shape; and as to colour, the rival
> monarchs of England and France opposed their persons to each other in
> scarlet and gold-lace, and white and silver. At the moment I am writing,
> King John has revived the exact habiliments of the 13th century, and either
> as to materials or elegance, the dresses of the mimic scene might have been
> admitted at the ancient court.[16]

Significantly, this feudal rectitude and discipline of the *mise-en-scène* was
conceived as the counterpart to the perceived politics of Shakespeare's
own work, being designed, in Planché's words, 'to render the dresses and
decorations of Shakespeare's plays, if possible, worthy of them.'[17]

In choosing *King John* as the vehicle for the historicisation and
authentication of Shakespeare, Kemble was making a further, very specific
political statement. Since the 1740s *King John* had, by and large, operated
as a highly patriotic play, a patriotism that had been underscored by
Richard Valpy's 1803 adaptation for schoolboys. This version, like
Kemble's, capitalised heavily upon pageantry and made much of the last
famous speech – 'nought can make us rue / If England to itself do rest but
true' – tellingly, a speech which had already turned up as a caption to at
least two anti-Jacobin and pro-Burke caricatures in the nineties: James
Sayers' *Loyalty Against Levelling*, and *Mr. Burke's Pair of Spectacles for
Short-Sighted Politicians*.[18] Such resonances also surface in the broadside
Shakespeare's Ghost! which features Shakespeare 'in the Character of A
TRUE ENGLISHMAN and A STURDY JOHN BULL, indignant that a
FRENCH ARMY should WAGE WAR IN OUR ISLE' speaking a mishmash of patriotic speeches drawn in part from *King John*.[19] That said,
despite a long pedigree as an impeccably patriotic play, *King John*
presented, as it had done earlier in the century,[20] certain obstacles to this
reading, difficulties registered by Crabb Robinson in a conversation with
Charles Lamb, recorded in Robinson's journal in December 1811; on

Robinson's objecting to 'King John and Lewis, as if Shakespeare meant like a Jacobin to shew how base and vile kings are,' Lamb commented in his turn that '*King John* [was] one of the plays he like[d] the least' praising instead *Richard II*.[21] The interesting substitution of *Richard II* for *King John* (which Scott repeats, as I shall show, in *Woodstock*) suggests that *King John* might well have retained some of its miscellaneously satirical and subversive character despite the patriotic tradition into which it had been assimilated. In this context Kemble's thoroughgoing historicisation of the play should perhaps be seen as an attempt to pre-empt any potential jacobinical appropriation, in the process dramatising even King John himself ('*not* a good man', as Milne pointed out a hundred years later) as part and parcel of Burke's 'age of chivalry'. As one contemporary commentator tellingly remarks of Kemble's reformation of costume, its purpose was not so much entire accuracy, but an erasure of 'modern associations', the substitution of a general sense of feudal splendour for any more dangerous topicality:

> [A]s the poet, carrying back his scene into remote days retains still to a certain extent the manners and sentiments of his own period, so it is sufficient for the purpose of costume if everything be avoided which can recall modern associations, and as much of the antique be assumed as will at once harmonise with the purpose of the exhibition and in so far awaken recollections of the days of yore as to give an air of truth to the scene.[22]

This sympathetic viewer of Kemble's project was in fact none other than Walter Scott himself. As a real-life antiquarian adviser on costume to his painter-friends, and indeed to Kemble himself,[23] as a collector of antiquarian books and rubble of all kinds, as a poet interested in simulating and assimilating the ancient poetry,[24] and, most importantly, as the Author of *Waverley*, Scott can be seen to be interested in the same games with historical fancy-dress that Kemble was playing. The radical Hazlitt bears sardonic witness once again to the emphatically counter-revolutionary bent of these nostalgic literary endeavours:

> The political bearing of the *Scotch Novels* has been a considerable recommendation to them. They are a relief to the mind, rarefied as it has been with modern philosophy, and heated with ultra-radicalism. At a time also, when we bid fair to revive the principles of the Stuarts, it is interesting to bring us acquainted with their persons and misfortunes . . . Sir Walter is a professed *clarifier* of the age from the vulgar and still lurking old-English antipathy to Popery and Slavery. Through some odd process of *servile* logic, it should seem, that in restoring the claims of the Stuarts by the courtesy of romance, the House of Brunswick are more firmly seated in point of fact, and the Bourbons, by collateral reasoning, become legitimate! In any other point of view, we cannot possibly conceive how Sir Walter imagines 'he has done something to revive the declining spirit of loyalty' by these novels. His

loyalty is founded on *would-be* treason: he props the actual throne by the shadow of rebellion.[25]

If it is true that both Kemble and Scott depend upon historicity to defuse contemporary radical politics and buttress Tory nationalism, it is no less true that both depend upon Shakespeare to sanction that strategy. Scott's appropriative quotation of Shakespearean plot and text to instate a vision of an Edenic, post-revolutionary Britain is so pervasive that a full account of it would have to encompass his entire *oeuvre*: for the purposes of this paper I propose to content myself with an analysis of his novel of the Civil Wars and Commonwealth, *Woodstock* (1826). *Woodstock* is of particular interest because, not content solely with repeating earlier strategies – plundering Shakespeare for authoritative tags, for instance, or inter-layering his novel's text with the residues of others to enact what amounts to a Burkean model of literary discourse – Scott in this late novel makes perhaps his conclusive statement upon the practice of appropriating Shakespeare through quotation. By exploiting the very concept of Shake-speare as a national institution, putting 'Shakespeare' (rather than the texts that go by that name) into quotation marks, Scott is enabled to purge the actual Shakespearean text of political ambivalence, selectively recon-stituting the plays within an unequivocally monarchical, loyalist, and nationalistic discourse.

II *Woodstock*: The Charles the First Folio

In *Woodstock* the generalised invocation of 'Shakespeare' functions at once as a marker of the political correctness of royalism and as the disciplinarian and reformer of royal peccadillo, here personified by the rakish Charles II. The novel takes as its subject the aid rendered to Charles II after Worcester by the loyalist Lee family, resident at Woodstock, who helped him escape Cromwell. The main action of the novel details the expulsion of the Commonwealth Commissioners from the house (carried out by means of some bogus supernatural hocus-pocus, enabled by a warren of secret passages), the subsequent residence of the disguised Charles, and his eventual escape, covered by the decoy 'King' Albert Lee, who leads the Commonwealth soldiers on a lengthy wild-goose chase through that same labyrinth. The novel aptly takes the house's name, for its architectural peculiarities are themselves loyalistic, smacking strongly of the ideal State imagined by Burke as the irregular but beautiful growth of ages:

The varied and multiplied fronts of this irregular building were . . . an absolute banquet to the architectural antiquary, as they certainly contained specimens of every style which existed, from the pure Norman of Henry of Anjou, down to the composite, half Gothic half classicial style of Elizabeth and her successor.[26]

At the very heart of this Tory architecture lies – what else? – the book which appears to function as the British Constitution's sacred text, Charles I's First Folio, marker of textual authenticity and monarchical legitimacy. Scott's happy amendment of history – for Charles I owned not the First Folio but the Second – is neatly glossed by Malone's lament in the opening pages of the 1790 edition:

> So little known indeed was the value of the early impressions of books [as the nearest approximation to the original intention of the author] . . . that King Charles the First, though a great admirer of our poet, was contented with the *Second* folio edition of his plays, unconscious of the numerous misrepresentations and interpolations by which every page of that copy is disfigured . . .'[27]

Since it could be said that Charles I's troubles were summed up in misrepresentation, interpolation, and disfigurement, it is strategic in Scott to restore him, thoroughly in the spirit of Malone, by way of the First Folio, the *editio princeps*, 'the only authentick edition'.[28] The elitism of Scott's choice of this particular edition of Shakespeare is highlighted by Lamb's much more democratic, though not less nationalistic, choice of edition:

> I do not care for a First Folio of Shakespeare . . . I have a community of feeling with my country-men about his Plays, and I like those editions of him best, which have been oftenest tumbled about and handled.[29]

Scott, by contrast, insists upon the association of the Folio with legitimacy by making Charles I the only expert and authentic interpreter of the text. In *Woodstock*, the more Royalist a character, the better they understand the Bard; hence the Royal Martyr, suitably re-equipped with F1, was the perfect text's perfect reader. As the present owner of this particular copy, the old loyalist Sir Henry Lee, says:

> '[Shakespeare's] book was the closet companion of my blessed master,' . . . 'after the Bible . . . he felt more comfort in it than in any other; and as I have shared his disease, why, it is natural I should take his medicine. Albeit, I pretend not to my master's art in explaining the dark passages . . .'[30]

This deliberate equation of Shakespeare with monarchism is again confirmed by Scott's inclusion of an opposing, 'jacobinical' view, which is equally convinced of Shakespeare's royalism but wholeheartedly rejects it:

> 'Here is the King and high priest of these vices and follies! . . . Here is he, whom princes chose for their cabinet-keeper, and whom maids of honour

take for their bed-fellow! . . . On thee, William Shakspeare, I charge whate'er of such lawless idleness and immodest folly hath defiled the land since thy day!'[31]

To speak in shreds and patches of Shakespeare, as Sir Henry Lee and his fellow-cavalier Wildrake consistently do, is to speak the language of royalist legitimacy; 'it would be as easy to convert [Sir Henry] to the Presbyterian form of government, or engage him to take the abjuration oath, as to shake his belief in Shakspeare.'[32] To be a devoted reader of Shakespeare therefore goes hand in hand with the ability to read accurately (that is to say, loyally) the novel's analogue to British history, the labyrinths or 'dark passages' of the Royal Lodge; Lee's map, the royal original, is thus pointedly comprehensive, while the map obtained by the rational revolutionary Cromwell from his Parliamentary spy is notably incomplete. The crucial authenticity of the map possessed by the royalist and Shakespeare-mad Lee ultimately enables the young king to escape capture and execution. It appears then that the reading of Shakespeare may stand for and ensure a proper understanding of the State as constituted within the counter-revolutionary cultural ideology of the early nineteenth century.

However, 'Shakespeare' functions in this novel as more than the underwriter of royalism's legitimacy, for the figure of the Bard is also invoked to reform the monarchy, a project that is at the core of this novel. The manifest inadequacy of the young libertine Charles II, *alias* Louis Kerneguy, to live up to Alice Lee's dignified ideal of a King is, for instance, refracted through an extended discussion of Shakespeare's own sexual practice. While the disguised King assimilates Shakespeare to his own libertine court culture by championing D'Avenant's pretensions to being the illegitimate son of Shakespeare (scrupulously footnoted by Scott to the Variorum edition), both Sir Henry and the virtuous republican Everard hotly defend Shakespeare as a perfect exemplar of the middle-class virtue of chastity, the latter weighing in with a reference to *King John* (I, i, 64–5) in which the Bastard is rebuked for dishonouring his mother by suggesting that he was illegitimate.[33] Given that the outcome of this opening scene is a confirmation of his bastardy, an illegitimacy that plays out, in little, King John's own very tenuous claim to the throne, this reference to *King John* serves to underline the importance of maintaining the closest links between legitimacy and the monarchy.

This privileging of a 'true', textual and moral Shakespeare – as opposed to the 'false' constructed by a corrupting tradition that appropriates him to cavalier libertinism – is mirrored in the privileging of the royalist antiquarian Dr Rochecliffe's new 'true' reading of the Lodge's architecture over that sanctioned by ancient tradition. Rochecliffe's archival researches (which are distinctly reminiscent of, even analogous to, Malone's) erase the historical scandal of royal illegitimate amours by insisting that Woodstock was not, despite tradition to the contrary, built as a love-nest for Henry II's mistress Fair Rosamund:

> . . . what was called Rosamund's Tower was merely an interior keep, or citadel, to which the lord or warden of the castle might retreat, when other points of safety failed him; and either protract his defence, or, at the worst, stipulate for reasonable terms of surrender.[34]

Significantly, those who cling to the more salacious version of the genesis of the Royal Lodge are identified with the revolutionaries:

> [I]t is even said that the Mayor . . . became Presbyterian in revenge of the doubts cast by the rector [Rochecliffe] upon this important subject, rather choosing to give up the Liturgy than his fixed belief in Rosamund's Tower, and Love's Ladder.[35]

Scott's joking tone apart, there is more invested in this arcane architectural wrangle than meets the eye. In the same way as Shakespeare is cleared of libertinism by an appeal to the inadequacy of the original evidence, so the libertine history of the monarchy is satisfactorily rewritten by an appeal to a similar antiquarianism. The action of the novel itself carries out this purge, for Rochecliffe's analysis of the use of the Tower is, after all, proved correct in the course of the plot when it functions as the last retreat of the supposed King; the 'love' in question turns out in the event to be the decorous and above-all legitimate love of the loyal subject Albert Lee, rather than the illegitimate *affaire* offered by the King (who makes eloquent use of the Rosamund parallel in his wooing) to Albert's sister Alice Lee. The young King's libertine tendencies are, furthermore, policed by recourse to a Shakespearean text when Lee attempts to subject Charles to a salutary reading of *Richard II* (reminiscent again of Malone's own polemical appropriation of this play),[36] Lee clearly occupying the position of the monitory John of Gaunt, Charles that of the feckless Richard under threat from the successful soldier and politician Bolingbroke/Cromwell.[37] The status of *Richard II* as an admonitory text is further reinforced when it is quoted three more times in the head-notes to provide an ominous parallel between Richard and the heir.[38]

But although Shakespeare is thus imagined to be in some sense more royalist than the Royal, capable of reforming by precept, the latently revolutionary character of *Richard II*[39] points to the potential subversiveness in applying to 'old Will's' histories to underwrite the Restoration, a restoration at once of the ideal within the King and the King himself.[40] Consequently the remainder of the novel is directed towards making sure that quotation from Shakespeare is always politically appropriate, that it does in fact support legitimacy, cutting off the threat posed by Sir Henry's sometimes indiscriminate conjurations of Shakespeare, 'whom, as many others do [Scott appears here to be indulging in a joke at his own expense], he was wont to quote from a sort of habit and respect, as a favourite of his unfortunate master, without having either much real taste for his works or great skill in applying the passages which he retained on his memory'.[41]

Not to take heed of Scott's half-warning would be foolish, particularly since *Woodstock* is remarkable for the level to which its language is saturated with casual Shakespeare snippets (insouciantly plundered from *Othello, A Midsummer Night's Dream, Much Ado About Nothing, King Lear, The Two Gentlemen of Verona, Twelfth Night, Macbeth,* and *Hamlet*). Such snippets serve in the main to Shakespeareanise the authorial discourse, and thus at once to legitimise it, conferring a pseudo-canonical status, and to identify it as the language of legitimacy. The authorial and authoritative voice thus dramatises itself as nearest in political tone to that of Sir Henry Lee.

Nevertheless, the novel's action is also presided over, as I have suggested in the case of *Richard II*, by more purposive tags drawn from history-plays: *Henry VIII, Henry IV, Richard II,* and *King John*. In parcelling these texts into apposite head-notes and quotation, Scott is able to persuade them to mime something approximating to his own politics. Once Charles II has been satisfactorily reformed, *Richard II* can be aborted and a more satisfactory text substituted. Thus the conclusion to the novel, the full panoply of the Restoration, can be endorsed by an unambiguously loyalist Shakespeare; Lee's last words to the King returned in triumph are borrowed from the last act of *King John*, reconstituted after Kemble as a paean to legitimate monarchy and rendered innocent of all lurking contextual irony to such an extent that the quotation is allowed to stand on its own:

> The King then turned once more to the knight, who seemed making an effort to speak. He took his aged hand in both his own, and stooped his head towards him to catch his accents, while the old man, detaining him with the other hand, said something faltering, of which Charles could only catch the quotation –
> 'Unthread the rude eye of rebellion,
> And welcome home discarded faith.'[42]

While Scott's activities in restructuring Shakespeare's texts into a nationalistic 'Shakespeare' innocent of political equivocation are hardly unprecedented, one of the effects of this appropriation was. The leakage between Scott and Shakespeare through the medium of the old cavalier that occurs in the footnote to the last sentence of *Woodstock* – '[i]t may interest some readers to know that Bevis, the gallant hound [belonging to Lee] . . . had his prototype in a dog called Maida, the gift of the late Chief of Glengarry to the author'[43] – was to characterise much of the critical discourse surrounding what Hazlitt called Scott's 'new edition of human nature'.[44] Through his convincing re-articulation of Shakespeare as a bulwark of reaction, 'that devoted Tory' Scott managed to become, in the eyes of a substantial majority of contemporary readers and critics (Hazlitt, of course, passionately dissenting), at least as 'Shakespearean', as Shakespeare, if not more so.

III *The Bard of Abbotsford and the Laird of Avon*

Scott himself, despite a disclaimer hard upon the heels of his success with *Woodstock* ('The blockheads talk of my being like Shakespeare – not fit to tie his brogues' – a very Scott-ish type of footwear nonetheless!),[45] seems to have identified his part-fictional, part-historical endeavours with those of Shakespeare. An enthusiastic expert witness against the Shakespeare forgeries,[46] a would-be editor of the Works, a contributor to the Boswell–Malone edition, a keen Stratford tourist, and the possessor of a bust of the Bard, Scott appears to have admired Shakespeare's supposedly slap-dash methods of composition – it was still a critical commonplace that Shakespeare had simply 'warbled his native wood-notes wild' – as in some sort of justification for his own habits of rapid, unrevised composition.[47] More tellingly, the famous speech given at a dinner of the Theatrical Fund, in which Scott finally confessed to being the Author of *Waverley*, is permeated with Shakespearean allusions. Scott casts himself firstly as a regicide figure, Macbeth, an illegitimate, even revolutionary father-king killer, perhaps imagining himself as a literary usurper, and then, with a resurgence of confidence, as the character by then regarded as Shakespeare's *alter ego*, Prospero:

> Like another Scottish criminal of more consequence – one
> Macbeth
>> I am afraid to think what I have done:
>> Look on't again, I dare not!
> The wand is now broken and the book buried. You will allow me further to say with Prospero, it is your breath that has filled my sails, and to crave one single toast in the capacity of author of these novels.[48]

It would be possible to accuse Scott of a certain amount of presumption in this appropriation of a speech commonly supposed to be Shakespeare's farewell to the stage, were it not that Scott was conceived with striking frequency in Shakespearean terms by his own contemporaries, and was later regularly personified as Prospero by the early Victorians.[49] So intimately was Scott associated with the figure of Shakespeare by as early as the 1820s that it was possible for William Allan, R.A. to produce a portrait of Scott 'on the occasion of his visit to Shakespeare's tomb in Holy Trinity Church, Stratford-upon-Avon on 8 April 1828.' (It is a measure of the decline in Scott's reputation that this portrait is now sold simply as a picture of Shakespeare's tomb.) Perhaps the crowning tribute to the age's successful reconstitution of Shakespeare as Scott came from Boaden, who in a flush of wishful thinking imagined Scott as the original for Shakespeare:

> I hope I may be allowed to add my feeble tribute of admiration to a genius not equalled since the days of Shakespeare . . . I rejoice . . . that so great and fertile a source of instruction and delight is reserved for my own times: but I can yet regret, that such a novelist did not exist in the days of Shakespeare; who, from tales which he could so easily have converted to the purposes of the stage, might have added even new features to his own vast range of dramatic excellence.[50]

The eulogy with which one Mr. H. G. Bell had favoured the company prior to the revelation of the Author of Waverley indicates some of the reasons for this common conflation:

> It had been said that, notwithstanding the mental supremacy of the present age, notwithstanding that the page of our history was studded with names destined also for the pages of immortality – that the genius of Shakespeare was extinct, and the fountain of his inspiration dried up. It might be that these observations were unfortunately correct, or it might be that we were bewildered with a name, not disappointed of the reality – for though Shakespeare had brought a Hamlet, an Othello, and a Macbeth, an Ariel, a Juliet, and a Rosalind, upon the stage, were there not authors living who had brought as varied, as exquisitely painted, and as undying a range of characters into our hearts? The shape of the mere mould into which genius poured its golden treasures was surely a matter of little moment – let it be called a Tragedy, a Comedy, or a Waverley Novel.[51]

Scott was held to have produced a set of characters, a 'new edition of human nature' as varied in scope, and most importantly, as original or 'natural', as that other 'great Expositor of Nature;'[52] as he himself immodestly put it in covertly reviewing his own *Tales of My Landlord*, '[t]he volume which this author has studied is the great book of Nature . . . The characters of Shakspeare are not more exclusively human, not more perfectly men and woman as they live and move, than those of this mysterious author.'[53] Scott was, in addition, thought to have successfully replicated something of the spirit of Shakespearean tragi-comedy;[54] he also, at least until that notable dinner, retained something of the mystique associated with Shakespeare by virtue of the similar obscurity that shrouded his identity. An incident that illustrates this conflation makes its way into Scott's journal soon after the Theatrical Fund dinner:

Funny thing at the theatre. Among the discourse in High Life below Stairs one of the Ladies' ladies asks who wrote Shakespeare. One says 'Ben Johnson' another 'Finis.' 'No' said Will Murray 'it is Sir Walter Scott; he confessed it at a publick meeting the other day.'[55]

Scott's obsessive games of peek-a-boo with his audience had successfully engineered a sort of ersatz 'negative capability'; if Hazlitt was grateful for the lack of biographical information about Shakespeare 'because it reinforced his own conception . . . of Shakespeare as the impersonal genius who exposed the limitations of contemporary egotists,' as Jonathan Bate puts it,[56] the same could be held true of 'the Great Unknown' by the hero of Maria Edgeworth's last novel, *Helen* (1834), who declares 'that he should be sorry to be personally acquainted with Scott, for fear of disturbing the agreeable picture in his own mind of the accomplished author.'[57] On the other hand, the new passion for intimate biography – a demand which both Ireland and Walter Savage Landor in their several ways sought to fill on behalf of Shakespeare – could be much more satisfactorily sated by details of Scott's well-documented life.[58] Finally, Scott's successful self-canonisation, his production of what might be imagined as his own self-authenticating Variorum edition, complete with prefaces, notes, and more notes, the Magnum Opus, must have also helped to assimilate the one to the other.

But perhaps the most weighty reason for the assimilation of Scott to Shakespeare was neither fortuitous, nor artistic, but political. The anonymous author of *A Parallel of Shakespeare and Scott* (1835), having listed those similarities I have already touched upon, adds certain arguments that have an unmistakably Tory, nationalistic and even imperialistic flavour. Shakespeare's 'universality' (*'the power of identifying himself with every kind and condition of existence'*)[59] here translates into Scott's comparable success, 'acknowledged in the humblest recesses of private life . . . heard in foreign lands – and the remotest parts of the civilised world.'[60] Above all, Shakespeare's supposedly Tory history was held to have found a worthy successor in Scott,[61] and in consequence of this perceived political correctness, Scott became a major competitor to Shakespeare as the Tory interpreter of British history. Scott's works became as popular as, or more popular than those of Shakespeare as sources for the highly prestigious and consciously nationalistic genre of history-painting, and it was by way of this avenue that Scott's versions of history were eventually installed alongside those of Shakespeare when subjects taken from the Waverley Novels were reproduced in school history books later in the century.[62] So intricately intertwined, indeed, did their versions of history become that it was possible to appeal to Shakespeare's history-plays in order to sanction the staging of Scott's historical novels; the epilogue to *Nigel; or The Crown Jewels* (1823), the theatrical adaptation of *The Fortunes of Nigel* (1822), makes James II invoke *Henry VIII* as the play's respectabilising precursor. Ironically equating himself with Shakespeare's own most famous passage of prophecy, the hapless Stuart predicts of the Spirit of the Future that:

> . . . in that year twenty-three,
> She'll make a stage-play of my Jewels and Me,
> (As Shakespeare serv'd Bessy, our great predecessor,
> Brought in on a crib, like a pig on a dresser.)[63]

British history was henceforth to become a matter of Scott grafted onto Shakespeare, and it would be true to say that, for the nineteenth century at any rate, Coleridge's insistence that Shakespeare's histories 'were the essential truth of history' and that they could accordingly serve as a primary source – 'Let no man blame his son for learning history from Shakespeare'[64] – could be extended without qualms to include Scott.

Modern critics and readers would be unlikely to rank Scott alongside Shakespeare, preferring in all probability to endorse the much less enthusiastic verdict of Hazlitt and his supporters on aesthetic grounds. But it should not be forgotten that Hazlitt, in giving an unfavourable estimate of the talents of Scott in comparison to Shakespeare, is conditioned by his political enmity to the Scott who 'administers charms and philtres to our love of Legitimacy, makes us conceive a horror of all reform, civil, political, or religious, and would fain put down the *Spirit of the Age.*'[65] Hazlitt goes out of his way to distinguish Shakespeare from Scott, notably in his essay 'Sir Walter Scott, Racine and Shakespear' of the genesis of which he writes:

> The subject occurred to me from some conversation with a French lady, who entertains a project of introducing Shakespear in France. As I demurred to the probability of this alteration in the national taste, she endeavoured to overcome my despondency by several lively arguments, and, among other things, urged the instantaneous and universal success of the Scotch Novels among all ranks and conditions of the French people. As Shakespear had been performing quarantine among them for a century and a half, I thought this difference rather proved the difference in the genius of the two writers than a change in the taste of the nation.[66]

Hazlitt here succeeds in opening up a gap between Shakespeare and Scott by inverting the commonplace suggestion that Scott was in some way as 'universal' as, if not more 'universal' than Shakespeare, as demonstrated by his exportability, suggesting instead that Scott is simply more 'French', which, in this context, simply means more barren, more like Racine. Hazlitt goes on to make his main charge: that Scott merely copies from nature ('nothing can be more like nature than facts, if you know where to find them')[67] without the (Shakespearean) power of 'invention'; that is to say, that Shakespeare is original and Scott a mere mechanical transcriber and compiler. Indeed Hazlitt at one point, even in the process of defending Scott's practice of borrowing from historical sources, assimilates him to Ireland, reinventing him as a forged Shakespeare:

> Such vexation [at the disclosure of Scott's sources] . . . would resemble the resentment of those who were deceived by the Shakespeare forgeries – they were annoyed that their want of penetration should be detected, and never forgave Ireland.[68]

Hazlitt insists further that Scott is simply local in time and place, whereas Shakespeare is timeless because he specialises in 'human nature'. This timelessness specifically negates the historicism specialised in by Kemble and Scott:

> Nobody from reading Shakespear would know . . . that Lear was an English king. He is merely a king and a father . . . The tradition is nothing, or a foolish one. There are no data in history to go upon; no advantage is taken of costume, no acquaintance with geography or architecture or dialect is necessary: but there is an old tradition, human nature – an old temple, the human mind – and Shakespear walks into it and looks about him with a lordly eye, and seizes on the sacred spoils as his own. The story is a thousand or two years old, and yet the tragedy has no smack of antiquarianism in it. I should like very well to see Sir Walter giving us a tragedy of this kind, a huge 'globose' of sorrow, swinging round in mid-air, independent of time, place and circumstance, sustained by its own weight and motion, and not propped up by the levers of custom, or patched up with quaint, old-fashioned dresses, or set off by grotesque backgrounds or rusty armour, but in which mere paraphernalia and accessories were left out of the question, and nothing but the soul of passion and the pith of imagination was to be found.[69]

Although nowadays it is fashionable in academic circles to insist that the concept of timelessly great literature is a profoundly conservative idea, Hazlitt is clearly using it here against Scott's nationalistic nostalgia, attempting thus to discredit the Tory 'Shakespeare' described in the course of this chapter.

Notwithstanding Hazlitt's best efforts, it was the Shakespeare of Scott and Kemble that dominated the stage throughout the remainder of the nineteenth century and through into the early twentieth century, embodied in a seemingly endless procession of 'historically accurate' productions.[70] Now that the hey-day of Shakespeare in contemporary costume seems to be well and truly past, and the RSC well on the way back to antiquarian authenticities (epitomised by one of their greatest successes of the 1980s, Bill Alexander's production of *Richard III* (1984) the set for which was fabricated from plaster-cast sections of Worcester Cathedral) – now, in fact, that Shakespearean theatre is partaking of the conservatism that dominated the eighties in Britain– it seems at least possible that Scott, pastmaster of post-modern pastiche, may be accorded once more at least something of his former canonical status under the spacious canopy of the Shakespearean umbrella.

Notes

1. *The Works of Charles and Mary Lamb* ed. E. V. Lucas (London: Methuen, 1912), I, p. 115. See also Jonathan Bate for a discussion of Lamb's privatisation of Shakespeare: *Shakespearean Constitutions* (Oxford: Clarendon Press, 1989), pp. 131–4. Bate, however, associates Scott's novelisation of Shakespeare with this impulse towards the privatisation of the Bard within the closet of the Romantic Imagination; while it is of course true that the novel privatises by comparison to the theatre, I shall be arguing here that Scott's project is not to 'Romanticise' Shakespeare in quite the fashion that Bate suggests.
2. Of his scheme to produce 'a national edition of Shakespeare' in the form of a series of history-paintings, Boydell found it necessary to apologise for the heresy of attempting to represent the unrepresentable (unrepresentable because more natural than nature and so inaccessible in some fundamental way to the imitating artist): 'it must always be remembered, that [Shakespeare] possessed powers which no pencil can reach; for such was the force of his creative imagination, that though he frequently goes beyond nature, he still continues to be natural, and seems only to do that which nature would have done, had she o'erstep'd her usual limits . . . what pencil can give to his airy beings "a local habitation and a name?" ' *The Boydell Shakespeare Prints*, introd. A. E. Santaniello (New York and London: Benjamin Blau Inc., 1968), Preface.
3. See especially Henry Fuseli's movement towards the unstageable in his paintings of the Macbeths, which move first towards the nude and then gesture towards virtual disembodiment.
4. See Hazlitt on *King Lear* as essentially unlocalised in time or space, a comment which springs, not incidentally, from a comparison of Shakespeare with Scott (see below). *The Complete Works of William Hazlitt* ed. P. P. Howe (London, 1930–4), XII, p. 341.
5. See Jonathan Bate's comment that 'it was above all Shakespeare who provided the Romantics . . . with "basic analogies for the poet and his poem," with crucial "tenets of poetical theory" and, most importantly, with raw materials for poetic practice.' *Shakespeare and the English Romantic Imagination* (Oxford: Clarendon Press, 1986), pp. 2–3.
6. This was also true of performance; Garrick's 1744 *Macbeth* marks the moment when it was for the first time asserted that the performance recovered the authentic Shakespeare, specifically that the play was being performed 'as written by Shakespeare'. The claim, at any rate as we would understand it, is not true. George C. D. Odell, *Shakespeare from Betterton to Irving* (New York, 1920), I, p. 340. For further discussion of this moment see Stephen Orgel, 'The Authentic Shakespeare,' *Representations*, XXI (Winter 1988), pp. 1–25, especially p. 15.
7. On Malone's project and its politics, see Margreta de Grazia, *Shakespeare Verbatim: The Reproduction of Authenticity and the 1790 Apparatus* (Oxford: Clarendon Press, 1991).

8. Edmond Malone, *An Inquiry into the Authenticity of certain Miscellaneous . . . Papers . . . Attributed to Shakspeare* (London: for Cadell and Davies, 1796), pp. 2-3.

9. Malone, *op. cit.*, pp. 40-2.

10. For the reactions of reviewers, see Peter Martin's forthcoming biography of Malone; for Burke's approving reaction, see [James Boswell the Younger], *A Biographical Memoir of the Late Edmond Malone Esq.* (London, 1814), p. 23. The practice of editing Shakespeare on the basis of an appeal to the 'original' and 'authentic' texts only became invariably connected with an antiquarian anti-Jacobinism after 1793 or so, as the skirmishes in the eighties and early nineties between Malone and the radical and frustrated Shakespearean editor Joseph Ritson demonstrate. Ritson's commentary has a potentially far more Jacobinical, or theoretical bent to it, fuelled as it is by an urge to clear away the 'corruptions' of past editions, and a refusal to fetishise the impediments of the past. Ritson's edition was, however, essentially suppressed. See Gary Taylor, *Reinventing Shakespeare* (New York: Wiedenfeld and Nicolson, 1989), pp. 144-7.

11. See Arthur Sherbo, *The Birth of Shakespeare Studies* (Michigan: Colleagues Press, 1986), pp. 177-9.

12. See *The Miscellaneous Prose Works of Sir Walter Scott, Bart.* (Edinburgh: Robert Cadell, 1849), XX ('Life of Kemble'), pp. 187-9; 202-5. Also Charles Shattuck, ed., *The Kemble Promptbooks* (Charlottesville: for Folger by University Press of Virginia, 1974), I, p. xiii and II, p. ii-iii.

13. James Robinson Planché, *Costume of Shakespeare's Historical Tragedy of King John . . . with Biographical, Critical, and Explanatory Notices* (London: John Miller, 1823), p. 4.

14. *Covent Garden Play-Bills 1823-4*, Bodleian Library, M. adds. 128 c. 10.

15. James Boaden, *Memoirs of the Life of John Philip Kemble, Esq. including A History of the Stage from the Time of Garrick to the present Period.* 4 vols in 2 (London: Longman, Hurst, Rees, Orme, Brown and Green, 1825), II, p. 279.

16. *Ibid.*, II, p. 279.

17. J. R. Planché, *op. cit.*, p. 4.

18. BMC 8138 and BMC 7858 respectively. Cited J. Bate (1989), *op. cit.*, p. 14.

19. The most spectacular borrowing from *King John* is, predictably, from the final speech, rendered as follows:

> THIS ENGLAND NEVER DID (NOR NEVER SHALL)
> LIE AT THE PROUD FOOT OF A CONQUEROR,
> But when it first doth help wound itself.
> Let come the three corners of the world in arms,
> And we shall shock them: *naught shall make us rue,*
> *If England to itself do rest but true.*

Gentleman's Magazine, LXXIII (1803), p. 664.

20. See J. Bate (1989), *op. cit.*, pp. 67-8.

21. Henry Crabb Robinson, *On Books and Their Writers*, ed. E. J. Morley (London: J. M. Dent, 1938), I, p. 55.

22. *The Prose Works of Sir Walter Scott, Bart., op. cit.*, XX ('Life of Kemble'), p. 204.

23. See Scott's anecdote of his improvements to Kemble's costume as Macbeth:

[H]e was delighted when, with our own critical hands . . . we divested his bonnet of sundry huge bunches of black feathers which made it look like an undertaker's cushion, and replaced them with the single broad quill feather of an eagle sloping across his noble brow; he told us afterwards that the change was worth to him three distinct rounds of applause as he came forwards in this improved and more genuine headgear. *The Prose Works of Sir Walter Scott, Bart.* (Edinburgh: Robert Cadell, 1849), XX ('Life of Kemble'), p. 205.

24. Tellingly, Planché extended his own antiquarian pleasures from historical costume design to collecting folk-ballads and legends in *The Lays and Legends of the Rhine*, dedicated, by permission, to Sir Walter Scott. Benjamin Webster, ed. *The Acting National Drama* (London: Chapman and Hall, 1837), I, p. 3.
25. John O. Hayden ed., *Scott: The Critical Heritage* (London: Routledge, Kegan Paul, 1970), pp. 286–7.
26. Sir Walter Scott, *Woodstock; or, The Cavalier, A Tale of the Year Sixteen Hundred and Forty-One* ed. with intro. Andrew Lang (Border edn) (London: John C. Nimmo, 1894), I, pp. 47–8.
27. Edmond Malone, ed., *The Plays and Poems of William Shakspeare, in Ten Volumes; collected VERBATIM with the most authentick Copies with the Corrections and Illustrations of Various Commentators* (London: for J. Rivington etc. etc., 1790), pp. xvii–iii.
28. *ibid.*, p. xix.
29. Charles Lamb, *op. cit.*, II, p. 197.
30. *Woodstock*, I, p. 29.
31. *ibid.*, I, p. 60.
32. *ibid.*, II, p. 121. Given the legitimist bias of the novel as a whole it is fitting that to speak 'Shakespeare', is also to speak in 'classic' or trans-historical language; in the confrontation staged between Shakespeare the royalist bard and Milton the republican poet, Milton is quite definitely marked as 'classic' only by the march of history; the lines quoted from *Comus* by Everard (by which even Henry Lee is captivated) are salvaged as 'classic' in the terms of the late eighteenth century only by history's erasure of Milton's jacobinical politics, 'lines now so well known, but which then had obtained no celebrity, the fame of the author resting upon the basis rather of his polemical and political publications, than on the poetry doomed in after years to support the eternal structure of his immortality.' *ibid.*, II, p. 123.
33. *ibid.*, II, pp. 119–20.
34. *ibid.*, I, p. 49.
35. *ibid.*, I, p. 149.
36. *ibid.*, II, p. 80.
37. Even Milton is pressed into this service: collapsing Milton from politician to poet and moralist, Scott appropriates him to the same ends as he appropriates Shakespeare, to police royal libertinism (after all, part of the original point of *comus*) in the service, however, of legitimacy. *ibid.*, II, pp. 123–4.
38. *ibid.*, I, p. 68, and II, pp. 38; 77; 110.
39. Tate's 1680 *Richard II*, for example, was perceived as pro-Whig in spite of his best efforts. See also the *Craftsman*, in which one 'C.C.P.L.' lists passages of Shakespeare which should be censored for their political subversiveness, and comments of *Richard II*, 'it not only represents an *obstinate, misguided Prince* deposed by his *People*, which is agreeable enough to the principles of the

Revolution; but likewise contains several Passages, which the *disaffected* may turn to their account.' The *Craftsman*, 2 July 1737. Quoted J. Bate (1989), *op. cit.*, pp. 67–8.

40. The contemporary analogue that infuses Scott's novel with some urgency was, of course, George IV, whose involvement in a series of sexual scandals during the 1820s was thought to bring the threat of revolution that much closer.

41. *Woodstock*, I, p. 80.

42. *ibid.*, II, p. 309.

43. *ibid.*, II, p. 364. In the original edition this note follows immediately at the bottom of the page.

44. John O. Hayden ed., *Scott: The Critical Heritage* (London: Routledge, Kegan Paul, 1970), p. 274.

45. Entry for 11 Dec. 1826. W. E. K. Anderson ed., *The Journal of Sir Walter Scott* (Oxford: Clarendon Press, 1972), p. 252.

46. Scott is listed as one of the experts who gave their verdicts against the Ireland papers in the *Gentleman's Magazine*, LXVI (April 1796), p. 267.

47. See for instance his comments on Shakespeare in the 'Essay on the Drama,' *The Miscellaneous Works of Sir Walter Scott, Bart.* (Edinburgh: Robert Cadell, 1850–9), VI, pp. 341–2.

48. Sir Walter Scott, *Chronicles of the Canongate* ed. with intro. Andrew Lang (Border edn) (London: John C. Nimmo, 1894), p. xlvii.

49. See, for example, *The Female Characters of Scott* (London: Stearns and Co., [1848]), p. 2.

50. James Boaden, *An Inquiry into the Authenticity of Various Pictures and Prints . . .* (London: for Robert Triphook, 1824), p. 104. A similar rating of Scott as the new Shakespeare appears in Nathan Drake's *Memorials of Shakespeare* (London, 1828), a substantial anthology of major writings on Shakespeare (arranged chronologically, from Heminge and Condell through Schiller) which culminates with Drake's own discussion of Shakespeare's similarity to Scott, his rightful heir; the Bard is praised as a master of what is recognisably a novelistic concept of character. For good measure, this discussion is refracted through a discussion of the legitimacy of Charles I and II.

51. Sir Walter Scott, *Chronicles of the Canongate etc.*, *op. cit.*, p. lv.

52. Unsigned review of *Ivanhoe*. *Eclectic Review* XIII (2nd series) (June 1820) pp. 526–40. Quoted in *Critical Heritage*, *op. cit.*, pp. 191–2.

53. *The Prose Works of Sir Walter Scott, Bart.* (Edinburgh: Robert Cadell, 1849), XIX, p. 65.

54. *Critical Heritage*, *op. cit.*, p. 231.

55. 2 Mar 1827. *The Journal of Sir Walter Scott*, *op. cit.*, p. 284.

56. J. Bate (1986), *op. cit.*, p. 164.

57. *A Parallel of Shakespeare and Scott; Being the Substance of Three Lectures on the Kindred Nature of Their Genius . . .* (London: Whitaker, Treacher, and Co., 1835), pp. iii–iv.

58. See Walter Savage Landor's extraordinary exercise in revivifying an (apocryphal) episode in Shakespeare's life, the deer-stealing at Charlecote Park: *Citation and Examination of Wil. Shakespeare . . . before the Worshipful Sir Thomas Lucy, Knight, touching deer-stalking . . . now first published from original papers.* For information regarding this composition see Malcolm Elwin, *Landor: A Replevin* (London: Macdonald, 1958), p. 268. For an instance of the contemporary interest in finding the author in his work see James Boaden's *An Inquiry into the Authenticity of various Pictures and Prints, which,*

from the Decease of the Poet to our own Times, Have been offered to the Public as Portraits of Shakespeare (London: for Robert Triphook, 1824), which project he explains as motivated by this same desire to excavate and authenticate by antiquarian means the 'true' Shakespeare, the author implied by and embodied within the ('authentic') text:

> [T]he plays sent me back to the portrait before them, and the portrait seldom failed to return me to the most ardent perusal of the plays. And as my love for his productions induced me to collect the most authentic copies of his Works, my fondness for the Writer led me to obtain the most accurate resemblance of his countenance. (p. ii). The inevitable conflation of Scott's mode of retrieving history into fiction and the rage for a biographised Shakespeare was left to Nathan Drake, who makes the Bard the protagonist of a historical novelette set in Jacobean Stratford and conducted entirely upon Scott's plan. *Noontide Leisure; or, sketches in Summer . . . including A Tale of the Days of Shakespeare* (London: for T. Cadell and W. Blackwood, 1824).

59. *A Parallel of Shakespeare and Scott, op. cit.*, p. 7.
60. *ibid.*, p. 3.
61. *ibid.*, pp. 11; 18.
62. Douglas Percy Bliss, *Sir Walter Scott and the Visual Arts* ([Glasgow]: The Foulis Archive Press, 1971), pp. 19; 21.
63. *Nigel; or, The Crown Jewels* (London, 1823), Epilogue.
64. R. A. Foakes, ed. *Coleridge on Shakespeare: The Text of the Lectures of 1811–12* (Charlottesville: for the Folger Library by the University Press of Virginia, 1971), p. 132.
65. *Critical Heritage, op. cit.*, pp. 275; 288.
66. *The Complete Works of William Hazlitt, op. cit.*, XII, p. 338.
67. *ibid.*, XII, p. 339.
68. Wm. Hazlitt, *op. cit.*, XX, p. 233.
69. *ibid.*, XII, pp. 340-1.
70. The most striking examples are perhaps Charles Kean's productions at the Princess's Theatre during the 1850s, the souvenir acting editions to which are at least as heavily footnoted (chiefly to artefacts faithfully copied from the British Museum for use as props) as Malone's edition itself.

6 Caught in the Act: Or, the Prosing of Juliet

John Glavin

'I should kill thee with much cherishing'
(*Romeo and Juliet* II, ii, 183–4)

The fact is – or, rather, the fiction, since I shall be dealing here primarily with novels – that by the end of the nineteenth century it had become very hard to play Juliet, and live. I am thinking specifically of: Mrs Humphry Ward's first novel, *Miss Bretherton*, published in December 1884; Henry James's *The Tragic Muse*, serialised 1888–9, and, in 1890, Oscar Wilde's *The Picture of Dorian Gray*. But I am also concerned with texts as various as Louisa May Alcott's 1865 story 'A Double Tragedy' and Soren Kierkegaard's long essay *The Crisis and a Crisis in The Life of an Actress* (1848), an account of an historical figure, the Scandinavian actress Johanne Luise Heiberg, returning to the role of Juliet in early middle-age. In each of the three novels, the leading female character plays Juliet, dangerously. And the danger involved seems to increase exponentially in relation to what the great actor Talma called 'that faculty of exaltation which agitates an actor . . . and enables him to enter into the most tragic situations, and the most terrible passions, *as if they were his own*.' (Emphases mine. Quoting this passage, Sir Henry Irving called it the 'perfect description of the art of acting.'[1]) Alcott's Juliet, a young actress called Clotilde Varian, also dies in and of the role. She stabs herself on stage in the play's finale, after she has killed her real husband, also with Romeo's dagger, just before the fatal performance begins. Only in Kierkegaard does the actress seem to survive the crisis Juliet entails. Fru Heiberg not only endures but triumphs in the role over time's depredations and her audience's devouring expectations.

In one sense, we recognize here a recuperation of the enormous and ultimately appalling violence locked into the play's dramatic structure and metaphoric texture. Ward, Wilde and James treat that impacted violence in different ways, shaped by the characteristic Victorian difference between the melodramatic (Ward, Wilde) and frivolous (James).[2] (Thus, James writes an ultimately comic novel and calls it with characteristic irony *The Tragic Muse*.) But in their shared strategy, intersecting the aesthetic and the erotic within the theatrical/female, they also uncover something crucial to the way in which the nineteenth century refigured the 'deeper structures of fear', embedded in Shakespeare's play.[3] We find a Victorian Juliet who is and is not continuous with her Elizabethan prototype.

Alan Sinfield reminds us that the extraordinary privilege attached to Shakespeare has made his plays 'an influential medium . . . a site of cultural struggle and change'.[4] a site at which, Kathleen McLuskie suggests, 'meaning is constructed every time the text is reproduced.'[5] As bourgeois culture through the course of the nineteenth century completes its enclosure of patriarchy, we can watch that change in action. Nostalgic sites of passion like the Forest of Arden, Ilyria, and most intensely Verona, now beckon with an almost unbearable poignancy beyond the new, high 'fences surrounding the sexual sphere of libidinal life.'[6] In its Elizabethan version, *Romeo and Juliet*'s fantasy of immediate, limitless affect focused on the libidinous energies of unyoked young men. Revised to suit the exigencies of bourgeois culture, the focus switches to the lady, to a Juliet who amidst continued violence is required to exert a power men understand themselves to have surrendered in all but fantasy. And when she cannot or will not supply such power, she must be ruthlessly scrapped. Nowhere is this refocusing of power and eros more clear than in the nineteenth-century prose which describes both Juliet and the play.

Within the play-script Juliet figures as the final, even the ultimate, victim of the family feuds that structure her world. She follows Romeo, Paris, Tybalt and Mercutio into the inescapable Veronese *liebestod* where 'death is a transcendent form of sexual consummation . . . [a] rebirth into a high stage of existence.'[7] But in Victorian fiction Juliet suffers not with the men who adore her, but for them. With that transformation, we move from the pleasure of seeing and showing, scopophilia, the fundamental pleasure of any theatre event, to its perversion, scopophobia, the fear of looking and being looked at. Juliet's conscription within the empire of the male gaze marks the crucial cultural swerve of the eighteenth to the nineteenth century, the swerve from exhibition to inhibition. Earlier anti-theatrical diatribes attack the public body of the actress who on stage exposes herself to the common gaze. Later, the novel shifts its focus to watching him who watches her, the male voyeur (connoisseur, impresario, lover). And in doubling the gaze, prose seeing play, reader watching the watcher who, at the same time, and often inside the same glance, sees the actress perform, Juliet's fantasy value mutates, from final to only victim, the expiatory, exemplary sexual sacrifice.

*   *   *   *   *

Despite Hazlitt's insistence (1819) that 'Of all Shakespeare's plays, this is perhaps the one that is acted, if not the oftenest, with most pleasure to the spectator,'[8] *Romeo and Juliet* was not as important for audiences at the beginning of the century as were tragedies like *Hamlet*, *Macbeth*, and *Richard III*. And yet, by the final decades of the nineteenth century, Juliet had been revalued as a key, if not the supreme, test of the first-rate young actress: 'this extremely difficult part (a part in which so few, if any, even of the greatest actresses, have been able to satisfy the imagination.)'[9] Earlier response to the role seems to acknowledge no such complexity. Kierkegaard, for instance, in his 1847 account of Fru Heiberg's performance sees in Juliet only an abundant *youthfulness*: 'the vivacious, abundant restlessness of youth, of which one always speaks with sponta-neous affection, as when it is said that a happily gifted child is the restless one in the family.'[10] But Kierkegaard's Scandinavian theatre seems almost naive and certainly *retardataire* in relation to the criticism emerging from contemporary French, German and British sources. These critics share an emphasis on the role's inherent difficulty, a difficulty attributed to the rapid transitions the role demanded. Juliet must move from childhood in the first scene with the Nurse, to adolescence in the first balcony scene, to passionate womanhood in the second balcony scene, and on to a fully tragic stature in the tomb. So, for example, in 1864 we find H. T. Rotscher writing:

> What a difference is there between the Juliet of the close of the Second Act and her first appearance in the second scene of the third! We no longer see the restless, anxious, half-unconstrained, half-love intoxicated being; the full fruit has ripened. The woman stands before us, in the unbroken energy of the blissful feeling to which the universe has become personified in her husband.[11]

It is this crucial requirement: to maintain Juliet as a coherent, consistent characterisation scene by scene, and at the same time to authenticate the fundamentally erotic transformation, between scenes, from innocent child to experienced woman, that so severely tested (and of course still tests) any actress's skill.

Our novels suggest, however, that by the end of the century, Juliet tried not only the actress's histrionic but her survival skills. In each text the crisis she endures is determined by the actress's coming into contact with a male connoisseur, whose gaze constitutes not only an erotic but ultimately an ontological demand. Wilde's Sybil Vane dies of that demand. Mrs Ward's Isabel Bretherton and Henry James's Miriam Roth find scapegoats, one female, the other male, who decline in their stead. But all three share the experience of rapture, of being seized as the heightened ground of sadomasochistic discourse: 'She is more than an individual! . . . she has genius. I love her, and I must make her love me . . . I want to make Romeo jealous. I want the dead lovers of the world to hear our laughter, and grow sad. I want a breath of passion to stir their dust into consciousness, to wake their ashes into pain.'[12] *To wake . . . into pain*: such an awakening, in one way or another, is the fundamental burden of a Victorian Juliet.

Good evidence suggests that James may actually have set out in *The Tragic Muse* to revise, or 'correct', his friend Mrs Ward's novel. And it seems at least plausible to hypothesise that Wilde, an inveterate plagiarist, may have borrowed the Ward-James scenario as the basis for the awkwardly conjoined Sybil Vane story in *Dorian Gray*. All three plots turn on a young, outsider actress (Miriam and Sybil are lower class and probably illegitimate; Isabel is a lady, but only an American lady) aspiring to Juliet. Each actress attracts through on-stage performance the erotic attention and artistic criticism of an aristocratic suitor, who prepares his Juliet for real theatrical eminence. Miriam's story varies, however, in one crucial way from that of her sister Juliets. Her patron does her suffering for her. While Sybil succumbs to Dorian Gray's cruelty and Isabel to Eustace Kendal's benignity, Miriam 'goes beyond' her patron, Peter Sherringham; 'she leaves him looking after her and wondering. She begins where he ends – soars away is lost to him.'[13] It is Sherringham who pays not only the economic but also the cultural costs of her triumph.

Sybil Vane's story is the best known of the three. 'Fancy, Jim, to be in love and play Juliet!', she rhapsodises to her brother, in love with Dorian Gray, and that evening to play Juliet for him (p. 94). The next morning, after a lacklustre performance, she is by her own hand dead. But the deep cause of her death is, of course, Gray himself, or rather her despair at discovering that the thwarted voyeur insists she live no life but Juliet's: 'Without your art you are nothing' (p. 116). Failing to fulfil the demands placed upon her by the ultimate connoisseur, she finds herself without a place either on stage or in life.

More fortunate than Sybil Vane, Isabel Bretherton finds someone else to do her dying for her. In the first part of the novel, she is taken up and then spurned as ignorant of real art by the dilettante Eustace Kendal, who is 'Bitten with a passion for that great, that fascinating French literature which absorbs – the interests of two-thirds of those who are sensitive to the things of letters.'[14] But she is saved from failure and then from death by the intervention of a quasi-angelic patroness. Marie de Chateauvieux, Kendal's sister, takes the limited, uncrafty actress under her protection, encouraging Isabel to study Diderot's *Paradox* with Marie's husband, Paul.

These lessons equip the young actress with the intellectual and vocal technique she sorely needs, until at the turning point of the novel, she performs Juliet by moonlight in the garden of the Chateauvieux's rented Venetian palazzo (almost but not quite Verona). In that triumphant, revelatory moment, Isabel becomes Juliet, just as Sybil was to have become Juliet in the shabby theatre Dorian patronized. 'When once I could reach the feeling of the Tybalt speech,' Isabel exclaims, 'when I could once *hate* him for killing Tybalt in the same breath in which I *loved* him for being Romeo, all was easy; gesture and movement came to me; I learnt them, and the thing was done' (p. 177).

And at the same moment, the curse of the part darkens the scene. 'She was quite worn out with the effort,' Marie writes to her brother (p. 177). Within weeks Miss Bretherton has begun to faint onstage, an experience which the novel assures us 'much alarmed the audience' (p. 244). From her all too likely fate, the actress is rescued by the deflected, expiatory death of her mentor. Exactly at the point when she is breaking down in London (p. 229), Marie in Paris mysteriously falls ill – of 'Internal chill' (p. 245) – and within two days is dead. Her dying words commit Isabel, and a miniature of herself, into Kendal's hands. As he is breaking the news of his sister's death, the couple suddenly find themselves drawn together in passion. The exchange is clear, not only to the reader but to Kendal himself: he 'had left Marie in the grave . . . But Isabel was still among the living . . . He took a strange, sad pleasure in making the contrast between the one picture and the other as vivid as possible' (p. 244). Staged forever in the surrogate proscenium of the miniaturised frame, Marie thus purchases Isabel's survival.

The equivocal complexity of this exchange surfaces as Kendal's musing continues. 'Death and silence on the one hand . . . But on the other, he forced on his imagination till it drew for him an image of youth and beauty so glowing that it almost charmed the sting out of his grief' (p. 244). The diminished image of the dead Marie contrasts poignantly a living Isabel, but she herself is also now merely an image, maintained by the male imagination, as Sybil Vane was maintained by Dorian's imaginative response to her performance. In this intricate transaction, Miss Bretherton's future as an actress is left opaque. In the last sequence she is found reading a playscript but still convalescent and weak from her fainting episodes. It may be that her health will never again suffice for the rigours of the stage. What is clear is that her own life, her own ability to determine that life, is gone forever. The final pages repeatedly station her as an 'image', held by Kendal 'within the "wind-warm space" of love' (p. 255). But that space, analogous to both the stage and the miniature frame, in turn depends upon, is protected by, in fact is produced by 'death and sorrow and parting – three grave and tender angels of benediction,' (these are the final words of the novel) who 'kept watch and ward without'. (p. 255). At the end then, even though she has not herself been forced to go down into death, the price Isabel pays for her vibrant, vital Juliet is reduction to the permanent status of revenant, 'fragile and worn' (p. 249). A final, ghost-like 'soft white cashmere shawl' seems to cancel any chance of development, insinuating that in the future she will only perform her debut role, The White Lady, a love-betrayed noblewoman, 'the most representative of all that is most poetical and romantic in physical beauty' (p. 54), who realises 'the utmost limits of the author's ideal . . . when she faded into the darkness beyond the moonlight in which she had first appeared' (p. 55).

In The Tragic Muse, Peter Sherringham, having tried in vain to resist her attractions, finally proposes to Miriam Roth out of weakness, in a scene full of 'vulgar, ghostly vibration'[15] (perhaps an ironic recollection of the ghostly madame de Chateauvieux hovering over Kendal's proposal to Isabel). Sherringham's desire, he confesses, is 'simply a need that consumes me' (p. 465). Here passion registers not as the harbinger of fatal illness (Dorian) or as its antidote (Kendal) but as illness itself, this time the man's illness: 'I've simply overrated my strength' (p. 462), he admits. And here it is the actress not her patron who embodies the force of the scene. Rejected by Miriam, Peter is 'flung back' by her 'histrionic hardness', back 'against a fifth-rate world', of tawdry, ironised theatrical imagery, 'against a bedimmed star-punctured nature which has no consolation – the bleared, irresponsive eyes of the London heaven' (p. 475). A year later, on the night her 'Juliet' opens, in the novel's concluding, climactic scene, he returns from the tropics 'how brown, how worn' (p. 523), willing now to throw over his career and manage hers, only to discover that three days before she has married her Mercutio. On stage 'Miriam Roth was sublime' (p. 527). In the audience, Sherringham collapses into 'a period of miserable madness' (p. 528). 'What a disaster,' an amiable cousin affirms (p. 523).

As in Miss Bretherton, the perilous price of playing Juliet is paid by another, one who lovingly gives a life (hers/his) to save the actress's future. But unlike the wan and wasted Isabel, the indestructible Miriam goes from strength to strength: 'both in public and in private she has a great deal more to show' (p. 530). Her ability to wedge open that space between her public and private life determines her survival as Juliet. All three actresses risk the encompassing contemporary crisis of representation itself, the crisis that determines the core of early modernism. But where European painting in the eighties breaks with mimesis, the theatre, necessarily loyal to the power of the gaze, embraces it. Kierkegaard, for instance, imagines the successful actress saying to the playwright: 'Here is the original you were trying to copy' (p. 131). Invariably the theatre audience finds itself directed toward a metonymic, not a metaphoric body, the performer's body in the character's clothing, rather than toward painting's new syntax of somatoid forms.[16] As we examine this 'realistic' push of late-Victorian theatre, toward erasing the recess between player and role, we can theorise what seems the critical gap through which Juliet's scripted pain inflicts and inflects the actress who stands in for her.

A new seriousness had overtaken the English-speaking theatre by the 1880s, as it competed for the patronage of the now dominant middle class, an audience 'which had vanished, it was always agreed, with the Puritan revolution.'[17] But to recover that audience, shaped by Puritanism's deeply ingrained hostility to artifice, the English theatre had to prove itself, despite its obvious artificiality, fundamentally sincere, indisputably – the supreme Victorian shibboleth – earnest. As Mrs Ward herself asked in her memoirs, and this question is for her both a technical and, even more importantly, a moral difficulty: 'What is the relation of the actor to the part represented?'[18] Behind that question couched the anxiety that lurks within all anti-theatrical prejudice, 'the fear that the theatre may so infuse and confuse reality that proper distinctions and the boundaries by which we make sense of life may no longer hold true.'[19]

A successful answer to Mrs Ward's question was debated throughout the eighties, by the likes of Matthew Arnold (Mrs Ward's uncle), Henry Irving, and Ibsen's influential, first English translator, William Archer. In 1883, the year before *Miss Bretherton*, an English translation appeared for both Diderot's *Paradox of the Actor* and Francois Joseph Talma's *Reflections on the Actor's Art*, both with prefaces by Henry Irving, himself busy during those years attempting to establish under his own direction a *de facto* National Theatre at the Lyceum. By 1887, when James began *The Tragic Muse*, writing about the theatre had become almost as popular as the theatre itself, activity that culminated in 1888 with William Archer's *Masks and Faces*, the definitive, late-Victorian compendium of performance theories and attitudes toward theatre.

The English proponents of this new realistic (read: sincere, sober) theatre united against the French authorities (read, as usual: craft, dishonest, not-English!), to insist that the actor must become one with the role. Archer called this emphasis, apologetically, *emotionalist*. For counter-text, he read Diderot's *Paradox* as the powerfully prestigious *locus classicus* of a theatricality to be superseded, the theatricality of the frivolous, aristocratic *ancien régime*, of both England and France. But here Archer's terms can be misleading if we associate emotion with Stanislavski and the Method. Diderot himself was not arguing for a cold or sterile style without affect. Diderot was not Brecht. (Neither was Brecht, as we are gradually beginning to realise.) Archer divided Diderot from Archer not on the absence or presence of feeling in a performance but on the degree to which the performer identifies himself or herself with the part during performance, the degree to which he or she becomes, in her or his own mind and in the audience's eyes, the character.

Writing for, and of, a theatre of idealised types, what he calls 'hippogriffs', Diderot insists that acting cannot be literally true to nature. For exactly that reason Rousseau, at roughly the same time, argued against the establishment of a theatre in Protestant Geneva (1758). His actor, the archetypally untrustworthy citizen, counterfeits and then evades liability: 'an actor on the stage, displaying other sentiments than his own, saying only what he is made to say, often representing a chimerical being, annihilates himself, as it were, and is lost in his hero.'[20] For Diderot, on the contrary, the actor makes himself a hero by triumphing over both his own limited individuality and the audience's credulity. Where Rousseau grounds acting in feeling, or more precisely in bad faith, Diderot grounds it in the brain, in an astute aping. Diderot's paradoxical actor observes nature, but, to play the theatrically conceived role, thoughtfully transposes what he has observed. 'The player's tears come from his brain,' the *Paradox* argues, in one of its most remarkable passages: the actor 'weeps as might weep an unbelieving priest preaching of the Passion; as a seducer might weep at the feet of a woman he does not love, but on whom he would impose; like a beggar in the street or at the door of a church – a beggar who substitutes insult for vain appeal; or like a courtesan who has no heart, and who abandons herself in your arms.'[21] That is exactly *comedie*-trained Miriam Roth's boast to Sherringham, when he asks her to marry him and become an Ambassador's wife: 'A nasty, prim "official" woman . . . I've seen them abroad, I could imitate them here . . . if I were not so tired' (pp. 470–1). 'I'm too clever,' she delightedly crows in her own facility, 'I'm a humbug' (p. 502).

Against such a shameless, un-English delight in shaming, the nine-teenth-century British theatre primly insisted on the primacy not simply of real feeling but of feeling real. Countering Diderot, Henry Irving appropriates the position of the French actor Talma who stressed that successful acting depends entirely upon *sensibility*: 'that faculty of exalta-tion which agitates an actor, takes possession of his senses, shakes even his soul, and enables him to enter into the most tragic situations, and the most terrible passions, as if they were his own.'[22] Such a passage echoes clearly in ill-fated Sybil Vane and fatally ill Isabel Bretherton, each of whom, as we saw earlier, boasts of becoming one with the Juliet she plays. Isabel in fact cries out in her Venetian triumph: 'Diderot is wrong, wrong, wrong!' (p. 177).

Louisa May Alcott's 'A Double Tragedy' seems, at first, to counter this anglophone stress by emphasising a liberating separation between performance and performer as the condition that makes not only theatre but self-realisation possible. Clotilde Varian is another actress who '[throws] herself into her part with an *abandon* that made her seem a beautiful embodiment of power and passion.'[23] Having fled from a brutal marriage, Clotilde becomes 'the rage that season' (p. 125), 'the reigning favorite' (p. 126) in a playhouse that seems francophile even if not francophone. The story's generating premiss implies that if she can play both on- and off-stage roles of her own choosing, the theatrical disjunction between self and role may free possibilities of desire forbidden in ordinary life. As Paul Lamar, the narrator, and Clotilde's lover/leading man, boasts: 'An actor learns to live a double life, so while Paul Lamar suffered torments of anxiety, Don Felix [his part in the play] fought a duel, killed his adversary, and was dragged to judgment' (pp. 127-8).

But even in the final words of Lamar's happy boast, theatrical weight swings from the liberating to the carceral. Self-invention cannot withstand the masterful scrutiny of the patriarchal gaze. Within a few lines doubleness has begun to register as duplicity, destabilised now by Clotilde's returning, vengeful husband, St. John, in a vertiginous paragraph in which all difference collapses into its contrary. Lamar finds himself watching Clotilde watching 'one of the stage-boxes, and at first I thought it was empty, but presently I caught the glitter of a glass turned apparently on myself . . . I searched the box with a keen glance. Nothing was visible, however, but a hand lying easily on the red cushion; a man's hand, white and shapely; on one finger shone a ring, evidently, a woman's ornament' (p. 128). The actors on the stage become at the same time audience gazing into the stage-box, as from the box the simultaneously concealed and revealed, ambivalently gendered, demonic St. John gazes back at them within the proscenium frame. 'Apparently' and 'evidently' cling to the possibility of identity surfacing in the crosscurrents of the gaze, to the actor's dream of resisting the all-encompassing scrutiny of the audience's 'keen glance'. But that dream has no hold on this now thoroughly theatricalised, that is, thoroughly acculturated space. The implications of Clotilde's status come clear: a 'reigning favorite' reigns only as long as its pleases her royal master to keep her in his glance.

Thus, despite its sympathy for Clotilde and its detestation of her husband, the story functions as agent for the 'keen glance' of the patriarchal gaze, steadily reducing the range of the actress's self-determination until it forces her to become entirely one with her role. When unbuttoned sword-play erupts between St. John and Lamar during rehearsal, Alcott's plot is overtaken by the *Romeo and Juliet* being prepared for public performance. The hitherto concealed St. John now reveals himself as the patriarchal kinsman, fighting to separate this Juliet from the object of her independent desire: 'Monsieur merely claims his own' (p. 135). This vertiginous circulation between stage and backstage creates what the text terms 'mimic tragedy' (p. 145): each side of Clotilde's life now doubles the other. The repeated emphasis on doubling has lost all its initial power to read doubleness as division, as a separation into alternatives. Clotilde's equipoise rebounds against her as the husband's gaze re-enrols her despite herself in a performance in which he takes redoubled sadistic pleasure. 'Much as [St. John] had admired her on the stage he was doubly charmed with her performance in private, for it was superb. They were among strangers, and she received him like one, playing her part with the utmost grace and self-control' (p. 134).

The logic of Alcott's plot works ruthlessly to the play's inevitable conclusion. As *Romeo and Juliet* begins, the only theatrical liberty left sides now with the gaze, in the audience, 'the gay crowd rustling before the curtain', contrasted against 'the dreadful scene transpiring behind it' (p. 142). Like Juliet's mock/real suicide within the play, Clotilde's attempt to control a path toward the fulfillment of desire in the end undoes her. Her murder of St. John with Romeo's dagger – she cuts the 'little platform, hastily built for the launching of an aerial-car in some grand spectacle' (p. 142) – alienates the self-righteous Lamar so that 'a wide gulf now lay between us' (p. 145). This 'Juliet's grave-clothes' are Clotilde's 'own' (p. 146) as onstage in the final paragraphs she stabs herself with Romeo's dagger, perfecting the identification the narration has striven so hard to subvert: 'the hapless Italian lovers never found better representatives than in us that night' (p. 146). Like demons, the roles demand to possess the actors who can not *merely* represent them: 'I had not played the lover to this beautiful woman many weeks before I found I was one in earnest' (p. 126). Bourgeois sincerity makes artifice, its adversary, echo back its own most characteristic term.

Thus, almost twenty-five years earlier than Wilde's novel, in a melodrama written for a popular family magazine, far from the aestheticist texts of the eighties, the insistence of the English-speaking theatre on identifying the actress with her role forces from Juliet both the repudiation of desire and the renunciation of life. It is especially intriguing to read Alcott's 'thriller' in this context. The heroine of the opening 'Spanish play' (p. 125) at the final curtain turns 'her head as if to glance triumphantly at the defeated Duke' (pp. 128–9). But in the surrounding story the possibility of a redemptive, innocent heroine, at the last 'bringing liberty and love as [the hero's] reward' (p. 128), diminishes into the ironised ostensible, behind which inevitable tragedy demands the meaningless deaths of heroine and villain and the 'long, lonely life' of the hero (p. 147). Forcibly torqued against its deep sympathy for the female, the earlier urgings of melodrama give way to newer imperatives.

In part, those imperatives derive from the new emotionalist code of isomorphic theatrical representation. But they also originate in the problematics of female desire that increasingly thematised, and traumatised, bourgeois narrative and drama in the final decades of the century: in Hardy's Tess, for example, as much as in Ibsen's Nora. Because bourgeois culture lacks 'any concept of female sexuality which is independent of men's,[24] a middle-class audience must stumble on a Juliet who had emerged as the acme of womanliness. She mirrors, and includes, the paradox of a realistic theatre in this age of self-restriction, an age that simultaneously demands and dreads strong feeling. Inevitably her successful representation precipitates a crucial crisis in cultural fantasy: where emotionalist theatre confronts and is confounded by the vortex of a doubly dangerous female eros, doubly dangerous because the woman Juliet must be, as the Victorian connoisseur insists, both beautiful and innocent,[25] extraordinarily desirable, powerfully desiring, yet incorrupt.[26]

For bourgeois culture the erotically perilous is always morally suspect. Juliet offers 'both the weakness and the strength of a woman', warns H. H. Hallam.[27] That weakness itself can imply viciousness, as in this characterisation of Juliet as 'an Italian girl, full of cunning self-command, of quiet, steady behaviour, equally clever at evasion and dissimulation.'[28] But for most of contemporary commentary weakness and strength seem to translate into a Juliet described simultaneously as 'both passionate and pure',[29] where passion figures somewhere in a continuum of weak, unvirtuous, erotic. Thus the usually balanced Hippolyte Taine (1866) can read Ophelia's and Juliet's deaths as not only psychologically inevitable but as morally synonymous, because each woman is, he insists, equally incapable of 'virtue'.[30] Ophelia, the other test-piece for the emerging actress, came to represent in nineteenth-century culture 'a study in sexual intimidation'[31] – that is, in the sexual intimidation of the young woman. Juliet, however, presented the Victorians with Ophelia's alarming *alter ego*, the archetype of that female eros that intimidates men: 'yielding to the touch of passion, she is thenceforth strong as a seraph.'[32] And thus Fru Heiberg, Kierkegaard's Juliet, in her *Memoirs* (1904) describes Juliet 'in the fourth act . . . as a fully-developed woman, powerful, energetic, who does not even shrink from the most terrible things, from that which would even make a man tremble. She knows what she wants, and she works her will with courage, with a courage that does not shrink even from the gates of death.'[33]

Of this powerful archetype Flaubert could claim that 'all other [female] characters in literature are . . . more or less happy imitations of Dido or of Juliet.'[34] The two count as the types, respectively, 'of the mature woman' and 'of the maiden in love'. And they are both equally dangerous to a really good man, because of the ways in which they destabilise what Tania Modleski has called 'the scopic regime of the male psychic economy'.[35] How dangerous that destabilisation could seem to a nineteenth-century critic we can see in Kreyszig's extraordinary 1859 commentary on the play. Kreyszig identifies the centre of the play as the 'most powerful of all the purely subjective passions . . . Love'.[36] But within the rigidly gendered forms of bourgeois patriarchy, this omnipotent passion registers in opposite ways for men and women. 'To woman this domain is her native home, while the healthily developed man enters it, so to speak, only as a guest, to wipe away the sweat of the battle-field . . . Woe to him if the place of rest unfits him for the battle!' (p. 459). As Kreyszig continues, we hear emerging the central problem of Romeo that bedevils the Victorian theatre. A reviewer in *The Dispatch* (13 January 1846) warned: 'There is no part more difficult to sustain efficiently than Romeo. At one time we have seen it a lifeless, sickly and repulsive conception; at another a rough, indelicate, animal picture.'[37] In the theatre of Irving, Kean and Macready, Charles Shattuck suggests, 'The regular actor of Macbeth or Othello would find embarrassingly womanish the passage in Friar Lawrence's cell where Romeo is called to tear his hair in grief and throw himself upon the ground.'[38] In a delightful irony it was the American actress Charlotte Cushman, *as Romeo*, who restored the play's popularity on stage, creating a sensation in the role in the London season of 1845–6. Romeo, 'the man to whom Love becomes the one aim of life' (Kreyszig (p. 459)), admirable in the twentieth century, a century earlier is scandalous, because he has forfeited his place in the phallic economy. 'Fallen away from the fundamental law of his being', Kreyszig thunders, 'he presents the unhandsome appearance of all that is discordant and contradictory, and . . . the greater his original strength, only the more surely does he succumb, not to fate, but to the Nemesis of the natural law which he has violated.' (p. 459). If Pius Aeneas has to abandon Dido for the good of Empire, so, patriarchal argument insists, should all good Englishmen, for comparable gain, in the patriarchal empire of the gaze. In Victorian eyes, falling for Juliet, a man, Romeo, any man, unmans himself: 'it is a weighty testimony to the massive healthiness of [Shakespeare] that among the heroes of his plays Romeo alone falls victim to love.' (p. 459).

This need to defend Shakespeare's 'massive healthiness' illustrates how far Kierkegaard's vivacious child has given way to a Victorian Juliet who is all about sickness, in an age which stressed 'the growing dominance of disease models as explanations for social phenomena'.[39] Hallam claims that 'the passion in which Juliet lives is most potently infectious: one can hardly venture near enough to see what and whence it is, without falling under its influence.'[40] And in the Alcott story, as St. John's sword wounds Lamar, 'A picture of Clotilde . . . Turned the thrust aside, else the force with which it was given might have rendered it fatal' (p. 139). The actress thus functions simultaneously as cause and cure of the hero's erotic wound. This doubleness the plot then unstrands as Clotilde prevents her lover from destroying himself by taking upon herself the burden of the revenge, the crime by which finally she also loses his trust and her own life. Here in 'A Double Tragedy,' as well as in our other fictions, Juliet's in-itself-innocent erotic power, must irresistibly infect those it attracts.

Juliet's epidemic potential seems to stir up the peculiar, late-Victorian, fascinated horror of all strong feeling, a fear that marks the difference between the first and the second half of the century. As Barbara Sicherman has shown: 'The thrust of advice on mental health in the Gilded Age was clearly toward self-restriction – of emotional attachment and expression, inspiration, imagination, creativity, and even individuality. Fears of going too far, having too much or too little, and losing control were . . . elevated into a rationale for designing a way of life.'[41] We hear those fears echoing inside Archer's admiration for great acting: 'the paroxysms of [the actor's] passion tend to communicate themselves to those not primarily affected through that subtle contagion which we call sympathy.'[42] In this complex medical metaphor, complex because this is, after all, the theatre Archer is urging on his countrymen, emotion is identified again, by 'paroxysm', as pain; its communication, epidemic; its problem, passion's abrogation of self-control. Juliet thus summons from the Victorians a cadence in which strong feeling leads to the strongest of feelings, not sexual desire merely, but sexual abandon: those 'Male fears of an engulfing femininity' in which 'The haunting specter of a loss of power combines with the fear of losing one's fortified and stable ego boundaries, which represent the *sine qua non* of male psychology in that bourgeois order.'[43]

Because of the deadliness and danger attached to Juliet, the attracted male must find a way to deflect back onto the source of the attraction, the expressive body of the actress, the dangers he risks in yielding to his excitement. Otherwise, with the erasure of the line between performer and role, the 'fetishistic attention to the actors' bodies' which forms 'the principal erotic pleasure of traditional theater', can engulf both text and audience.[44] The connoisseur comes to believe he must either control the actress's power to sustain Juliet or be destroyed by that power. Dorian abandons Sybil to her ugly death. Kendal harshly assigns Isabel to the Chateauvieux and Venice: 'Because I thought you [Isabel] must inevitably be absorbed, swallowed up by the great, new future before you; because my own life looked so gray and dull beside yours . . . So I went away' (p. 254). And when Sherringham returns to London, having decided to resign his position and thereby destroy his career, it is because, in his cousin's 'fantastic words', 'He has come home to marry Juliet' (p. 523).

In Shakespeare's script Juliet's attraction is so powerful, 'none but the sternest readers can well resist' it;[45] in the 'virtual theater' of fiction it becomes overwhelming. (Evlyn Gould coins this useful term *virtual theater* as 'a paradox that proposes the externalization of internal and energetic optical phenomena in the physical space of textual representation.'[46] As a result, the novels reread the play even as they stage it by resighting Romeo as voyeur. Within the play Romeo initiates the sexual relation between himself and Juliet, and he dies of it. The commentary, both fictional and critical, rereads the texts, and recuperates the hero. Juliet supplants Romeo as prime erotic figure. Romeo is now not so much the experienced seducer who scales Juliet's wall, but much more Kreyszig's fallen 'victim' of Love, or, in more benign language, a mere 'idolater' whom 'Juliet converts . . . into a true worshipper'.[47] It thus becomes possible for patriarchal culture as a whole, as well as for the novels' representative male connoisseurs, to feel the sexual excitement the actress arouses, and which, indeed, they have come to the theatre to experience. But at the same time the novels see to it that we see the female, not the male, punished for this transgression of the approved bounds, and bonds, of feeling, which 'whether in the form of shame or sense of honour . . . assures the habitual reproduction of distinctive conduct, and the strict drive-control underlying it, in individual people'.[48] These virtual stagings save the male gazer by recirculating through their plots the cardinal scenario of individual scopophilia. In his classic study of voyeurism, *The Fear of Looking*, David Allen demonstrates how 'In the repeated scopophilia' of his male subjects 'an essential element was the defensive use of fantasy'.[49] This fantasy reverses the actual experience of a young male whose initiation of sexual activity is discovered and punished by the mother. 'In the fantasy the girl is the seducer and he participates. And the girl, also representing the mother and superego, is not punitive.' As a result, the 'imagined acceptance of his looking and showing impulses . . . permit[s] escalation of sexual feeling'. In the novels, the punishment, in different ways, redounds not only from male to female, but from Juliet to the actress who embodies her, and who lovingly accepts her victim's status. Only Miriam Roth the actress who knows and cherishes her Diderot, can survive by refusing throughout to identify with this, or indeed with any role. But, of course, in her case Peter Sherringham must bear the suffering such *différance* generates.

Juliet has thus become by the end of the Victorian era a sight of suffering, a sadistic fantasy of masochism freely chosen and exquisitely endured. Lord Lytton, reviewing Mary Anderson's Juliet – the actress on whose life Isabel Bretherton is based – rhapsodised that 'with the accurate instinct of a true artist', in the final scene 'all revolting indications of physical torture are . . . suppressed.' 'Miss Anderson . . . avoids all that is painful and concentrates our attention upon all that is beautiful, in the situation.' The situation? A 'martyrdom depicted by Raphael'.[50]

That dependable access to a tranquillity beyond excitation links the martyred Juliet of the connoisseurs to the nostalgia at the core of any Shakespearean revival. In the nosology of the gaze, nostalgia designates that disease of sight which tries in vain to visualize a desired past the seeker has in fact never seen, or seen, at best, incorrectly. She retrieves a culturally earlier moment, Renaissance Verona/the Shakespearean text, a moment of 'simpler societies [in which] affect directly engages affect' because there 'Everything seems directly related to feeling.'[51] The voyeuristic connoisseur, sighting in Juliet a past and therefore non-threatening eros, thus retrieves in her performance a sort of souvenir, one which 'plays in the distance between the present and an imagined, prelapsarian experience as it might be "directly lived."'[52] Taking into herself the wound of male desire, Juliet releases patriarchy to the, in every sense, pure pleasures of the unburdened gaze.

*   *   *   *   *

Norbert Elias has shown how western civilization means at heart the internalisation of restraint. 'It always veers towards a more or less automatic self-control, to the subordination of short-term impulses to the commands of an ingrained long-term view, and to the formation of a more complex and secure "super-ego" agency.'[53] The novel in the same process emerges, despite its Bakhtinian complexities, as the paramount form for the display of human life under that 'Advancing division of functions and their daily involvement in long human chains', 'a chain of events that need to be contemplated dispassionately over long stretches if their connections are to be disclosed.'[54] Against such a paradigm we can theorise drama itself and particularly Shakespearean drama as the nostalgic other: the pure play of high and unmediated feeling. Even as nineteenth-century drama went to school to the novel to leech away fiction's bourgeois readership and bourgeois subject, Shakespeare seemed to open up the counter dream of lost immediacy and a fantasy of unrestricted desire. In rereading Juliet, even when it reads her as diversely as Kierkegaard and Wilde do, the nineteenth century thus recuperates for itself lost fields of feeling, closed to experience now, and limited exclusively to the scopic regime of the gaze.

Notes

1. Henry Irving, 'Preface' to Denis Diderot, *The Paradox of Acting*, trans. Walter Herries Pollock (London, 1883), p. 8.

2. I use 'frivolous' here as Jacques Derrida defines it in *The Archeology of the Frivolous*: 'Frivolity originates from the deviation or gap of the signifier, but also from its folding back on itself in its closed and nonrepresentative identity' (p. 128).

3. Madelon Gohlke, ' "I wooed thee with my sword": Shakespeare's Tragic Paradigms' in *The Woman's Part: Feminist Criticism of Shakespeare*, ed. Carolyn Ruth Swift Lenz, Gayle Greene, Carol Thomas Neely (Urbana: University of Illinois Press, 1983), p. 153.

4. Alan Sinfield, 'Introduction: Reproductions, Interventions,' *Political Shakespeare: New Essays in Cultural Materialism*, ed. Jonathan Dollimore and Alan Sinfield (Manchester: Manchester University Press, 1985), p. 131.

5. Kathleen McLuskie, 'The Patriarchal Bard: Feminist Criticism and Shakespeare: *King Lear* and *Measure for Measure*,' *Political Shakespeare, op. cit.*, p. 93.

6. Norbert Elias, *Power and Civility*, trans. Edmund Jephcott (New York: Pantheon, 1978), p. 315.

7. Coppélia Kahn, 'Coming of Age in Verona,' *The Woman's Part, op. cit.*, p. 188.

8. Quoted by Jill L. Levenson, *Romeo and Juliet* (Manchester: Manchester University Press, 1987), p. 17.

9. Owen Meredith, Lord Lytton, 'Miss Anderson's Juliet,' *Nineteenth Century* (December 1884), p. 885.

10. Soren Kierkegaard, *Crisis in the Life of An Actress and Other Essays on Drama* (1847) trans. with an Introduction by Stephen Crites (London: Collins, 1967), p. 74. All further references are to this edition.

11. Quoted in *Romeo and Juliet: A New Variorum Edition of Shakespeare*, ed. Horace Howard Furness (Philadelphia: Lippincott, 1878), pp. 464–5.

12. Oscar Wilde, *The Picture of Dorian Gray*, ed. Peter Ackroyd (New York: Penguin, 1985), p. 80. All further references are to this edition.

13. D. J. Gordon and John Stokes, 'The Reference of *The Tragic Muse*,' *The Air of Reality: New Essays on Henry James*, ed. John Goode (London: Methuen, 1972), p. 119.

14. Mrs Humphry Ward, *Miss Bretherton* (London: 1884), p. 26. All further references are to this edition.

15. Henry James, *The Tragic Muse* (New York: Penguin, 1982), p. 461. All further references are to this edition.

16. Thus while European painting works toward Matisse, European theatre at the same time is moving toward Stanislavski, born six years earlier. It is because the ballet treats the body as a syntax of forms that it enters modernism with painting and music, originally under the tutelage of Diaghilev, and ultimately with Balanchine. We can feel the break between the drama and the ballet if we remember that in the 1950s in New York, a morning spent at the Museum of Modern Art looking at Picassos, and an afternoon spent at the New York City Ballet watching Balanchine choreography to a Stravinski score, would have ended with a theatre evening of Arthur Miller. It is only with Beckett that the theatre's bondage to the body is broken, and only for the avant garde.

17. John Stokes, *Resistible Theatres: Enterprise and Experiment in the Late Nineteenth Century* (London: Elek, 1972), p. 5.

18. Mrs Humphry Ward, *A Writer's Recollections*, (London, 1918), p. 193.

19. Tania Modleski, *The Women Who Knew Too Much* (New York: Methuen, 1988), p. 32.

20. Jacques Rousseau, *Politics and the Arts. Letter to M. D'Alembert on the Theatre*, trans. with an Introduction by Allan Bloom (Illinois: The Free Press of Glencoe, 1960), p. 81.
21. Denis Diderot, *The Paradox of Acting*, op. cit., p. 20.
22. Sir Henry Irving, 'Preface' to *The Paradox of Acting*, op. cit., p. 8.
23. Lousia May Alcott, 'A Double Tragedy. An Actor's Story,' *A Double Life*, ed. Madeleine Stern (Boston: Little Brown, 1988), p. 125. All further references are to this edition.
24. Jeffrey Weeks, *Sex, Politics and Society: The Regulation of Sexuality since 1800* (London: Longman, 1981), p. 42.
25. Lytton, op. cit., 'Miss Anderson's Juliet', p. 887.
26. It may seem strange to a twentieth-century reader, used to Lady Macbeth as the powerful Shakespearean figure for untrammelled female sexuality, to have the same thing said of so different a character as Juliet. Macbeth's fiend-queen represented for the Victorians, of course, as for ourselves the supreme 'icon of divine-demonic woman' (Nina Auerbach, *Woman and the Demon* (Cambridge: Harvard University Press, 1982) p. 207. But that doubling marks where a crucial difference divides her and her fate from that of Juliet. Lady Macbeth is devilish, and we see her in the sleep-walking scene suffer her appropriate devil's fate. Juliet, however, is good: beautiful and good, virtuous and sexual. That virtue, ironically, seems to make her for a Victorian audience much more terrifying than a moralised figure like Lady Macbeth. This combination renders her, as in certain kinds of theophany which unite love and fear, authentically terrible.
27. In *The Variorum Romeo and Juliet*, op. cit., p. 221.
28. Gervinius, quoted in *The Variorum Romeo and Juliet*, op. cit., p. 456.
29. Chasles, quoted in *The Variorium Romeo and Juliet*, op. cit., p. 434.
30. Quoted in *The Variorum Romeo and Juliet*, op. cit., p. 443.
31. Elaine Showalter, *The Female Malady* (New York: Pantheon, 1985), p. 89.
32. H. H. Hallam, quoted in the Rev. H. H. Hudson, *Shakespeare: His Life, Art and Characters* (New York: Haskell House, 1970), p. 221.
33. Fru Heiberg, quoted in Stephen Crites, 'Introduction' to S. Kierkegaard, *Crisis in the Life of An Actress*, op. cit., p. 8.
34. Clara Longworth de Chambrun, *Shakespeare Actor-Poet* (New York: Appleton, 1927), p. 57.
35. T. Modleski, *The Women Who Knew Too much*, op. cit., p. 13.
36. Kreyszig, quoted in *The Variorum Romeo and Juliet*, op. cit., p. 459.
37. Quoted in J. L. Levenson, op. cit., *Romeo and Juliet*, p. 31.
38. Charles H. Shattuck, *Shakespeare on the American Stage* (Washington: Folger Shakespeare Library, 1976), p. 893.
39. J. Weeks, *Sex, Politics and Society*, op. cit., p. 42.
40. Quoted in H. H. Hudson, *Shakespeare: His Life, Art and Characters*, op. cit., p. 219.
41. Barbara Sicherman, 'The Paradox of Prudence: Mental Health in the Gilded Age,' *Madhouses, Mad-Doctors, and Madmen: The Social History of Psychiatry in the Victorian Age*, ed. Andrew Scull (Philadelphia: University of Pennsylvania Press, 1981), p. 224.
42. William Archer, *Masks or Faces?* (1888), ed. Lee Strasberg (New York: Hill and Wang, 1957), p. 220.
43. Andreas Huyssen, 'Mass Culture as Woman: Modernism's Other,' *Studies in*

Entertainment, ed. Tania Modleski (Bloomington: Indiana University Press, 1986), p. 196.

44. Leo Bersani, *A Future for Astyanax* (New York: Columbia University Press, 1984), pp. 269-70.

45. H. H. Hudson, *Shakespeare: His Life, Art and Characters, op. cit.*, p. 219.

46. Evlyn Gould, *Virtual Theater from Diderot to Mallarme* (Baltimore: The Johns Hopkins University Press, 1989), p. 1.

47. H. H. Hudson, *Shakespeare: His Life, Art and Characters, op. cit.*, p. 215.

48. N. Elias, *Power and Civility, op. cit.*, pp. 254-5.

49. David W. Allen, *The Fear of Looking* (Charlottesville: University of Virginia Press, 1974), p. 41.

50. Lytton, 'Miss Anderson's Juliet,' *op. cit.*, pp. 899-900.

51. N. Elias, *Power and Civility, op. cit.*, p. 273.

52. Susan Stewart, *On Longing, Narratives of the Miniature, the Gigantic, the Souvenir, the Collection* (Baltimore: The Johns Hopkins University Press, 1984), p. 139.

53. N. Elias, *Power and Civility, op. cit.*, p. 248.

54. N. Elias, *Power and Civility, op. cit.*, p. 273.

7 Disintegration and its Reverberations

Hugh Grady

If contemporary students and scholars of Shakespeare have heard the term *disintegration*, it is likely that they know it from one of two quite disparate contexts. For historians of Shakespeare criticism, disintegration may recall the by now all but forgotten branch of Victorian Shakespeare scholarship which in its day created a series of notable scandals by arguing for the presence of other writers' words within the Shakespeare canon. On the other hand, contemporary literary theorists might find something suggestive of post-structuralism in the term, which is in fact a subsidiary one in Foucault's terminology.[1]

It is this apparently coincidental double meaning of the term *disintegration* which I mean to consider in the following chapter: the apparently contingent use of the term at two disparate moments of critical history deserves exploration. And there are, indeed, I will argue, certain parallels between the disintegrating Victorian Shakespeareans and contemporary post-structuralist theorists: each tendency has taken aim in its own way at that over-determined structure of modernised societies that Raymond Williams called 'culture'. The impasses in which the Victorian disintegrators became involved are suggestive of similar impasses encountered by the insurgent cultural theory of the 1980s. And if these impasses persist because of certain cultural contradictions of late capitalism to be discussed below, they can at least now be clearly conceptualised in theory, through contemporary post-structuralism's development of simultaneous critique of objectivism and subjectivism.

Disintegration as the term has been used in Shakespeare studies is quite obviously intertwined with the complex history of textual scholarship. Suspicions that certain of the Folio texts contained matter from non-Shakespearean writers arose as early as 1678, and the next century saw the creation of a general climate of what was later called 'bibliographical pessimism' concerning the accuracy of the Folio texts.[2] That pioneering entrepreneur of letters, Samuel Johnson, for example, wrote:

> Copied for the actors, and multiplied by transcript after transcript, vitiated
> by the blunders of the penman, or changed by the affectation of the player;
> perhaps enlarged to introduce a jest, or mutilated to shorten the represen-
> tation; and printed at last without the concurrence of the author, without
> the consent of the proprietor, from compilations made by chance or by
> stealth out of the separate parts written for the theatre: and thus thrust into
> the world surreptitiously and hastily, they suffered another depravation
> from the ignorance and negligence of the printers . . . It is not easy for
> invention to bring together so many causes concurring to vitiate a text.[3]

This pessimistic tendency, verging toward but not quite yet fully disintegrationist, was partially checked by Edmund Malone's highly
influential late Enlightenment scholarship, which, as Margreta de Grazia
has demonstrated, accomplished in many ways the production of the
modern scholarly paradigm of a transcendent author, an accepted canon, a
chronology of the works, a biography based on facts and records, and an
interest in chronological development.[4] In terms of disintegration, Malone
saw extra-Shakespearean style only in *Titus Andronicus* and the Henry VI
plays. He accepted *Pericles* as Shakespearean and concentrated on
establishing a chronology of the works rather than seeking to identify
alien matter within the canon.

The heyday of disintegration as a critical tendency came in a series of
Victorian developments of and challenges to Malone's work, developments which were centred in the New Shakspere Society – the very
spelling of the society's name suggesting several of its cardinal traits:
suspicion toward the received Folio texts, a new reliance on documentary
evidence,[5] and a general 'progressive' interest in reform, including the
reform of spelling. The Society was founded in London in 1873 by F. J.
Furnivall and disbanded in 1894 after a stormy and controversial tenure.
To the extent that memory of this group survives, it is associated with its
attempt at using scansion and versification analysis to invent a 'scientific'
approach to questions of chronology and authorship in the Shakespeare
canon. The movement persisted into the twentieth century most vigorously in the writings of J. M. Robertson, who became a lonely and isolated
voice in a period of Shakespeare scholarship when organic unity and
authorial agency were the very unexamined enabling propositions for the
vast majority of Shakespeareans.[6]

The society's founder, the enormously energetic literary amateur
Frederick James Furnivall (1825–1910), was only indirectly connected
with disintegration proper. In the founding prospectus of the New
Shakspere Society he outlined a programme of research which would use
versification analysis as a tool to perfect the chronology of the composition of the works in order to develop an evolutionary account of

Shakespeare's artistic and philosophical development. He specifically cited the work of the German Hegelian critic G. G. Gervinus as a model for what he had in mind,[7] and when Edward Dowden's 1875 *Shakspere: A Critical Study of his Mind and Art* appeared, the Society's purposes as Furnivall had defined them were in a sense fulfilled. Dowden, reportedly an avid reader of the society's *Transactions* in Dublin but never a direct participant in the Society, in fact used Furnivall's division of Shakespeare's career into four divisions in his immensely influential narrativisation of the plays and life.[8]

Furnivall, however, could not control the dynamics which resulted from the attempt at 'scientific' versification analysis. While he wished to confine such analysis to questions of the chronology of the works, others were prepared to go further and raised questions over the authorship of certain passages, parts of plays, and whole plays in the canon. Here the leading figure was undoubtedly Frederick Gard Fleay (1831–1909), school-master and Anglican priest (he resigned his ministry in 1884), who devoted many years of his life to scanning Shakespeare's works and reporting on the results of his research in Society meetings and various Victorian periodicals. It was Fleay who first 'disintegrated' the received Shakespearean texts through metrical tests in a systematic way,[9] and his tables were often reprinted, well into the twentieth century. Few attempted to match Fleay's industriousness in this regard: he had been dubbed 'the industrious flea' even before this undertaking, in his undergraduate days, and the task was certainly immense. His only rival on this scale was the German professor G. Koenig, whose *Vers in Shakespeares Dramen* appeared in 1888 but unlike Fleay's work did not include actual counts of lines for the plays, but instead a table of ratios.[10] In any case several others produced analyses of single plays or occasionally multiple plays, but Fleay and Koenig alone attempted the complete canon, so far as I am able to discover.

The results of Fleay's 'disintegration' were organised in his *Shakespeare Manual*. He found three plays to be non-canonical: *Titus Andronicus* and *2 and 3 Henry VI* (a not uncommon view before the twentieth century, in line with Malone's doubts about the plays); two plays for which Shakespeare was said to have contributed isolated scenes: *1 Henry VI* and *Edward III*; three plays held to be Shakespeare's revisions of others' works (producing 'bad' quartos), which then were revised again by Shakespeare (producing the Folio texts): *Romeo and Juliet, Richard III*, and *The Taming of the Shrew*; three plays said to have been drafted by Shakespeare but revised by others: *Timon of Athens, Pericles*, and *Troilus and Cressida*; two plays jointly written with Fletcher: *The Two Noble Kinsmen* and *Henry VIII*; three plays said to have been abridged: *Macbeth, The Tempest*, and *Julius Caesar*; two plays said to include interpolations from other playwrights:

Macbeth and *Cymbeline* – with three others suspected of similar interpolations: *The Tempest, Henry V*, and *The Merry Wives of Windsor*.[11]

In addition, Fleay believed that Shakespeare had freely revised his own
work and that it was possible to detect which portions of the texts had
been written earlier, which revised later. For the case of *Hamlet*, to be
sure, there had to be more complexity: he posited a lost 1589 version
jointly written by Marlowe and Shakespeare, traces of which were said to
have made their way into the 'bad' quarto, then two wholly Shakespearean versions in 1601 and 1603 (Fleay p. 41). In general, Fleay's treatment
of the so-called bad quartos was unsystematic. As indicated above, he
thought three of them to be revisions of others' plays; others, like that of
Henry V, he thought were pirated and garbled transmissions; others
records of early Shakespearean versions of the plays; and still others
mixtures of the last two types (Fleay pp. 61–3).

For most of the twentieth century, these findings seemed laughable and
beneath the consideration of serious scholars. But recent developments in
contemporary scholarship provide a radically different perspective.
Fleay's results, in fact, are not all that different from those of the first
'Postmodern' edition of the works, the new Oxford Shakespeare. The
Oxford editors, Stanley Wells and Gary Taylor, assign *Titus* and *2 and 3
Henry VI*[12] to Shakespeare, unlike Fleay, but they do suggest there were
possible unknown collaborators for all three plays[13]; they concur with
Fleay's view of collaborators with Shakespeare in *1 Henry VI*, if not
necessarily with his exact division of the work among the authors; they
reject Fleay's hypotheses that Shakespeare used portions of another's
work in quarto texts of *Romeo and Juliet, Richard III*, and *The Taming of the
Shrew*; they concur on the thesis of joint authorship for *Timon* and *Pericles*
(differing on the identity of the other authors), but not for *Troilus and
Cressida*; they agree that the 'good' quarto and Folio texts of *Hamlet*
represent respectively an earlier and later Shakespearean version of the
play – but refuse to speculate about the authorship of an *Ur-Hamlet*; they
agree that *Henry VIII* and *The Two Noble Kinsmen* were jointly written with
Fletcher (as have editors for some time); they agree that *Macbeth* contains
interpolations by another writer and was probably abridged ('adapted by
Thomas Middleton' is the formula used) but are silent on *Cymbeline, The
Tempest, Henry V, Julius Caesar*, and *The Merry Wives* (for three of which
Fleay had made only claims for 'probable' interpolation).

Ironically, while the Oxford editors adopted Fleay's view that Shakespeare revised his work, only the case of differing quarto and Folio *Lear*
texts was represented in the new edition by separate textual versions[14];
Fleay in contrast had rejected the authenticity of the *Lear* quarto, seeing it
as a 'bad' version taken from theatre notes (Fleay p. 62). Nevertheless the
new Oxford edition comes off nearly as disintegrationist as Fleay, if not

following the letter of Fleay's findings and still less his methods of versification analysis. In a comparison of the two, Fleay seems much less cautious than contemporary scholarship, and uneven, particularly in dealing with the 'bad' quartos, but hardly as completely wrong-headed as he seemed a generation ago, when organic unity and single authorship ruled the day. What happened to Fleay's reputation had less to do with deficiencies in his logic or arithmetic than with the cultural politics which lay just below the surface of the dispute over disintegration. To begin to understand the rise, fall, and now partial revival of disintegration, therefore, it will be helpful to place these very specialised concerns in a broader social context in which those political issues can be defined.

As numerous commentators have pointed out, Victorian scholarship shows clear influence from the dynamics of a rapidly modernising nineteenth-century economy. The rise of industrial monopolies, the development of professionalism and bureaucratisation, and the organisation of science and technology into the systems of economic expansion created a complex social reaction that Jürgen Habermas has termed differentiation. On the one hand there was a new prestige for science, technology, and bureaucratic rationality in all the leading Western countries; simultaneously, there was a reaction against these tendencies, in forms as various as Luddite workers' attacks on machinery, Matthew Arnold's prescriptions for a post-religious West, and – to name the remarkable figure whose work encompassed both of the previous strands – William Morris's Socialist aestheticism. This culturalist reaction against Victorian scientism led to the formation of the new social strata and institutions, themselves becoming increasingly specialised and autonomous, which Raymond Williams and Antonio Gramsci have called the forces of culture.[15] The divide between humanist culture and scientific technology became partially conceptualised in such key twentieth-century ideological notions as Eliot's 'dissociation of sensibility' and C. P. Snow's 'two cultures', and it conditioned the emergence of Romanticism, Symbolism, and Modernism as movements in which art and poetry were henceforth always defined in opposition to the instrumental rationality of industrial capitalism. In response, not only was culture in the older, broader sense divided; so too were many individual psyches.[16]

Victorian disintegration and the disputes which it occasioned were complexly over-determined and symptomatic of the newly heightened tension between the bureaucratic–technical and the cultural.[17] Clearly, disintegration was an assertion of the claims of the scientific and technical within a domain that had been constituted by the previous generation of Romantics as a preserve of culture against the rapid encroachments of modernisation. At its heart was the positivist[18] belief that applications of the scientific method to textual analysis could yield new, positive knowledge, not only of the chronology of the plays but also of their authorship. To be sure, in retrospect, the choice of scansion as the main analytic weapon hardly seems 'scientific' today and was clearly influenced by nineteenth-century classical education more than anything else. Disagreement over scansion would in fact prove to be one of the downfalls of the movement. To Fleay and Furnivall, however, the scanning, counting, and tabulating of metrical characteristics was a direct application of scientific method. Furnivall, for example, claimed, 'The study of Shakespeare's work must be made natural and scientific . . . and I claim that the method I have pursued is that of a man of science.' [19] Fleay wrote: 'The great need for any critic who attempts to use these tests is to have had a thorough training in the Natural Sciences, especially in Mineralogy, classificatory Botany, and above all, in Chemical Analysis. The methods of all these sciences are applicable to this kind of criticism which, indeed, can scarcely be understood without them.' [20]

This stance toward Shakespeare certainly shares many features of Enlightenment and Romantic bardolatry, in particular an intensification and further development of the sacralisation of Shakespeare.[21] The labour-intensive lucubrations involved in compiling the statistics were of course an index of the central importance of the texts subjected to such scrutiny; one has to look to contemporaneous Continental Biblical or Homeric analysis for anything equivalent. On the other hand, if we use Habermas's analysis of the interests that underlie the various disciplinary methodologies of modern culture, the sharp contrast between the aesthetic and cultural Shakespeare criticism of Coleridge, Hazlitt, Dowden, or Swinburne, and the scientistic analyses of Furnivall and Fleay becomes obvious. The first group of critics approach the text with what Habermas called a hermeneutic attitude, based on an interest in understanding.[22] In such a stance the value – even in a certain sense the sacredness – of the text is presupposed, more or less consciously. The interpretation takes the form of a mediation between reader and text in which the text is poured into the empty container of the reader for his/her edification, or, where the creative role of the reader is recognised at least partially, meaning is seen as renewed through some 'translation' into contemporary idiom or culture through glosses, notes, or 'illustrations'.

There is always a certain sleight of hand involved here, of course, precisely because no reader is an empty receptacle and because there is no translation without difference. In retrospect, it always becomes clear how any culture's readings of its classic artefacts is in effect a re-writing of them as well – witness the *I Ching*, Talmudic commentary, American constitutional law, or the history of Shakespearian criticism. For Schlegel, Coleridge, and Hazlitt, Shakespeare was the great English Romantic poet, just as for Bradley he was the great realist dramatist and for G. Wilson

Knight and Cleanth Brooks the great Symbolist poet. Nevertheless, inherent in the traditional hermeneutic stance is the potentiality of an attitude of humble submission by the reader to the authority of the text and the appearance that the interpretation is always simply a revelation of a latent meaning, a further testimony to the Nature-like fecundity of the Great Author. The authority of the critic is, in appearance at any rate, strictly secondary, dependent on the critic's skill as an interpreter of an absent master.[23]

The disintegrationists implicitly claimed to share in this reverential attitude toward Shakespeare, through purifying a sacred text whose 'authentic' message had been adulterated with non-authentic matter: J. M. Robertson, after all, entitled his summary work *The Genuine in Shakespeare*. The unexpected response to their enterprise, however (violent objection, disagreement and disarray) suggests that there was something inherent in their methods which worked against the grain of their stated reverential attitude. To define the unstated logic of that method, Habermas's analysis of what he calls instrumental–bureaucratic reason is apposite. Underneath the rhetoric of neutrality, objectivity, and technological dispassion, Habermas inferred an interest of control and domination. The logic of what he calls instrumental–administrative reason involves an abstraction of the perceived object out of the cultural matrix of traditions and values in which it is inscribed in and through ordinary language. This abstraction creates a 'value-free' sphere in which the object is opened to the laws of synthetic and deductive logic, tamed and made subject to human desire. But as both Habermas and Foucault have argued in their different ways, the supposedly value-free domain thus created is in reality a theatre of wills-to-power contesting for an autotelic supremacy under the masks of various ideologies.

The Victorian disintegrationists, in their turn to scientific methodology in textual criticism, managed to create a virtual parody of those dynamics, leaving the New Shakspere Society to dissolve amid mutual polemical accusations. The shift in methodology entailed a subtle but decisive shift, from the authority of the text to the authority of the critic. But they were never able to achieve that *sine qua non* of scientific method, a shared paradigm with testable results. With the disintegrators, will-to-power was never successfully displaced from the individual ego to a collective, impersonal agency of domination, as is the case in 'ordinary science'. The normally obscured role of will-to-power in the operations of instrumental reason became all too apparent, at least to observers, if not always to the disintegrationists themselves. Disintegration came to grief over the elusive goal of agreement in observation. Even so apparently simple a matter as counting the syllables in a line of poetry proved, over the course of entire plays, to present numerous ambiguities and uncertainties, and the matter of stressed and unstressed syllables and the placement of the caesura proved even more divisive. Fleay, for example, published a second, 'corrected' version of his tables in 1881 without explanation, but raising doubts over the supposedly objective criteria of his first attempt.[24] The last of the verse-analysing disintegrators, J. M. Robertson, as we shall see shortly, simply threw up his hands over the question of reproducible results and opted for informed subjectivity. But this leaching of authority from author to critic was a transgression unpalatable to many contemporaries, a subversion of the sense of settled tradition and received wisdom which, in reaction to the French revolution, had become a central component of the national culture.

If the culturally corrosive nature of disintegration was not always apparent to the disintegrators, it was certainly a major concern of their enemies. One of the most astonishing things about disintegration retrospectively, given especially the completeness of its effacement from contemporary Shakespeare studies, is the nearly hysterical level of objection which it occasioned in its own time and place. As the bringer of the instrumental into the hitherto privileged area of poetry within Victorian culture, it had violated a major cultural taboo, and it produced outraged reaction, most memorably through the eccentric but symptomatic indignation of the poet and critic A. C. Swinburne:

> For all the counting up of numbers and casting up of figures that a whole university – nay, a whole universe of pedants could accomplish, no teacher and no learner will ever be a whit the nearer to the haven where they would be. In spite of all tabulated statements and regulated summaries of research, the music which will not be dissected or defined, the 'spirit of sense' which is one and indivisible from the body or the raiment of speech that clothes it, keeps safe the secret of its sound . . . It is useless to pretend or to protest that they work by any rule but the rule of thumb and finger: that they have no ear to work by, whatever outward show they may make of unmistakable ears, the very nature of their project gives full and damning proof.[25]

Swinburne devoted the entirety of the book from which this passage is taken to the refutation of versification tests – appending for good measure a skilfully malicious parody of a New Shakspere Society meeting. But Furnivall, not the man to meet this silently, retaliated with *ad hominem* polemics, to which Swinburne heartily rejoined. In a battle of philological punning to names, Furnivall dubbed Swinburne 'Pig's-Brook', while Swinburne retaliated against Furnivall with 'Brothel-Dyke'. Eventually, Furnivall and Fleay had a separate falling out, and membership in the Society, and its prestige, began to decline.

Clearly, the two sides of the divided Victorian sensibility had declared war over this supremely important piece of cultural turf known as Shakespeare. In the next generation, peace was established when a new 'scientific' textual criticism claimed to be able to refute the disintegrators on 'scientific' grounds and 'saved' the authenticity of the Folio texts of Shakespeare's plays with results that would have given great joy to Swinburne. Disintegration all but disappeared, save for the lonely but undaunted voice of J. M. Robertson.

The self-educated Robertson, a Liberal journalist and Member of Parliament who prided himself as a free-thinker, had in effect capitulated to the culturalists in his own way, bringing disintegration over to Swinburne's side by giving up all pretence to 'scientific objectivity'. He argued that while versification tables could serve as a rough guide to disintegration, ultimately the genuine in Shakespeare is discernible only through a cultivated aesthetic appreciation of poetic rhythm. 'All counting of double-endings is somewhat insecure,' he wrote, 'inasmuch as there are a number of doubtful words, capable of being read either as monosyllables or as dissyllables; a number more which may be read as either dissyllabes or trisyllables; and a number of lines of which the scansion may be varied, so as to make them either irregular or regular.' [26]

In the conclusion of his summarising work *The Genuine in Shakespeare*, he grappled with the great cultural divide between science and the humanities, metonymised for him by an opposition between Darwin and Shakespeare, in an attempt to understand the 'ultimate valuations of life'.[27] And that ultimate valuation is captured for him, not in the scientific genius of Darwin, but in the great rhythms of Shakespeare's verse, just as it had been for Swinburne. Of course, in arriving at his own God-in-the-iambic-pentameter, Robertson found himself, in the familiar tradition of Protestant (and free-thinking) sectarianism, taking great pains to insist on what was *not* of value in Shakespeare: Shakespeare as dramatist, as plot-maker, as original thinker. In fact, Robertson asserts, only one play was wholly and entirely Shakespeare's – *A Midsummer Night's Dream*. In all the others Shakespeare was re-writing an earlier work, with various degrees of completeness. It was Robertson's claim to have separated out the truly Shakespearean from the unaltered source material and through such a disintegration to have presented the world with the key to ultimate values. But Robertson's arguments fell on an increasingly deaf audience. Disintegration was simply no longer viable. The culturalists had triumphed, and disintegration was no longer a threat.

It was not that the divide between the differentiated fragments of modernity had been somehow overcome, although there were claims in this direction. Rather, disintegration succumbed to two separate but inter-related developments. The first was the production of the 'scientific bibliography' of Greg, McKerrow, and Pollard, who developed a set of arguments which essentially authenticated the Folio texts and made unfashionable the earnest attempts of the late Victorians to identify various alien hands in the canonical Shakespeare. Science was now the guarantor of the integrity of the national culture, a guard standing outside the sacred arena. In this new guise it became not only uncontroversial, but welcomed and honoured, complementing as it did the transformation of Shakespeare on the 'culturalist' side by a new generation of Modernist critics, the second of the two developments which brought about disintegration's demise.

This is not the place to analyse the strengths and weaknesses of the vastly influential enterprise of the 'new' or 'scientific' bibliography.[28] Suffice it to say here that the unanimity with which the salvation of the received texts was hailed and implemented in subsequent editions of the works is remarkable and bespeaks powerful cultural forces at work, beyond whatever force of reason we care to assign to the new bibliographers. Certainly, the fissures of Victorian culture were entirely too fundamental to the processes of capitalist modernisation to be healed by Eliot's claims that Symbolist and Modernist poetry had overcome them in a return to medieval and Renaissance unified sensibility. But the redeemed text complemented beautifully – suspiciously so, one might say – the new emphasis on organic unity and the autonomy of art presupposed in a new generation of Modernist critics led by T. S. Eliot, I. A. Richards, William Empson, and G. Wilson Knight in Britain and by John Crowe Ransom, Cleanth Brooks, Allen Tate, Robert Heilman, and their numerous New Critical followers in America. For these new critics the Shakespearean plays were privileged aesthetic spaces in which often previously unsuspected image-patterns and themes were traced in intricate textual choreography, the play of meaning held to be inherent within the texts themselves and a prima-facie indication of single authorship, that is, when such considerations were allowed to intrude into the critical discussion at all, for one of the hallmarks of the new methods was an attempt to re-contextualise the plays within Modernist aesthetics, outside their original cultural matrix. This was known as dealing with 'the plays themselves'. The topic of artistic unity was always either explicit or silently tangible in these discussions, built as it was into the Modernist aesthetic paradigm which all these critics deployed. In plays like *Pericles* or *Timon of Athens*, whose loose ends and disparate styles had made them prime cases for the disintegrators' briefs, the triumphant Modernist readings simply asserted what G. Wilson Knight called a 'spatial' unity of image and theme. In these analyses questions of textual authenticity simply had no place; everything was subordinated to the critics' skill at organising the scores of images into thematic and artistic coherence, and success at such organisation was assumed to underwrite their canonical status as unified artefacts by a single author. Perhaps the most startling of these new readings was G. Wilson Knight's revaluation of *Timon of Athens*, a play praised in the past but hardly seen as a major Shakespearean masterpiece, and often taken as an incoherent mishmash. But for Knight *Timon* merited nothing less than the status of major masterpiece:

> There is no tragic movement so swift, so clean-cut, so daring and so terrible in all Shakespeare as this of Timon. We pity Lear, we dread for Macbeth: but the awfulness of Timon, dwarfing pity and out-topping sympathy, is as the grandeur and menace of the naked rock of a sky-lined mountain, whither we look and tremble . . . This unswerving majesty is a grander thing than the barbaric fury of Othello, or the faltering ire of Lear.[29]

In the course of his bravura reading, the authorship question, which had dominated discussion of the play in the previous generation, and which would be re-asserted again in the 1970s and 1980s (the new consensus is of double authorship by Shakespeare and Middleton), simply never arose.

Within Modernist criticism, then (of which Knight can be seen as one of the originators within Shakespeare studies), disintegration was routed by the most devastating and effective tactics of newer critical movements: it was ignored out of existence. But when corroboration was desired from 'scientific' methodology, the 'new' or 'scientific' bibliography could be brought to bear. The Victorian sensibility, which had been divided into separate aesthetic and scientific spheres, thus seemed to be unified in the Age of Modernism. But the unity was contingent; certainly not based on any confluence of methodology between hermeneutic New Critics and instrumental new bibiographers. As with Eliot's own claim for a modern 'unification of sensibility,' it is a unity of appearance only, perhaps a unity of convenience.

Since about 1980 in Shakespeare studies (with intimations of change going back before that point, of course), a palpable change in critical paradigms has taken place, and precisely the set of suppositions which had laughed disintegration off the playing field in the early decades of our century have themselves been called into question. Organic unity has been replaced by a Postmodern poetics of de-centring. The idea of the author has been shown to be historical and contingent. As a result, disintegration, although not that particular term, has reappeared in Shakespeare studies in a quiet way: in some ways, given the new suppositions, it seems never to have completely left.

Twenty years ago, to read Eliot's appropriation of J. M. Robertson's disintegrating theses on *Hamlet* was to encounter unaccountably anachronistic matter in what was otherwise a seminal Modernist document:

> Mr. Robertson points out, very pertinently, how critics have failed in their 'interpretations' of *Hamlet* by ignoring what ought to be very obvious: that *Hamlet* is a stratification, that it represents the efforts of a series of men, each making what he could out of the work of his predecessors. The *Hamlet* of Shakespeare will appear to us very differently if, instead of treating the

> whole action of the play as due to Shakespeare's design, we perceive his *Hamlet* to be superposed upon much cruder material which persists even in the final form.[30]

Today the passage may simply be obscure. How many readers, even specialists, can place J. M. Robertson? But with the gloss provided by this essay, I want to suggest that this passage can now be read as an unaccountably prescient attempt, in an otherwise hopelessly High Modernist essay, at capturing the processes of non-authorial cultural inscription, almost as if Eliot had been reading Foucault's 'What is an Author?' But is there more than fancy behind such a perception of Postmodern prescience in Eliot's anachronistic Victorianism?

While the older disintegration's positivist side has in recent years also had a modest revival through positivist stylistic analysis, sometimes aided by the computer,[31] the more interesting development, as I suggested above, is the influence of deconstruction and other forms of post-structuralism in Shakespeare studies. These methods share with Post-modernist art-works a clear 'disintegrating' component, through a rejection of the concept and practice of organic unity, and a critique of the notion of the author in the old Romantic and Modernist sense as the transcendental unifying subject creative of the organic unity of the art-work. Such new tendencies have clearly influenced, if they have not directly defined, the way we now think of the status of the plays' texts. Instead of the single, authentic text from Shakespeare's hand which the new bibliographers dreamed of establishing – they would clear away all encrustations until only a central, essential and purified text remained – we can now think of the Shakespearean play, in Terence Hawkes' figure, as analogous to jazz music, never existing in any pure form, existing only in specific *interpretations*.[32] Similarly, the Oxford editors see as their goal not the presentation of the final, definitive and canonical edition of a work of literature, but rather the re-creation of a moment from the changing world of theatrical production. They seek to present *a* version of the play as it was sometimes enacted by Shakespeare's troupe, with the understanding that even then revision must have been freely practised. The symbolic case of *Lear* in the Oxford edition underlines the new assumption of revisions and different versions. In a world where the author is dead, it is no great scandal to allow the possibility in some cases and the definite ascription in others of 'disintegration' in the old-fashioned sense. As we saw earlier, it is no exaggeration to see the Oxford edition as a belated vindication of Fleay and the New Shakspere Society, if not in letter, then in spirit. But it is a return with some enormously important differences.

It would certainly be mistaken simply to reverse the binary oppositions of the Modernist critics and turn Fleay and Co. into anti-culturalist heroes because they once had been victims in a Modernist *Dunciad*. If their

iconoclasm revealed the subservient and uncritical proclivities of traditional hermeneutics and of the cultural tradition in general, their own
experience with instrumentalising positivism revealed that a shift in
authority from author to critic and in interest from understanding to
control simply introduces a new set of problems to replace the old ones,
ultimately solving nothing.

One of the most telling reverberations of disintegration concerns the
insurgent critical theory of the early 80s in English studies. Using a post-
structuralist vocabulary of de-centring and de-emphasising the author, it
tended, in its eagerness to critique Modernist notions of culture, to
appropriate one of Modernism's most questionable assumptions: that
'culture' had in fact provided the lost centre of modern civilization in the
wake of the failure of religion to do so. For many radicals, it followed that
an attack on the cultural 'centre' was somehow strategic.[33] Overlooked in
the eagerness to take on the Modernist father-figures, however, was the
central question of whether 'culture' had ever in fact achieved such
centrality in modern society, particularly in the United States. There
remains the legacy of Raymond Williams and Gramsci to suggest that
some Postmodern re-functioning of 'culture' – without the Modernist
baggage of elitism and male chauvinism – might be possible. I have
invoked Habermas in this connection, in spite of the problems of his
recent attempts to ground critical theory in a re-defined universal
rationality, precisely because his diagnosis of the basic differentiations of
modern society is so sorely needed by a contemporary criticism still
haunted by the ghost of unified culture.[34]

Few in contemporary literary studies will be tempted to revive the
disintegrators' 'metrical tests': even today's experiments in computerised
stylistic analyses seem to eschew them in favour of more easily measurable
data-bits, such as word frequency. More importantly, the critical revolution associated with deconstruction and its aftermath has been resolutely
anti-positivist and anti-empiricist in ways completely opposed to Fleay's
and Furnivall's basic project. The reverberation I speak of is quieter, but
nevertheless suggestive. One of the over-determinations of Victorian
disintegration can be described through Freud's figure of displacement: in
some sense the disintegration of Shakespeare's canon represented for
many, *pace* Swinburne, the processes of modernisation and differentiation
that threatened to level and even annihilate those areas of resistance to
commodification and bureaucratisation contained in art and literature.
But critics on both sides of this debate were caught on the horns of the
dilemma of dissociated sensibility and could only oscillate between, and
perhaps attempt to demarcate the boundaries of, two disparate realms: a
sphere of corrosive instrumental rationality and a sentimental, de-
rationalised sphere of art, poetry, and culture. Nowadays new forms of

critical rationality have revealed all the ways in which two generations of
Modernist attempts to create unsentimental, tough-minded, and ratio-
cinative art and poetry have disguised but not changed the differentiation
of modernised society, and in the late twentieth-century who can believe
that indefinitely repeating these Modernist gestures has any point at all?
Granting this depletion of Modernism, we need nevertheless to recognise
that those 'culturalist' positions that have been the targets of much of
post-structuralist criticism to date were among the few viable alternatives
to the bureaucratic institutions and instrumental mentalities which dominated mid-twentieth-century Western society. As Foucault toward the
end of his life began to suspect was the case with structuralism, there is a
real danger that a one-sided critique of culture could accelerate the already
powerful tendency within late-capitalist society to subordinate all other
values to impersonal domination and power.

If disintegration was a displaced symbolisation of the fact of cultural
differentiation's being constructed in the Victorian era, its partial return
now can be seen as a displacement of a new, deeper consciousness of
Postmodern de-centred selves which have developed out of, among other
forces, the fact of long-standing societal differentiations such as I have
discussed. If we are condemned to work in, through, and against such
divisions, it is at least possible to insist within Shakespeare studies that we
are still about what has been central to cultural studies since the
Romantics: producing meanings out of a social situation of increasing
cultural disintegration, which we both lament and celebrate.

Notes

1. Foucault writes in a strategic passage, 'One must give rise to thought as
   intensive irregularity – disintegration of the subject.' See Michel Foucault,
   Language, Counter-Memory, Practice: Selected Essays and Interviews, p. 183. The
   term has also been used in the title of Peter Dews' study of the intersections of
   Derrida and an earlier generation of Frankfurt critical theorists, *The Logics of
   Disintegration: Post-Structuralist Thought and the Claims of Critical Theory*
   (London: Verson, 1987).
2. 'Disintegration,' *The Reader's Encyclopedia of Shakespeare*, eds. O. J. Campbell
   and E. G. Quinn (New York: Cromwell, 1966).
3. Samuel Johnson, *Proposals* (1756), quoted in Frank P. Wilson, *Shakespeare
   and the New Bibliography*. ed. Helen Gardner (Oxford: Clarendon, 1970), p.
   11.
4. Margreta de Grazia, *Shakespeare Verbatim: The Reproduction of Authenticity*
   (Oxford, Clarendon 1991).
5. Furnivall preferred the spelling 'Shakspere' because, he said, it was that used
   by Shakespeare in his will and Stratford mortgages; but if one reads a bit

further into his explanation, it emerges that the spelling 'Shakspere' is rather an ideal type of the variant spellings in those documents. See 'The New Shakspere Society (The Founder's Prospectus Revised)' (1875), n. 1, p. 6, a pamphlet bound in at the end of *Transactions of the New Shakspere Society*, ser. 1, vol. 1. The last word on the question seems to have been had by E. K. Chambers, who recorded 83 variant spellings of the family name. See his *William Shakespeare: A Study of the Facts and Problems* (Oxford: Clarendon, 1930), vol. II, pp. 371-5.

6. See my *The Modernist Shakespeare: Critical Texts in a Material World* (Oxford, 1991) for an account of the shift toward Modernist aesthetic presuppositions within Shakespeare scholarship in the twentieth century, a shift which made disintegration almost literally unthinkable.

7. 'The New Shakspere Society: (The Founder's Prospectus Revised),' *op. cit.*, p. 6.

8. Furnivall had adapted them in turn from Gervinus. See Gary Taylor, *Reinventing Shakespeare: A Cultural History, 1642-1986* (New York: Weidenfeld & Nicolson, 1989), p. 160.

9. There were earlier verse tests in Shakespeare studies. Richard Roderick was apparently the earliest in 1758, and Malone counted rhymes – one of the several tabulated bits of data for Fleay and others – as evidence for his chronology. William Spalding used a more elaborate set of tests in 1833, while the New Shakspere Society credited James Spedding as the true founder of the method in his article 'Who Wrote Henry VIII?' *Gentleman's Magazine*, August 1850). For this chronology, I draw from J. Isaacs, 'Shakespearean Scholarship,' in *A Companion to Shakespeare Studies*, eds. Harley Granville-Barker and G. B. Harrison (Cambridge: Cambridge UP, 1949), p. 316. For a more recent account, see Taylor, *op. cit.*, pp. 153-60.

10. E. K. Chambers, *The Disintegration of Shakespeare* (London: Oxford University Press, 1924), p. 11.

11. F. G. Fleay, *Shakespeare Manual* (London: Macmillan, 1878), pp. 58-60.

12. I am ignoring the new edition's re-titlings of some plays.

13. Stanley Wells and Gary Taylor (eds), *William Shakespeare: The Complete Works* (Oxford: Clarendon, 1988), p. xx. For detailed arguments on the complete gamut of textual problems, see their *William Shakespeare: A Textual Companion* (Oxford: Clarendon, 1987).

14. In presentations made at the 1990 Annual Meeting of the Shakespeare Association of America, Wells and Taylor regretted that *Hamlet* had not been similarly treated with two separate textual versions.

15. Raymond Williams, *Culture and Society, 1780-1950* (New York: Columbia University Press, 1958) and Antonio Gramsci, *Selections from the Prison Notebooks* (New York: International, 1971).

16. The classic instance is provided by Raymond William's analysis of John Stuart Mill's own description of how the poetry of Wordsworth saved him from the overly severe and arid education imposed by his father. '. . .the normal method of intellectual organization, in minds of this kind', Williams writes, 'is a method which tends to deny the substance of feelings, to dismiss them as "subjective" and therefore likely to obscure or hinder the ordinary march of thought. If the mind is a "machine for thinking", then feeling, in the ordinary sense, is irrelevant to its operations. Yet the "machine for thinking" inhabits a whole personality, which is subject, as in Mill's case, to complex stresses, and even to breakdown. Observing this situation, a mind organized in

such a way conceives the need for an additional "department", a special reserve area in which feeling can be tended and organized. It supposes, immediately, that such a "department" exists in poetry and art, and it considers that recourse to this reserve area is in fact an "enlargement" of the mind. Such a disposition has become characteristic. . .,' Raymond Williams, *Culture and Society, 1780–1950* (1958; reprint New York: Harper Torchbacks, 1966), pp. 67–8.

17. I discussed these issues at greater length in a somewhat different context, including the rise of professionalism and professionalism's relation to capitalist modernisation, in *The Modernist Shakespeare, op. cit.*, pp. 28–43.

18. Fleay's leaving of the Church of England was greatly influenced by his reading of positivism's ideologue Auguste Comte. See DNB.

19. Quoted in 'Furnivall, Frederick James,' *The Reader's Encyclopedia of Shakespeare*, ed. O. J. Campbell (New York: Crowell, 1966).

20. F. G. Fleay, *Shakespeare Manual, op. cit.*, p. 108.

21. See the Howard Felperin essay elsewhere in this volume for an elaboration of this valid perception.

22. The distinction between instrumental and hermeneutic reason is from Jürgen Habermas, *Knowledge and Human Interests*, trans. Jeremy Shapiro (Boston: Beacon, 1971). In the communicative turn of his more recent work, the hermeneutic as a separate epistemological orientation disappears, replaced by an attempt to ground all knowledge in intersubjective communication. But I find the earlier distinction continues to have validity, especially in the disintegrationist context.

23. Clearly, a more self-conscious approach to hermeneutics might entail less conservative, less displaced, and more egalitarian relations between reader and author than the traditional dynamics I am describing which prevailed in the mainstream of nineteenth- and twentieth-century Shakespeare criticism. Habermas, for example, argued that the interest underlying hermeneutics is not submission but understanding, with implications of mutuality, equality, and respect for differences. In the period I am examining, however (and even in our own), deeply reverential attitudes toward Shakespeare as a secularly sacred oracle were the rule.

24. E. K. Chambers tended to believe carelessness was at work or even a perverse delight in fluttering literary sensibilities on Fleay's part. He wrote: 'Fleay adds up wrongly, puts figures in the wrong columns, misses bits of prose, omits a whole scene in T. C., and the like.' Chambers nevertheless re-produced several uncorrected tables from Fleay. In addition to the pamphlet *The Disintegration of Shakespeare* cited above, see E. K. Chambers, *William Shakespeare: A Study of the Facts and Problems* (Oxford: Clarendon, 1930) vol. II, pp. 397–408.

25. Algernon Charles Swinburne, *A Study of Shakespeare* (1909; reprint New York: AMS, 1965), pp. 5–6.

26. J. M. Robertson, *The Shakespeare Canon* (London: Routledge, 1922), p. 7.

27. J. M. Robertson, *The Genuine in Shakespeare* (London: Routledge, 1930), pp. 159–63.

28. For some recent attempts at such analysis, see Margreta de Grazia, 'The Essential Shakespeare and the Material Book,' *Textual Practice* 2, no. 1 (Spring 1988), pp. 69–87; Gary Taylor, *Reinventing Shakespeare, op. cit.*, pp. 234–8; and my *The Modernist Shakespeare, op. cit.*, pp. 57–63.

29. G. Wilson Knight, *The Wheel of Fire: Interpretations of Shakespearian Tragedy*, rev. edn (London: Methuen, 1949), pp. 222–3.

30. T. S. Eliot, 'Hamlet and His Problems,' in *The Sacred Wood* (1920; rpt. New York: Barnes, 1964), pp. 96–7.

31. In the 1989 Modern Languages Association Convention, for example, one of the sessions was devoted to computer-aided stylistic analyses ('Computers in Reader-Response Theory and Literary Analysis'), which included a paper by D. H. Craig of the University of Newcastle, Australia, in which word frequency analysis of texts by Jonson and Shakespeare was used to re-ascribe a series of additions to *The Spanish Tragedy*. Craig argued that passages which had been thought to be Jonson's on the basis of external attribution were in fact Shakespeare's on the basis of internal word-frequency tests which differentiated Jonson and Shakespeare.

32. Terence Hawkes, *That Shakesperian Rag: Essays on a Critical Process* (London: Methuen, 1986), pp. 117–18.

33. I am thinking particularly in this connection of such otherwise path-breaking works as Peter Widdowson, ed., *Re-Reading English* (London: Methuen, 1982); William Spanos, 'The Apollonian Investment of Modern Humanist Education: The Examples of Matthew Arnold, Irving Babbitt, and I. A. Richards', *Cultural Critique* 1 and 2 (Fall 1985 and Winter 1985–86): pp. 7–72; 105–34; Paul Bové, *Intellectuals in Power: A Genealogy of Critical Humanism* (New York: Columbia UP, 1986); Janet Batsleer, *et. al*, eds, *Rewriting English: Cultural Politics of Gender and Class* (London: Methuen, 1985).

34. I do not mean to imply that Habermas is the only figure on which such a re-functioning of 'culture' could be based; indeed, the stylistic aridity of much of his writing (I believe it to be the aridity of one who is attempting to securely anchor Utopia through a penitential prosaism) can be daunting. Another similar strategy would stress the importance of feminist attempts to provide alternative values.

8 Bardolatry Then and Now

Howard Felperin

> Tis mad idolatry
> To make the service greater than the god!
> Shakespeare

I The Idealisation of Shakespeare

It is now all but a commonplace that the idealisation of Shakespeare in the later eighteenth century, instinct as it was with an emerging romantic ideology of the timeless and universal Author, worked to obscure the historicity of his plays and thereby contain any present political charge they might have carried.[1] This legacy of 'bardolatry' – the term coined by Bernard Shaw in 1901 – doubtless has its own ideological dimension, but one susceptible of definition in terms quite different from, even opposite to, those currently in favour. While the 'idealist' or 'essentialist' appropriation of Shakespeare in the course of the nineteenth century remains a function of cultural ideology, it may be seen as more than singly motivated, a reflex not simply of conservative recuperation or hegemonic repression but of new and heterogeneous interests and impulses arising from historical change of unprecedented sweep and rapidity.

The nineteenth-century transformation of Shakespeare into an object of world-cultural idolatry might alternatively be read, from a 'left'-political standpoint, as the 'success story' of his liberation from proprietorship of an aristocratic and literary elite and the first realisation of the democratic potential of his work.[2] If the Shakespeare of Coleridge's lectures had taken on the idealised, and thereby dehistoricised, form of a universal genius through whose creation the inner workings of our natures are essentially displayed in their full clarity, it was no longer necessary to be either an established man of letters, like Pope or Johnson, or a gentleman-scholar with access to great libraries, like Edmond Malone, to comment significantly on his works, or even to edit them. One does not have to be a gentleman, a scholar, or a poet-critic, after all, merely to

129

report on one's consciousness, the newly established site of the plays' signification, in their presence. What else, for example, is De Quincey's celebrated essay 'On the Knocking at the Gate in *Macbeth*'?

From the moment Shakespeare became the paragon of a romantic subjectivity in which we all have a share, a new multiplicity of subjective readings became possible, potentially as many as there were reading and theatregoing subjects among the newly dominant bourgeoisie. Yet this idealisation of Shakespeare's work, with its potential for a democratic multiplicity of self-expressive readings, could have become the victim of its own success. With the falling away of such older constraints on commentary as social position, neoclassical doctrine, and historical erudition, how was the potential relativism of this new and burgeoning subjectivity to be avoided? To account for his own gift for Shakespearean recitation, Coleridge's fictional contemporary, Henry Crawford in *Mansfield Park* (1814), styles Shakespeare 'part of an Englishman's constitution'.[3] Coleridge's idealism may have secured the constitutional right of everyone, and not just Englishmen, to read and comment on Shakespeare, but this only meant that new criteria of validity would have to be found to anchor critical discourse in something more than the mere right to perform it.

If the older criteria, located for the Augustans in a social and literary aristocracy of taste, judgement and erudition, could no longer maintain themselves in place under 'democratic' pressures, then new sources and sites of cultural authority would have to be established. Coleridge himself envisioned these new constraints and principles arising from an as yet unborn pyschological and ethical science of the universal laws of our natures, a larger, systematic, and enlightened project of which his lectures on literature formed only a preliminary stage, a new 'interdisciplinary' knowledge that would hold in check and balance the untrammelled subjectivity in which he was also expert. But what institutional forms, embodying their own constraints, would such a new science take in elucidating this newly idealised part of an Englishman's constitution? Would they be analogous to those adopted by the legal and medical professions (now in the process of taking on their modern form) to maintain its more material parts?

The analogy points to the process of 'professionalisation', through which established vocations were to grow increasingly technical, specialist, and routinised, in response to accelerating scientific advance and social mobility in the course of the century, and issuing in newly centralised bodies of certification and control.[4] At the beginning of the nineteenth century, for example, physicians and surgeons were separate groups, representing different social and educational backgrounds; by the end of the century, they were not. In certain respects, the interpretation of

Shakespeare was to undergo an analogous process of professionalisation, becoming in time a central part of the new 'subject' of academic 'English'. The increasing academicisation of Shakespeare should not be ignored, and we shall have to return to it; but it only gives a local habitation and a name to the broader cultural currents of modernisation and specialisation which do not fully converge until the present century. Through most of the nineteenth century, the study of Shakespeare was still diffused within a 'public sphere' at once wider than the universities, and more 'evangelical' than specialist or technical in character.

II *Shakespeare Societies*

These mixed motives and interests are very much in evidence in the various Shakespeare societies that sprang up on both sides of the Atlantic, and on the Continent, in the middle of the century. The Shakespeare Society, for example, was founded in 1840 – like others, by a lawyer of sorts – 'for the purpose of collecting materials, or of circulating information, by which he [Shakespeare] may be thoroughly understood and fully appreciated'. Its 'prospectus' deemed it 'remarkable' that no such 'Literary Association' had been formed previously.[5] Perhaps it is less 'remarkable' in retrospect, from a vantage point when the very idea of the 'literary' as a form of institutionalised subjectivity seems a distinctly romantic innovation.

Nor is it surprising in retrospect to find a deeply conservative emphasis on documentary evidence and historical scholarship qualifying an otherwise missionary purpose with no apparent sense of contradiction. While the aim of extending 'appreciation' and 'understanding' might smack of the subjective universalism promulgated by Coleridge, Emerson, and other romantic critics, the activities of the Society were still guided by the historical empiricism pioneered by Edmond Malone: 'It will produce a spirit of inquiry and examination, the result of which may be the discovery of much curious and valuable information, in private hands and among family papers.' Significantly too, its 'constitution' limited membership, very like a gentleman's club, to 'one thousand Subscribers . . . on the introduction of one of the Council, or by application to the Secretary or Treasurer'. A 'parsimonious pluralism' indeed.[6]

The career of its founder, John Payne Collier, dramatically illustrates not only the divided social and philosophical purposes of nineteenth-century Shakespeare studies, but the ambiguous destiny of subsequent literary scholarship as well. The spirits of both the evangelical Coleridge, who was a friend of his father, and of the historicising Malone, whose scholarship he set out to supplement and correct, must have attended at his birth. Like the latter, Collier was an assiduous antiquary, in many ways a child of the previous century. As librarian to the Duke of Devonshire, with access to the Bridgewater Library and the Henslowe–Alleyn papers housed at Dulwich College, he was well-placed to carry out his mission of finding and filling out the evidence, textual and documentary, on which to reconstruct the history of the Elizabethan stage and the biographies of its leading figures.

But like Shakespeare's Autolycus, Collier also seems to have been 'littered under Mercury', god of such intermediaries as thieves and scholars. For whenever the authentic documents proved incomplete or inadequate – which was often – Collier fabricated new ones or augmented the old with notes and interlineations in a pseudo-antique hand. His most elaborate forgery, and the subject of controversy for a decade, appeared in 1853 in the form of a volume entitled *Notes and Emendations to the text of Shakespeare's Plays, from Early Manuscript corrections to A Copy of the Folio, 1632*, which accompanied his new edition. The distended title was portentous, for the volume contained some 1300 major corrections of the second folio, as well as nine lines altogether new, 'in a handwriting of the time' by one close to the early production of the plays, identified by Collier as the folio's owner, a certain 'Thomas Perkins'. In publishing only 1300 of this persona's major 'corrections', Collier actually showed restraint, since he had claimed in a pre-publication announcement that the folio contained over 20,000.[7]

The significance for our purposes of poor Payne Collier is the way he seems to have been in the grip of the very forces to which he was ostensibly opposed. Nothing could have been further from the potentially untrammelled subjectivity of the romantic idealists than his, and his Society's, historical and documentary empiricism. Yet this same emphasis, going back to Malone, on recovering and reconstructing the 'authentic' Shakespeare was rooted in and inspired by the new romantic sense of the playwright's contemporary and universal meaning. After all, Collier's was only another in the series of literary–historical fabrications that had occurred over the previous half-century, two of which had been exposed by none other than Malone himself.[8] In the case of Collier, unlike that of Malone, the forger and the scholar overlapped within a single personality.

After all, the exposure of literary fakes depended and drew on the very same antiquarian impulses and archeological skills as the production of them, both of these distinctly romantic developments having been underwritten by that idealist logic through which the historical text had become transhistorically present. Even the reproduction of ancient, native verse forms in *The Lyrical Ballads*, as well as the antique gloss of 'The

Ancient Mariner', can be read as a kind of 'open' fake inspired by a transhistorical subjectivity at once national and universal, a radical extension into poetic practice of the principles underlying Coleridge's criticism. If the thoughts of every man are anticipated and expressed by the Bard, what is to stop every man from recovering and expressing the thoughts of the Bard?

III *Disintegrators and Dissenters*

The contemporary answer to this unsettling question could only be an historical and interpretive empiricism based on principles of objectivity, that is, on verifiable *science* as distinct from the aristocratic taste and genteel antiquarianism of an earlier age. In 1875, the New Shakspere Society was formed by Frederick J. Furnivall. Though not without his own missionary side – he had been a Christian socialist in his youth and founded numerous other societies devoted to promoting the causes of literary and cultural nationalism[9] – Furnivall was more responsive than Collier to the challenge posed by empirical science to traditional forms of cultural transmission, and better equipped to accommodate it. Furnivall believed that Shakespeare's works should be examined 'as the geologist treats the earth's crust, as the comparative anatomist treats the world', that is, 'as the product of a mind working in successive periods'.[10]

The evolutionary model he adopts led to the 'verse-test', an analytic procedure devised to authenticate and date the texts of the Shakespearean canon, and thereby enable an accurate description of the development of the playwright's imagination in its integrity and totality. Yet Furnivall's 'scientific' attempt to discriminate knowledge from opinion in dating the plays and charting the playwright's artistic development was undermined from the start by the radical circularity of his method. In order to explain the metrical and grammatical variations across Shakespeare's work, he posited a series of characteristic chronological styles themselves derived from those variations. When the stylistic features of a given play were not homogeneous, it was ascribed to later revision or mixed authorship.

The Shakespearean canon was thus broken down into the 'Sunny-or-Sweet-Time' Group, the 'Unfit-Nature-or-Under-Burden-Falling' Group, the 'Lust-or-False-Love' Group, the 'Ingratitude-and-Cursing' Group, the 'Reunion-or-Reconciliation-and-Forgiveness' Group, and so on. On the basis of features derived from the plays, this schema was then projected back onto the plays to determine their chronology and authenticity. Not surprisingly, Furnivall's procedures provoked many arguments with those who did not share his faith in them, and some with those who did, such as those members of his own society whose findings differed from his own. Why not more or other groups, such as the 'Danger-of-Leaving-Your-Wife-to-Entertain-Strangers' Group to include *The Rape of Lucrece?*[11] A procedure designed to establish the authenticity of the plays of the canon and their integrity with the life of their 'author' thus issued in their increasing 'disintegration'.

Before returning to the activities of the disintegrators, let us look briefly askance at the still more bizarre labours of another society whose beginnings are traceable to the same period. In 1853, the year in which Collier published his monumental rewriting of Shakespeare, another fantast was in England gathering material for an article entitled 'William Shakespeare and his Plays. An Inquiry Concerning Them'. Its author was an American autodidact named Delia Bacon; she argued that the plays were not by Shakespeare at all, but by Francis Bacon, from whom she later claimed descent. The thesis was greatly elaborated in her 582-page study, *The Philosophy of the Plays of Shakespeare Unfolded*, which appeared in America in 1857, just after a pamphlet by William Smith, entitled *Was Lord Bacon the Author of Shakespeare's Plays?*, appeared in England.[12] To make the case for Bacon, they rely respectively on feverish textual parallel-hunting and strenuous biographical and historical speculation.

But these labours of scholarly fantasy seem almost casual compared with those of the American polymath Ignatius Donnelly, whose 1000-page *The Great Cryptogram* of 1888 advanced a theory of ciphers – cunningly occulted signatures in anagram – that would dominate anti-Stratfordian thinking well into this century. So powerful was his theory of ciphers that in the hands of other members of the Baconian Society it would subsequently be used to prove that Bacon wrote not only Shakespeare's works but those of Milton, Swift, Addison, Steele, Carlyle, and even the King James Bible. And so flexible is cipher-decipherment as a device for determining authorship that Shakespeare's (or are they Bacon's?) works have in turn been re-attributed to Marlowe, Raleigh, the Earls of Oxford, Derby, and Rutland, and even to Queen Elizabeth (the First).

It might seem strange, in the face of their persistent and promiscuous denial of Shakespeare's authorship, to recall the anti-Stratfordians – or, for that matter, the disintegrators – in a discussion of 'bardolatry'. Does not 'bardolatry' refer to that worship of Shakespeare as the source of timeless and universal wisdom which begins in the eighteenth century, gathers strength with the romantics, and reaches its height among Shaw's Victorian predecessors, in, for example, Edward Dowden's *Shakspere: His Mind and Art* (1875)? So what are such eccentric nay-sayers as these doing in an account of what is, after all, a mainstream of orthodox Shakespeare criticism and a mainspring of that continuing monumentalisation of Shakespeare of which the present volume is a late and self-conscious example?

Yet when we examine their assumptions, aims, and methods, such movements, for all their apparent difference and eccentricity, turn out to have a great deal in common with the more orthodox bardolatry of the period. It would be strange indeed, historically speaking, if they did not. And they might even have something to tell us – thither my argument tends – about the continuing cultural appropriation of Shakespeare in which we are complicit. One thing they have in common with orthodox bardolatry is fairly obvious: an overriding, even obsessive, concern with the 'author'. For even though the Baconians deny Shakespeare's author-ship *in toto*, and the disintegrators in part, both sects fully accept the massive cultural authority of the plays.

This is, in effect, the enabling pre-supposition of their respective projects, precisely what necessitates their strenuous labours in the first place. The consummate knowledge of man and society embodied in the plays requires for the Baconians a more respectable author than the half-educated son of a provincial tradesman. The very depth, breadth, and accuracy of their framing of the world, likened repeatedly to 'nature' itself, cries out for an author who would have been in a position, social, professional, and philosophical, to attain and impart it. Who might such a 'star of England' actually be? Enter Francis Bacon, Lord Verulam, Viscount St Albans, Lord High Chancellor of the Realm, classicist, scientist, and philosopher, as the first and likeliest alternative for author-ship, and, as it turns out, not only of Shakespeare's plays, but the King James Bible and much else. But even his claim to the role of 'Shakespeare' has been contested and succeeded by a train of aristocrats culminating in Queen Elizabeth herself.[13]

What might be dismissed as the extreme or limiting cases of anti-Stratfordian fantasy – that Elizabeth was Shakespeare, and that Bacon authored not only the plays but the Bible (or at least edited the Authorised Version) – can be seen as its paradigm-cases. Early anti-Stratfordianism had two distinct but related dimensions: to confirm the genius of the works not only in national but in universal terms; and to identify that genius with a figure worthier of its possession than the low-born and ill-educated poacher from Stratford. The simple snobbery that motivates the latter project is obvious and has often been remarked. (Even Marlowe, though far from an aristocrat, had at least been to Cambridge.) But snobbery is itself historically conditioned, and in this case it serves the clearly ideological function of reinforcing nostalgic notions of correspon-dence between artistic and social hierarchy in a period of sweeping, and threatening, democratic reform.

It seems more than accidental, for example, that so many anti-

Stratfordians, from Delia Bacon to Dorothy and Charlton Ogburn, have been Americans, disinherited at birth from an established social hierarchy, which could appropriate artistic and intellectual merit to its own sense of 'natural order'. Never mind that Marlowe died in 1593, or that Bacon's life, not to mention Elizabeth's, is well documented, including the fact that he left no offspring through whom Delia could have descended. More important to the Baconians than the empirical verification of their historical and biographical narratives was the ideological function these essentially 'Jacobite' narratives served, a residually reactionary function within the nineteenth-century ideology of the author, one that retained both royalist and religious dimensions in what is usually and otherwise regarded as a desacralising age of 'progress'.

From the time of William Smith and Delia Bacon, the establishment of Bacon's – or Elizabeth's – claim to the authorship of Shakespeare's plays has involved both a freely revisionist historicism and a strenuous textualism of a parallel- and precedent-hunting kind. It is often remarked by more sober and orthodox Shakespeareans that the anti-Stratfordians' byzantine hypotheses of authorship exemplify a kind of religious fanaticism. What is not usually noticed is the extent to which the heretical historicism and textualism they practise actually parallel and parody those forms of critical attention focused on the Bible itself in the same period. The rise of anti-Stratfordian speculation in the later nineteenth century coincides with the rise of what has been termed 'critical history' in the study of the New Testament.[14]

This is not the place to explore such parallels and continuities in detail; but it might be worth mentioning in this connection that Delia Bacon came from a family of ministers and was married to one. Her writings are certainly suffused with that air of 'inside knowledge' characteristic of the literature of 'faith communities' in general, and replete with scriptural allusion in particular. Nor is her work eccentric in this respect, at least not within the Baconian tradition. Anti-Stratfordian tracts often strain after biblical resonances to create a tonality of inspired knowingness and a concomitant illusion of hermeneutic depth, piety, and rigour. Whether or not Bacon edited the Bible, many of his adherents had read it, and brought to their study of 'his' work highly methodical practices of institutionalised overreading already in place.

IV *Filling the Gaps*

In the cases of both scriptural and Shakespearean scholarship in the period, the strenuousness of hermeneutic and historical practice seems to arise out of a felt discrepancy between the massive cultural value invested in these texts and the slender present understanding of how they actually came into being. For the anti-Stratfordians in particular, a pre-condition of their project, and one on which they were quick to capitalise, is the paucity of biographical information surrounding Shakespeare. This actually served to reinforce, as well as motivate, their project. As well as offering little resistance to their rich fantasies of authorship, the lack of much first-hand biographical detail enabled the argument, frequently made, that if Shakespeare was the author of the great plays he is supposed to have written, why was there so little contemporary interest in documenting the record of his life and work? The assumption that the lives of the poets, particularly the lives of popular dramatists, must always have been regarded as worth preserving is itself the outcome of a distinctly romantic bardolatry.

This thinness of Elizabethan documentation is, after all, what had tempted Collier's misguided labours – what he could not find, he fabricated – as well as the rather different activities of Furnivall, Fleay, and the other disintegrators. What with such slight and unreliable external documentation of chronology, printing and production practices, collaboration and revision, and even attribution, the way was open for renewed scrutiny, on systematic principles, of internal evidence. A new 'professionalism' of approach, enlisting the growing influence and prestige of science, was required. Enter the new verse-testers. For like the Baconians, for whose wacky theories and methods they had no time at all – Furnivall called their work 'crakt, idiotic, tomfoolery', and James Spedding, who, as his biographer, knew Bacon's work better than anyone else, remained unconvinced by their parallels[15] – the disintegrators' unstated assumption was that Shakespeare's work was too important to leave, in the obviously imperfect state we have it, to Shakespeare. Here was the beginning of a specialised bibliographical industry, still very much with us, based upon a textual technology repeatedly updated and reinvented to realise the dream of definitive knowledge.

The same objective of filling the gaps in our knowledge is to be found in the work of the mainstream bardolaters; only the gap to be filled, the new technology they employed, and the kind of 'knowledge' they sought are different. For unlike the labours of the verse-testers and cipher-constructors, those of the bardolaters proper required no specialised knowledge of an historical or textual kind, nor any technical protocol, arcane or scientific, to gain access to the author. The method of mainstream bardolatry was in no way elitist or nostalgic but democratic and progressive, drawing as it did on emerging paradigms of a universally human subjectivity, common to the historical author, his timeless characters, and the contemporary audience. How could such a project fail to become dominant in the nineteenth-century institutionalisation of Shakespeare, when it coincided with the rise of liberal-democratic ideology in the wider culture of Anglo-America and the concomitant ascendance of a new depth-psychology of the private self?

The author was still very much the centre of attention, though not in the local or empirical senses of bibliographical attribution or biographical identity, but in the universal form of the 'inner life' he shared with everyone else, albeit on a mythic scale. In the influential work of Edward Dowden, the 'object' of knowledge was now well and truly the 'subject'. While drawing on the verse-testers' construction of a Shakespeare who passes through stages of development, Dowden's *Shakspere: His Mind and Art* announces reversed priorities and elaborates a fully universalised pattern of development: 'In the Workshop', 'In the World', 'Out of the Depths', and finally 'On the Heights'. In foregrounding the 'mind' of the poet, Dowden and his followers were attempting to fill the biggest gap of all: the hidden depths whence his great work flowed.

In so doing, Dowden effectively displaced the source of Shakespeare's authority from the specifically Elizabethan cultural and theatrical provenance in which it had been sought and relocated it in a transcendental psychology in which we all, at least potentially, have a stake: a romantic psychology of passionate struggle and hard-won triumph. By relocating Shakespeare's authority in his subjectivity, Dowden established a newly inward frame of reference for the 'universality' that had been increasingly ascribed to Shakespeare's work from the eighteenth century onwards. At the same time, Dowden's laying bare of Shakespeare's 'mind' was a powerfully, if implicitly, political move. It furthered the Enlightenment, specifically Kantian and Coleridgean, project of removing high culture from the exclusive possession of aristocrats and scholars and making it available to the ever-expanding middle class.

This could of course be achieved only at the price of idealising and dehistoricising art; but it also conferred upon 'art' an unprecedented prestige by illustrating in full dress, as it were, the romantic mythology of the artist as inhabiting the spiritual centre of society, whether or not he is relegated to its material margins. Keats' famous remark that 'Shakespeare led a life of Allegory, his works are the comments on it' might have served as epigraph to Dowden's book.[16] Dowden's construction of Shakespeare as a type of 'universal subject', and of his inner struggle and development as the source and subtext, the allegorical 'other', of his work, was paradigmatic of the aesthetic of lonely, self-expressive creativity that came to dominate the high bourgeois culture of the Victorian era and is still with us today, albeit in the degraded or residual forms of best-selling *Kunstleromane*, television mini-series made from them, and one-man retrospects mounted by museums and galleries.

In the procedure Dowden adopts, Keats's metaphor has been strangely literalised. The works are now subordinated to the life, as commentary to text, so that any actual commentary on the works, as commentary on commentary, exists at a third remove from the 'reality', the life of the author, which is its goal. This life of allegory is exalted into a transcendent, extra-textual form, while the text is demoted into a secondary epiphenomenon, an afterglow, the trace of ash left over from the gem-like flame of mental life. With such revised priorities in place, a certain reductive circularity in dealing with the text was bound to occur. If the text is no more than the means to an end located outside the text in the author's mind, almost anything may be imposed upon the text in the interest of getting beyond it to where the action really is. Dowden's reading of Shakespeare licenses the interpretation of the plays in terms of a preconception of what they mean with only the most gestural recourse to what they say.

V *Closing the Circle*

In each of the movements we have traced – whether the emphasis is textual or historical, critical or celebratory, empirical or idealist – the objective has been to 'fill the gaps'. This is of course basic to all hermeneutic practice. In the age of the 'author', the biggest gap to be filled was framed in the form of the question, 'Who was the author of the extraordinary plays ascribed to "William Shakespeare"?', and as we have begun to see, it received a number of answers at variously literal and allegorical levels. After all, it is not really one question but many, and it cannot help but register the range of social and ideological inflections of those who frame it. For the 'Jacobite' nostalgia of the anti-Stratfordians, the question is biographical and sociohistorical, and its answers more or less royalist and conservative. For the disintegrators, it is a much more narrowly professional and positivist question of bibliographical ascription, and its answers textual and technical, despite an underlying speculative biographism. For progressive liberal humanists like Dowden – the heirs of Coleridge and the main line of descent of orthodox bardolatry – the answer is at once individualistic and universalising: 'Shakespeare' is, at base, 'everyman'.

It is worth pointing out, however, that these 'answers', and the methods deployed to arrive at them, tend to contradict, or at least to conflict with, one another. We have already sampled the disintegrators' views on the findings of the Baconians. Similarly, the bardolaters' idealist construction of an inspired genius expressing his inner experience was not shared by the

Baconians. For theirs was actually an *historicist* Shakespeare constructed on the assumption that the authorship of the plays was *socially* conditioned, and their composition only possible within certain biographical, educational, and cultural circumstances. 'Unless Shakespeare be the sole example', writes T. W. White in 1892, 'the history of mankind affords no instance of a man without education having produced a literary work of the highest excellence. Yet that is what we are required to believe in the case of Shakespeare'.[17] Inner struggle, however intense, is not enough; neither the creation nor the understanding of great art is open to anyone. In their emphasis on the social conditioning of 'great art', as well as their 'demystifying' irreverence towards scholarly orthodoxy, the anti-Stratfordians actually anticipate certain recent developments in criticism, particularly that of the 'new-historicism'.[18]

This uncanny resonance should caution us against thinking we have left behind the vitiating circularities and vulgar errors of nineteenth-century commentary by virtue of our having turned away from the 'author' as the centre of critical attention, the point of origin and reference for Shakespearean signification. Though the search for the 'author' as the 'signified' – biographical, bibliographical, transcendental – of Shakespeare's plays has been all but abandoned, we are still caught up in hermeneutic toils that might some day seem no less problematic or absurd. Despite further shifts of critical focus in our century from author to text (the new bibliography), from teller to tale (the new-criticism), and more recently, from inspired individual genius to the discursive structures that sponsor and contain it (the new historicisms and feminisms), we have not so much escaped or transcended the institutionalised circularities of our precursors as extended and enlarged them. For where the 'author' was, there is now the text, or the context, or the reader and his or her 'interpretive community' as the no less transcendental signified of critical discourse, however 'historicist' or 'professionalised' it might have become.

Any criticism that seeks, projects, and delivers in a single gesture a centre privileged in advance as its first principle and final justification is predisposed to circularity, because it already knows what it wants to find in the texts it takes up, and gets out of them only what it puts in. It is also predisposed to idolatry, in that its very centredness enables and invites the formation of self-reinforcing circles, schools, institutions around it, whose teachable routines and regimens work to reproduce what remains a communally generated and constrained 'knowledge', a thoroughly 'conventional knowledge' in the popular as well as philosophical sense: what Francis Bacon described from the viewpoint of early empiricism as idols of the tribe, cave, theatre, and marketplace.[19] As Bacon, and indeed Shakespeare, recognised, idolatry is not a function of the particular idol erected by the community for worship, but of the promotion of its own cognitive processes to sacred status in the first place, the worship of the 'self' in the name of the 'other'.

We are thus led to the admittedly weird and worrying conclusion that John Payne Collier's early activities, his literal re-writings of Shakespeare and his formation of a Society to legitimate them, stand as a kind of paradigm-case for the institutionalised hermeneutic circularity within which we still labour. After all, Collier merely claimed, as have all schools since, to have discovered a Shakespeare he had actually invented. Yet this deception is paradoxically more honest and straightforward, or at least less self-deceived, than the byzantine manoeuvres devised by subsequent schools to get out of the text only what they too had put into it, but without appearing to do so: the panoply of communally sanctioned rituals designed to promote the illusion that we are doing something else and something more. How curious that these illusions seem in retrospect such transparent self-deceptions, when viewed from the standpoint of a 'different' community busily engaged in doing the same thing!

Is there any way out of the circularities that characterise 'centred', 'founded', in a word, *institutionalised* interpretation? Must all 'conventionalist', i.e. socially generated and constrained, knowledge sooner or later collapse into the idolatry of collective self-projection? According to Heidegger, its foremost modern theorist, all hermeneutic activity is circular in its essence. But there is a kind of reading, or more accurately, of re-reading that can be opposed to the presuppositious, self-interested, idolatrous reading we have identified with institutionalised interpretation. Such re-reading would have to be not 'centred' in advance but decentred or eccentric; not the projection of merely sectional or sectarian, or even of larger communal or communitarian, interests, but properly Utopian; that is, a projection of the interests of a community and a politics that does not yet exist. Such re-reading is obliged to counter what the text has been taken or made to mean in the name of what it can mean, to submit its supposed signifieds to the renewed scrutiny of its actual signifiers.

The inevitable outcome of such anti-suppositions, though not presuppositionless, re-reading must be a degree of aporia, of impasse and undecidability before the text that is the very opposite of the positivist or conventionalist 'knowledge' traditionally pursued by institutionalised interpretation. Indeed, this has been the main objection mounted against deconstruction by those schools anxious to 'get on with it' – as if the textual difference and discontinuity they themselves recognise and to which they pay lip-service did not entail the aporia they wish to 'move beyond'. Yet this deconstructive 'vortex' of interpretation,[20] while an impediment to the dubious progress of more politicised and evangelical movements, is certainly less hermeneutically reductive – ultimately it might even be more politically productive – than the self-reinforcing and ever-diminishing circles characteristic of the institutionalised – one is tempted to say 'rotarian' – interpretation currently in fashion.

At a moment when the institutionalisation of a pseudo-professional and pseudo-political pluralism is all but complete, and the new-historicist paradigm is increasingly dominant as the 'normal science' of the academy, the need for a strong form of anti-institutional re-reading to counter the weak forms of ideological critique now in place is more pressing than ever. Perhaps in the 'newer' historicism now under way, that concerned with Shakespeare's reception and reinscription within successive cultures, the self-conscious insights of deconstruction – currently repressed, demonised, or domesticated but by no means refuted or superseded – will perform the indispensable work of defamiliarisation and destabilisation of current idolatries that they performed on the older idolatries of literary studies that now seem so outmoded.

Notes

1. This 'new-historicist' orthodoxy is expounded at some length by John Drakakis in his introduction to *Alternative Shakespeares* (London: Methuen, 1985).
2. See the opening chapter, 'Historicizing Bardolatry, or Where Could Coleridge Have Been Coming From?', of my *The Uses of the Canon* (Oxford: Clarendon Press, 1990), pp. 1–15.
3. Cited crucially by Jonathan Bate, *Shakespearean Constitutions: Politics, Theatre, Criticism 1730–1830* (Oxford: Clarendon Press, 1989).
4. A number of recent studies of professionalisation bear directly on these issues. See, for example, Burton J. Bledstein, *The Culture of Professionalism* (New York: Norton, 1976); Magali Sarfati Larson, *The Rise of Professionalism: A Sociological Analysis* (Berkeley: University of California Press, 1977); and Gerald Graff, *Professing Literature: An Institutional History* (Chicago: University of Chicago Press, 1981).
5. 'Prospectus of the Shakespeare Society' (London, 1842).
6. The phrase, coined by Roland Barthes to describe the constrained interpretive potential offered by classic realism, is not out of place in this context. See his *S/Z*, trans. Richard Miller (New York: Hill and Wang, 1974). Dues in the Society of £1 annually were high enough to ensure that its membership was distinctly middle class.
7. Collier's advance notice of his impending publication of the so-called 'Perkins Folio' occurred in the *Atheneum* of 31 January, 1852. The edition appeared the following year as a 'Supplemental Volume' to the edition he had prepared ten years earlier, 'formed', as he claimed on its title-page, 'from an entirely new Collation of the Old Editions'.
8. I refer to the archaising fabrications of Thomas Chatterton and William Henry Ireland, which were preceded by those of James Macpherson. Malone's

role in exposing the fakes of Chatterton and Ireland is discussed by Louis Marder, *His Exits and His Entrances* (London: John Murray, 1964); and by Bernard Grebanier, *The Great Shakespeare Forgery* (New York: Crowell, 1960). The controversy surrounding the 'Perkins Folio' and the evidence against its authenticity was set out by C. Mansfield Ingleby, *The Shakespeare Fabrications* (London: John Russell Smith, 1859).

9. Including the Chaucer Society and the Early English Text Society. The spelling of 'Shakspere', which he imposed on his Society, was a hobby-horse of Furnivall's.

10. See his *The Succession of Shakspere's Works* (London Smith, Elder, 1874). At the opening meeting of the New Shakspere Society, Furnivall announced its purpose as 'setting on foot a fresh institution for the study of Shakspere, on what I hope will prove the soundest basis that has yet been laid for the structure of criticism and study'. *New Shakspere Society's Transactions*, ser.1, vol. 1 (1874). Fourteen years later, at the 136th meeting of the Society, this spirit was as strong as ever, and defined by Thomas Tyler as 'Shaksperology': 'The word . . . represents a just and true idea, namely that there is a science concerned with Shakspere – a science proceeding on principles analogous to those by which Astronomy is guided in dealing with the phenomena of the heavenly bodies, or Geology in investigating the formation of the earth's crust . . . The science of Shakspere seeks to ascertain, in view of all the facts, the truth about Shakspere himself and his works . . . [and] resembles in these respects most other departments of science'. Tyler opposes 'Shaksperology' to 'Shakspere-idolatry', little suspecting that the former might be only another version of the latter. See 'Shakspere Idolatry', *Transactions of the New Shakspere Society*, ser.1, vol. 12, Part 2 (1887–92), pp. 191–212.

11. This satirical suggestion was put by Appleton Morgan of the New York Shakespeare Society in *The Literary World* of Boston in 1887, and amplified in his *Shakespeare in Fact and Criticism* (New York: W. E. Benjamin, 1888).

12. Still the most useful account of the controversies over Shakespearean authorship is that of Frank W. Wadsworth, *The Poacher from Stratford* (Berkeley and Los Angeles: University of California Press, 1958). See also Alfred Harbage, *Conceptions of Shakespeare* (Cambridge, Mass.: Harvard University Press, 1966).

13. Elizabeth's claims were first put forward by W. R. Titterton in 1913, but developed in greater detail by George Elliot Sweet in *Shake-speare the Mystery* (Palo Alto: Stanford University Press, 1956); the case for Bacon's editorship of the Bible was first made by the cryptologist William L. Gaines in the *Indianapolis Star* in January, 1956. Gaines also advances the hypothesis, elegant in its economy, that Bacon was Elizabeth's illegitimate son. See Wadsworth, *op. cit.*, pp. 157 ff. and 91 ff.

14. For a helpful introduction to nineteenth-century Biblical studies, see Stephen Neill, *The Interpretation of the New Testament 1861-1961* (London: Oxford University Press, 1966); and Van A. Harvey, *The Historian and the Believer* (London: SCM Press, 1967).

15. See L. Marder, *op. cit.*, p. 169.

16. Keats to George and Georgiana Keats, 14 Feb.–3 May, 1819 in *The Letters of John Keats*, ed. Maurice Buxton Forman (London: Oxford University Press, 1947, 3rd edn), p. 305.

17. *Our English Homer, or Shakespeare Historically Considered* (London: Sampson, Low, Marston, 1892), p. vi.

18. The demystifying 'historicist' thrust of much anti-Stratfordian commentary is often evident in the titles under which it mounts its case. Consider, for example, the selection of letters reprinted from *The Daily Telegraph* pending the appearance of Donnelly's massive work in 1888: *Dethroning Shakspere*, ed. R. M. Theobald (London: Sampson, Low, Marston, Searle, and Rivington, 1888). How closely such a title chimes with those of recent cultural-materialist production! The pseudo-historicist basis of anti-Stratfordian thinking is explicitly discussed by Dorothy and Charlton Ogburn in their preface to *This Star of England* (New York: Coward-McCann, 1952), pp. xi-xiii: 'We have been prone to believe that the artist may be no more than a pipeline between a source of divine inspiration and a pad of paper . . . This fiction corresponds with no valid human experience . . . Yet one must accept it if one is to believe that the dramas of Shakespeare were written by a man who – if he could write at all – could have had no possible experience of what he was writing about, and to whom the point of view from which he wrote would have been foreign to a degree almost impossible for us to comprehend in these days of social fluidity and classlessness.'

19. *Novum Organum* (1620), sections 50–68.

20. This happy phrase was coined by, of all critics, John Middleton Murry, and redeemed for contemporary theory by Geoffrey Hartman, 'Shakespeare's Poetical Character in *Twelfth Night*' in *Shakespeare and the Question of Theory*, eds. Patricia Parker and Geoffrey Hartman (New York and London: Methuen, 1985), pp. 38 ff. Murry presciently wrote: 'The moment comes in our experience of Shakespeare when we are dimly conscious of a choice to be made: either we must turn away (whether by leaving him in silence, or by substituting for his reality some comfortable intellectual fiction of our own), or we must suffer ourselves to be drawn into the vortex.'

9 The Transvestite's Progress: Rosalind the Yeshiva Boy*

Marjorie Garber

Rosalind's transvestism . . . functions to allow Rosalind to live out a freer, more assertive and independent role than she could otherwise . . . In male garb, Rosalind automatically becomes the dominant figure . . . It is she who deals with the outside world, who can meet and converse with men, speak and act assertively, even authoritatively . . . In short, she can be a person.

Marilyn French, *Shakespeare's
Division of Experience*[1]

In a quintessential version of the transvestite progress narrative,[2] Shakespeare's cross-dressed female characters were often seen in the early years of feminist criticism as role models for modern (and postmodern) women. Resourceful, ambitious, passionate, smart, looking good in pants, these women – Rosalind, Viola, Portia, Julia, Imogen – provided authority and reassurance. Even Beatrice and Katharina, without benefit of breeches, spoke out in protest against patriarchy, and both were rewarded with desirable marriages.

All the more striking were the transvestite heroines, whether dressed as pages, country boys, or clerks. Theirs was a recuperative pattern: however outspoken they were, however much they challenged authority in the form of wicked dukes or moneylenders, they took pains to let their femaleness show. Rosalind and Julia swoon at moments of stress, Viola, facing the prospect of a duel, laments 'a little thing would make me tell them how much I lack of a man' (*Twelfth Night*, III, iv, 307–9), and Portia remarks to Nerissa that in their male disguise 'they shall think we are accomplished/With that we lack' (*The Merchant of Venice*, III, iv, 61–3). 'They', and 'them', are of course the onstage (and offstage) audience of

*This essay is part of a considerably longer chapter on 'The Transvestite's Progress' which appears in *Vested Interests: Cross-Dressing and Cultural Anxiety* (New York: Routledge, 1991).

men, who ostensibly 'have' what the cross-dressed women 'lack'. And if, as materialist critics of the eighties were quick to point out, these *double entendres* were in fact triple, because the transvestite women who 'lacked' were in fact always already men, boy actors, with the audience very much in on the joke, this did not mitigate, but rather confirmed, the remanding of women back to their proper places at the end of the play. Cross-dressing, as contrasted with 'masculinity' (like that detected by some critics in Goneril, or Lady Macbeth, or Volumnia) was playful and liminal, and also ameliorative and educational, whether for the 'women' in the plays (Rosalind *et al.*) or for the audience.

We are accustomed to Shakespeare being fetishised in Western culture, made the touchstone (if not the Touchstone) of issues literary, philosophical, and social, the surety and verification of the issues of our – or any – time. But it is striking to note that of all Shakespeare's cross-dressed heroines it is Rosalind who is almost always chosen as the normative case by nineteenth- and twentieth-century authors. When, for example, Oscar Wilde's Dorian Gray falls in love, it is with an actress playing the part of Rosalind – or rather, the part of Ganymede: 'You should have seen her! When she came on in her boy's clothes she was perfectly wonderful. She wore a moss-coloured velvet jerkin with cinnamon sleeves, slim brown cross-gartered hose, a dainty little green cap with a hawk's feather caught in a jewel, and a hooded cloak lined with dull red. She had never seemed to me more beautiful.' [3]

'Rosalind' appears, in fact, in a surprising number of modern texts as a kind of shorthand for the cross-dressed woman, or the enigma that she represents. Why Rosalind rather than Viola, or Portia, or Julia, or Imogen? Why is it so often Rosalind who is singled out as the exemplary early modern cross-dresser, the Katherine Hepburn (if not the Marlene Dietrich or the Annie Lennox) of her time? To approach this question, which has some larger implications for the cultural construction of transvestism, let us look at a few diverse and fascinating examples.

Théophile Gautier's 1835 novel *Mademoiselle de Maupin* is a remarkable text about gender undecidability in which the sexually enigmatic Théodore de Serannes is beloved by both the narrator d'Albert and his mistress, Rosette. The dramatic and the psychological plots of *Mademoiselle de Maupin* turn on a production of *As You Like It* in which Théodore appears in the part of Rosalind.

D'Albert the narrator, it is almost needless to say, is cast as Orlando. When he first sees Théodore dressed as Rosalind, he is enchanted: this is the answer to his prayers. 'You would think he had never worn any other costume in his life! He is not in the very least awkward in his movements, he walks very well and he doesn't get caught up in his train; he uses his eyes and his fan to admiration; and what a slim waist he has! . . . Oh, lovely Rosalind! Who would not want to be her Orlando?' [4] Bear in mind that d'Albert at least thinks of himself as heterosexual; his desire is for Théodore to turn out to *be* a woman, so that he can safely love her. Thus his consternation when, in the third act, Rosalind cross-dresses, and appears as Ganymede:

> I grew all sombre when Théodore reappeared in masculine dress, more sombre than I had been before; for happiness only serves to make one more aware of grief. . . . And yet he was dressed in a way that suggested that this masculine attire had a feminine lining; something broader about the hips and fuller in the chest, some sort of flow which materials don't have on a man's body, left little doubt of the person's sex. . . . My serenity began to return, and I persuaded myself again that it was quite definitely a woman. (Gautier, p. 249)

Playing out the scene, in which Orlando tries to persuade the 'fair youth' that he is really in love, and 'Ganymede' reproves him for this mode of address, saying, 'Nay, you must call me Rosalind,' d'Albert feels that the play has been written for the express purpose of verbalising his own situation. 'No doubt there is some important reason, which I cannot know, which obliges this beautiful woman to adopt this accursed disguise' (Gautier, p. 252).

As for his rival in love, his mistress Rosette, *she* is also – again, needless to say – a member of the play's cast. Having refused the part of Rosalind for herself because she was reluctant to dress up as a man (a fact that surprises the self-absorbed and narcissistic d'Albert: 'prudery is hardly one of her failings. If I had not been sure of the contrary, I would have thought that she had ugly legs' [Gautier, p. 235]) Rosette has accepted the role of Phebe, the shepherdess who falls hopelessly and fruitlessly in love with the fictive 'Ganymede'. As d'Albert observes complacently:

> the history of Phebe is her own, as that of Orlando is mine with this difference, that everything ends happily for Orlando, and that Phebe, disappointed in love, is reduced to marrying Sylvius [sic] instead of the delightful ideal she wanted to embrace. Life is like that: one person's happiness is bound to be someone else's misfortune. It is very fortunate for me that Théodore is a woman; it is very unfortunate for Rosette that Théodore isn't a man, and that she now finds herself cast into the amorous impossibilities in which I went astray not long ago. (Gautier, p. 257)

There is much more in this vein. Shakespeare's play serves as a *mise en abîme* into which Gautier's characters avidly hurl themselves, and the conundrum of gender undecidability is given a local habitation and a name. D'Albert's assertion, 'I have no proofs, and I cannot remain in this state of uncertainty any longer' (Gautier, p. 257), mirrors Orlando's decisive 'I can live no longer by thinking' (*As You Like It*, V, ii, 50) and is equally self-delusive about the possibility of 'proof' in matters of gender, identity, and role. 'Théodore – Rosalind – for I don't know what name to call you by' (Gautier, p. 294). 'Rosalind, you who have so many prescriptions for curing the malady of love, cure me, for I am very ill. Play your part to the end, cast off the clothes of the beautiful page Ganymede, and hold out your white hand to the youngest son of the brave Sir Rowland de Boys' (Gautier, p. 301). So ends d'Albert's narrative.

But this is not the end of the novel. Théodore now picks up the narration (this is very near the end of the book, Chapter 14 of 17) and 'explains' the subterfuge. 'Her' plan is in fact a 'real life' version of the story of *As You Like It*:

> This was my plan. In my male attire I should make the acquaintance of some young man whose appearance pleased me; I should live familiarly with him; by skilful questions and by false confidences which elicited true ones, I should soon acquire a complete understanding of his feelings and his thoughts. . . . I should make a pretext of some journey, and . . . come back in my women's clothes . . . then I should so arrange things that he met me and wooed me. (Gautier, p. 315)

The mystery would seem to be solved. Théodore, like 'Rosalind' in the play, is a woman. Yet in the next moment she puts that identification, and the binarism of gender, in question:

> I was imperceptibly losing the idea of my sex, and I hardly remembered, at long intervals, that I was a woman; at the beginning, I'd often let slip some phrase or other which didn't fit in with the male attire that I was wearing. . . . If ever the fancy takes me to go and find my skirts again in the drawer where I left them, which I very much doubt, unless I fall in love with some young beau, I shall find it hard to lose this habit, and, instead of a woman disguised as a man, I shall look like a man disguised as a woman. In truth, neither sex is really mine . . . I belong to a third sex, a sex apart, which has as yet no name . . . My dream would be to have each sex in turn, and to satisfy my dual nature: man today, woman tomorrow. (Gautier, pp. 329–30)

At the close of the novel, however, even this certainty about transvestism and the third kind is undermined. A new narrative voice takes over in the sixteenth chapter, recording visits by Théodore to the rooms of d'Albert and Rosette, and Théodore's departure the next morning. The novel's last chapter takes the form of a letter from Théodore to d'Albert, offered as a substitute and an 'explanation': a letter which establishes 'her' as the locus of desire: 'Your unassuaged desire will still open its wings to fly to me; I shall always be for you something desirable, to which your fancy loves to return' (Gautier, p. 347). The transvestite here articulates herself/himself as *that which escapes*, what Lacan describes in his essay on 'The Signification of the Phallus' as 'desire':

desire is neither the appetite for satisfaction, nor the demand for love, but the difference that results from the subtraction of the first from the second, the phenomenon of their splitting (*Spaltung*).[5]

Thus desire is by definition that which cannot be satisfied: it is what is left of absolute demand when all possible satisfaction has been subtracted from it. And this is another definition of the transvestite, exemplified in Shakespeare as in Gautier. The transvestite is the space of desire.

In a way this space is denied by readings of Shakespearean transvestism such as that of Stephen Greenblatt, who writes that 'the unique qualities of [Rosalind's] identity – those that give Rosalind her independence, her sharply etched individuality – will not, as Shakespeare conceives the play, endure: they are bound up with exile, disguise, and freedom from ordinary constraint, and they will vanish, along with the playful chafing, when the play is done'.[6] But 'vanishing' here is the converse of escaping. Greenblatt describes this as 'an improvisational self-fashioning that longs for self-effacement and reabsorption in the community', and attributes that 'longing' to 'a social system that marks out singularity, particularly in women, as prodigious'.

Whose longing is it, really, that is being described here under the cover of a social and cultural constraint? If Rosalind's 'unique qualities' – which is to say, her capacity for becoming or constructing Ganymede – will not endure, will 'vanish' when the play is done, so too will Rosalind and Orlando and all the rest of the dramatis personae who are part of how 'Shakespeare conceives the play.' But in fact what lingers, like the smile of the Cheshire Cat, is precisely that residue, that supplement: Ganymede.

The 'longing' for self-effacement and reabsorption is a domesticated and, I would suggest, partriarchal or masculinist longing, which is transferred onto the figure of the transvestite in a gesture of denial or fending off. Not to endure, to vanish, these are the negative reformulations of desire, which instead *escapes*, goes everywhere rather than nowhere, for the transvestite is the space of desire.

Let us look now at another recent fictional appropriation of Rosalind, this time from the twentieth rather than the nineteenth century: Angela Carter's novel *The Passion of New Eve*. First published in 1977, Carter's postmodern novel tells the story of Evelyn, a young Englishman who undergoes transsexual surgery to become Eve, and the woman of his dreams, Tristessa, a former Hollywood star who turns out to be literally a phallic 'woman', a male transvestite. The plot is intricate and unnecessary to summarise here, but the wedding scene between Eve and Tristessa is one that finds both participants cross-dressed. Tristessa wears 'the white satin bridal gown he'd last worn thirty years before in . . . *Wuthering Heights*,' and Eve appears in a costume once intended for an actor playing Frédéric Chopin in the story of George Sand. (Sand was herself a famous cross-dresser, and Chopin, her lover, was notoriously described by his critics not only as 'effeminate' but also as 'the only female musician',[7] so that Carter's plot of inverted inversion has yet further refractions, a cultural ripple effect.)

Here is Eve – formerly Evelyn – reflecting on her own reflection in the mirror:

> the transformation that an endless series of reflections showed me was a double drag. This young buck, this Baudelairean dandy so elegant and trim in his evening clothes – it seemed at first glance, I had become my old self again in the inverted world of mirrors. But this masquerade was more than skin deep. Under the mask of maleness I wore another mask of femaleness but a mask that now I never would be able to remove, no matter how hard I tried, although I was a boy disguised as a girl and now disguised as a boy again, like Rosalind in Elizabethan Arden.[8]

The evocation of Rosalind, so similar, in a way, to that of Gautier's Théodore, produces similar ruminations on the questions of constructed and essential gender identity. 'Rosalind' becomes here a sign word for that reflecting mirror, that infinite regress of representation, of which the transvestite (*always*, in one sense, in 'double drag') is a powerful and inescapable reminder.

Why, then, is Rosalind the favourite among Shakespeare's cross-dressers; the shorthand term for benign female-to-male cross-dressing in literature and culture?

Rosalind differs from Viola in a crucial way: she returns to the stage dressed as a woman. In the last scene of the play she leaves the stage as Ganymede and returns, led by Hymen, in a 'sight and shape' so unmistakably female as to give joy to Orlando and consternation to Phebe. In the Epilogue that follows 'she' deliberately breaks the frame to acknowledge the 'real' gender of the actor ('If I were a woman, I would kiss as many of you as had beards that pleased me, complexions that liked me, and breaths that I defied not' *As You Like It*, V, iv, 214–7), and by calling attention to her underlying male 'identity' as an actor ('*If* I were a woman') Rosalind opens up the possibility of a male/male homo-eroticism between male audience member and male actor which is the counterpart of the male/'male' homoeroticism that animates Orlando's conversations with Ganymede, as well as the converse of the female/female homoeroticism figured in the play by Phebe's infatuation.

But in returning dressed as a woman she also allows for the possibility of a recuperative interpretation (of which Greenblatt's is a very subtle and powerful version) that suggests a transformed woman now 'reabsorbed' into the community and thus capable of 'vanishing'. Rosalind, according to this recuperative fantasy, has now finished her job of education and self-instruction (Greenblatt calls it 'improvisation', but it is clearly very temporary indeed), and can now take up her wifely role. There is no more need for Ganymede, who would have been very inconvenient if he had stayed around. As for the male Rosalind of the Epilogue, he does not need or want Ganymede either, except as an Ovidian reminder that gods and boys often go well together. ('Ganymede' was also Elizabethan slang, usually pejorative in tone, for a male prostitute or a servant kept for sexual purposes.[9]) Neither ending – that of the onstage pairs in marital ranks, nor that of the epilogue and its wink to certain members of the audience – acknowledges the 'other' transvestite, the one who is *not* there in either final scene or epilogue. Yet it is *Ganymede* who is the play's locus of desire, *Ganymede*, not Rosalind, with whom Phebe falls so hopelessly in love, *Ganymede* who enchants the audience. How are we to account for *Ganymede*? For the erotic?

Here, then, is the paradox. Only by looking at the transvestite on the stage, in the literary text, can we see clearly that he or she is not there. Only by regarding Ganymede, and Cesario and Dorothy Michaels in *Tootsie* as instated presences, not as other versions of Rosalind, or Viola, or Michael Dorsey, or Dustin Hoffman, but as constructs that have a subjectivity and an agency, can we understand something of their relation to narcissism, desire, and possibility. To appropriate them to a social and historical discourse is to understand their politics and their history, but not their power. For that power resides elsewhere.

*   *   *   *   *

What a strange power there is in clothing.
    I. B. Singer, 'Yentl the Yeshiva Boy'

The point is made remarkably in the contrast between I. B. Singer's short story, 'Yentl the Yeshiva Boy,' published in 1962, and the 1983 Barbra Streisand film, *Yentl*, adapted from Singer's work. For Streisand makes her film a classic progress narrative or role-model allegory for the eighties, the story of a woman's liberation from old-world patriarchy, the emigration of a Jewish princess to the new world of Hollywood. Singer's story, by contrast, insists not only upon the quasi-mystical otherness of his nineteenth-century old-world setting, but also upon the transvestite as a subject rather than a 'stage'. The 'Anshel' of his tale escapes, is not converted but dispersed and reborn.

In Streisand's film, jokingly described by Hollywood sceptics as 'Tootsie on the Roof,' [10] Yentl is a young girl who is more interested in studying the Hebrew scriptures with her scholar father than in buying fish with the local housewives. When her father dies, she faces herself in the mirror (in an important narcissistic moment), cuts off her long hair, and, dressed as a boy, sets off to become a scholar and spend her life reading the Torah. She takes the name 'Anshel', which, since it was the name of her brother who died in childhood, represents her fantasied male self. (Compare this to Viola/Cesario's affecting little story in *Twelfth Night* about a mythical 'sister' who never told her love, and pined away; or, equally pertinent, Viola's decision to dress herself, in her guise as 'Cesario,' exactly like her brother, Sebastian.)

Inevitably, Yentl/Anshel meets a young man, Avigdor (Mandy Patinkin) with whom she falls in love, though he himself is in love with Hadass (Amy Irving). When Avigdor's marriage is prevented (his brother had committed suicide, rendering the whole family outcast and unsuitable for alliance) he urges 'Anshel' to marry Hadass. A comic series of episodes follows, including one rather pointed scene at the tailor's, where the terrified husband-to-be is being fitted for a wedding suit. In the course of a long, determinedly broad song-and-dance number the audience is invited to speculate on 'Anshel's' trousers, and on what the tailors see – and don't see – beneath them in the course of their work.

These tailors, like the tailors who intimidated Freud's Wolf-Man, are *Schneiders*, cutters, a word related, as Freud points out, to the verb *beschneiden*, 'to circumcise'.[11] Are Orthodox Jewish men, ritually circumcised, really any different from women? Streisand-Yentl-'Anshel,' re-enacting in comic (and musical) terms the always-already of castration/circumcision, draws attention to her quandary – the heterosexual female transvestite facing the prospect of marriage to a woman – as incapacity. In the next scenes, of the wedding and its remarkably eroticised aftermath, she will triumph over that apparent obstacle.

On the wedding night, 'Anshel' persuades Hadass that there is no rush to consummate their marriage, that Hadass should choose sex rather than having it forced upon her. In an extraordinarily tender and erotic scene of instruction, the forbidden sexual energy is deflected into a mutual reading of the Talmud, with Streisand (the woman playing a woman dressed as a man) teaching Irving how to understand the Law. This is one of the scenes that most reminds me of Rosalind in *As You Like It*, in her guise as 'Ganymede' teaching Orlando how to show his love.

Streisand's film is, at least on the surface, normatively heterosexual, so that this dangerous liminal moment in which Hadass falls in love with Yentl/Anshel is flanked, so to speak, on the one side by an early, comic episode in which Yentl/Anshel has to share a bed with Avigdor (who of course thinks she's a boy, and doesn't therefore understand her reluctance to strip and get under the covers) and on the other side by the revelation scene, in which Yentl declares her 'true' sexual identity to Avigdor, ultimately baring her breasts to resolve his doubt.

Yet the scene between Streisand and Amy Irving smoulders with repressed sexuality. Irving later declared that she was 'pretty excited. I mean, I'm the first female to have a screen kiss with Barbra Streisand! She refused to rehearse, but after the first take she said, "It's not so bad. It's like kissing an arm." I was a little insulted, because I believed so much that she was a boy that I'd sort of fallen in love with her.' (Considine, p. 344). In another interview she explained that Streisand 'was like the male lead, and she gave me the feminine lead. No problems'.[12] Is Irving's 'like' a comparative, or 'eighties babble-speak punctuation for emphasis? *Was* Streisand the male lead – or just an impersonator? Her own response to 'Anshel's' undecidable and overdetermined eroticism was, predictably, a kind of appropriative denial. When Hollywood producer Howard Rosenman, attending a private screening of *Yentl*, told her 'You were fabulous as a boy. Anshel was very sexy,' she replied, he says, 'very cutelike, in that nasal voice, "Howard! Anshel is taken."' (Considine, p. 351).

Mandy Patinkin, the ('other') male lead, remarked of Streisand's performance, 'I never thought of her as a girl. She was a guy, period'. On the other hand, he said Streisand-as-director was 'demanding, yet flexible and compassionate, with the gentleness of a woman'. (Considine, p. 344). On screen, Patinkin's Avigdor is at first horrified, then attracted, as is the norm in contemporary cross-dressing films (compare James Garner's King Marchand in *Victor/Victoria*). 'I should have known,' he says, as he admits his love for her. An active, learned, acceptably transgressive figure (as contrasted with the unliberated Hadass, who cooks, bakes and smilingly serves the men their favourite dishes) Yentl is the 'new woman' of the 'eighties, a fit partner for a scholar – if she will only renounce her ambitions.

But the mechanism of substitution which is almost always a textual or dramatic effect of the transvestite in literature is again in force. Streisand as Yentl declines to marry Avigdor because she wants to be a scholar more than she wants to be anyone's wife. Happily, however, Avigdor's first love Hadass is still around, now educated through her 'romantic friendship' or homoerotic transferential reading experiences with 'Anshel'. As the film ends, the transvestite 'vanishes' and is dispersed; Avigdor and Hadass will marry and have a better – i.e., more modern and more equal – marriage than they would have if both had not fallen in love with 'Anshel'; Yentl herself, now dressed like a woman, is on a boat going to America, where she can presumably live the life of a scholar without disguising her gender identity.

Thus instead of *class* substituting for gender *national culture* does so. The transvestite is a sign of the category crisis of the immigrant, between nations, forced out of one role that no longer fits (here, on the surface, because a woman cannot be a scholar; but not very far beneath the surface, because of poverty, antisemitism, and pogrom – Jewish as well as female) and into another role, that of a stranger in a strange land.

Streisand's own cultural identity as a Jewish musical star, with unWASPy looks, a big nose, and a reputation in the business for shrewdness (read, in the ethnic stereotype, 'pushy') redoubles this already doubled story. As a Jewish woman in a star category usually occupied by gentiles (despite, or because of, the fact that many *male* movie moguls were Jews) she is Yentl/ Anshel in another sense as well, 'masquerading' as a regular movie star when in fact she differed from them in an important way.

Critics of the film have wished that it could be more progressively feminist than it is, given its date. 'It is not', writes one observer, 'so much a film about women's right to an education as it is a personal statement by Streisand about her own determination to exert influence in a world still dominated by male power structures'.[13] The glee in certain quarters when Streisand was 'stiffed' in the Oscar nominations, nominated for neither Best Actress nor Best Director (though she had campaigned for the attention of both Jewish and women voters in the Motion Picture Academy, and had earlier been given the Golden Globe award for Best Director) seemed to reinforce this male ambivalence about her career path, and to emphasise her insider–outsider position. 'The Oscar nominations are out and Barbra Streisand didn't get any,' gloated Johnny Carson on the *Tonight Show*. 'Today she found out the true meaning of *The Big Chill*.'[14]

Yet this analysis leaves out her Jewishness, which, in a plot line chosen presumably for its at least glancing relevance to her personal situation, is extremely striking. The unusual spelling of Streisand's first name, 'Barbra' without the conventional third 'a', is a kind of marker of her implicitly defiant difference. Nor is it surprising that the expression of difference should manifest itself in a transvestite vehicle. In fact, that transvestism here should be not only a sign of itself, and its attendant anxieties, including paneroticism (both Avigdor and Hadass fall in love with 'Anshel', the transferential object of desire, who then strategically and inevitably subtracts 'himself') but also of other contingent and contiguous category crises (oppression of Jews in Eastern Europe, and the need or desire to emigrate; oppression or at least a certain 'attitude' about female Jewish artists in Hollywood, and about women in the producer's role, the role so often occupied by Jewish men) is a compelling illustration of what I take to be the power of the transvestite in literature and culture. Streisand, who displaces both WASP women and Jewish men in her dual roles as star and producer, lobbied long and hard to get this particular property to work as a film. Her first public appearance on behalf of the film took place, perhaps significantly, at the annual United Jewish Appeal dinner in New York, where she was designated the UJA Man of the Year.

Yet on the surface Streisand's *Yentl* presents itself not as a disruption but as a progress narrative, the story of a woman's quest for education; in fact, the story of two women's quests. For Hadass is another version of the 'normalised' Yentl, a sympathetic figure who – like Celia in *As You Like It* – comes to conclusions about the gender dissymmetries of love and power very similar to those of the cross-dressed woman. According to this reading, Yentl learns something both *for* and *from* Hadass, just as Celia profits from Rosalind's cross-dressing, and Nerissa from Portia's. *Yentl* thus becomes a story of female bonding or sisterhood, as well as a story of heterosexual love in conflict with professional fulfilment. As we have noted, Streisand aggressively denied any *non*-heterosexual possibilities encrypted in her text ('It was like kissing an arm'; 'Howard! Anshel is taken').

Although her film makes much of the threat of cutting implied in the tailor scene, Streisand herself refused the unkindest cut, the loss of her long hair. Despite the alacrity with which many film actresses shed their locks on the way to movie stardom (Bette Davis and Glenda Jackson as the bald Elizabeth I, Meryl Streep in *Sophie's Choice*, Vanessa Redgrave with her scalp shaved as Fania Fenelon in *Playing for Time*) Streisand wore a wig, and cut *it*, not her own hair, when she transformed herself in the play's key scene into a boy. 'As a boy', reported a makeup artist who was on the scene, 'She wore a short wig throughout the entire movie. There was no way she was going to part with those Medusa curls of hers. She loved her long hair' (Considine, pp. 361–2).

The barb in 'Medusa curls' is clear, whatever the makeup artist's knowledge of Freud. Streisand was . . . in this view – a self-made phallic woman, and one who refused to decapitate or castrate herself. Freud, writing of 'the *phallic* mother, of whom we are afraid,' notes that 'the mythological creation, Medusa's head, can be traced back to the same *motif* of fright at castration,' [15] and remarks upon the paradoxical empowerment of the terrifying spectacle:

> The sight of Medusa's head makes the spectator stiff with terror, turns him to stone. Observe that we have here once again the same origin from the castration complex and the same transformation of affect! For becoming stiff means an erection. Thus in the original situation it offers consolation to the spectator: he is still in possession of a penis, and the stiffening reassures him of the fact. [16]

Streisand herself offered a physiological interpretation of orthodox Judaism's division of labour between men and women. 'I think it has to do with erections,' she said. 'A man is so capable of feeling impotent that what makes him able to have an erection a lot of the time is the weakness of women' (Considine, p. 341). 'It's not law,' she said, 'It's bullshit. Men have used these things to put women in their place.' In view of these comments, it is perhaps not surprising that I. B. Singer failed to admire her interpretation of his tale.

Singer spoke out angrily in the 'Arts and Leisure' section of the Sunday *New York Times*, lamenting the addition of music to his story and singling out the star for blame: 'My story was in no way material for a musical, certainly not the kind Miss Streisand has given us. Let me say: one cannot cover up with songs the shortcomings of the direction and acting.' Above all he criticised the ending, which differed sharply from the original.

'Was going to America Miss Streisand's idea of a happy ending for *Yentl?*', he asked with withering contempt. 'What would Yentl have done in America? Worked in a sweatshop twelve hours a day when there is no time for learning? Would she try to marry a salesman in New York, move to the Bronx or Brooklyn and rent an apartment with an icebox and dumbwaiter?' 'Weren't there enough yeshivas in Poland or in Lithuania where she could continue to study?'[17] The gravamen of his change was that the film was too commercial, and that Streisand was no Yentl, lacking 'her character, her ideals, her sacrifice, her great passion for spiritual achievement.'

The Yentl of Singer's 1984 blast at Streisand was, then, apparently a nice Jewish girl with a passion for Talmud, who needed, above all, a time and place for study, not the spoiled and materialistic Jewish Princess that he (and Johnny Carson) perceived in Streisand. But the Yentl of Singer's 1962 story is something rather different: a figure of ambivalence, complex subjectivity, and erotic power, who 'disrupts the system of differences on which sexual stereotyping depends,' to cite Catherine Belsey on Shakespeare's cross-dressed women; a figure who resembles a scholarly version of Gautier's Théodore as Rosalind. In fact, Yentl as transvestite contravenes both Streisand's reading of the story and Singer's own. To see how that happens, and what its theoretical consequences may be for the progress narrative, it may be useful to return to the text of I. B. Singer's story, 'Yentl the Yeshiva Boy.'

In Singer's story, Yentl, the daughter of a Jewish scholar, longs to study the Torah. Forbidden to do so by Jewish law, she studies secretly with her father until he dies. 'She had proved so apt a pupil that her father used to say: "Yentl – you have the soul of a man." ' ' "So why was I born a woman?" ' she asks, and he answers, ' "Even heaven makes mistakes." ' 'There was no doubt about it,' says the narrator:

> Yentl was unlike any of the girls in Yanev – tall, thin, bony, with small breasts and narrow hips. On Sabbath afternoons, when her father slept, she would dress up in his trousers, his fringed garment, his silk coat, his skull-cap, his velvet hat, and study her reflection in the mirror. She looked like a dark, handsome young man. There was even a slight down on her upper lip.[18]

After her father's death Yentl cuts her hair, dresses herself in her father's clothes, and sets off for Lubin. She takes a new name, 'Anshel', after an uncle who had died, and joins up with a group of young students. (The replacement of Singer's 'uncle' with Streisand's 'brother' adds pathos – since her brother would have to have died in childhood – and allows for the possibility of a ghostly 'double' on the model of Viola's brother Sebastian.) Befriended by Avigdor, who takes 'Anshel' with him to his yeshiva and chooses 'him' for a study partner, she soon finds herself in a characteristic and problematic predicament: secretly in love with Avigdor, she is urged by him to marry his former fiancée Hadass.

'Stripped of gaberdine and trousers she was once more Yentl, a girl of marriageable age, in love with a young man who was betrothed to another' (Singer, p. 169). In this situation Yentl/Anshel sounds once again a little like Rosalind – 'Alas the day, what shall I do with my doublet and hose?' (*As You Like It*, III, ii, 219) – and even more like Viola – '. . . and I (poor monster) fond as much on him' (*Twelfth Night*, II, ii, 34) – but with a disconcerting psychosexual twist. For she dreams that 'she had been at the same time a man and a woman, wearing both a woman's bodice and a man's fringed garment . . . Only now did Yentl grasp the meaning of the Torah's prohibition against wearing the clothes of the other sex. By doing so one deceived not only others but also oneself' (Singer, pp. 169–70). With consternation, Anshel (as Singer refers to the cross-dressed protagonist throughout his tale) finds herself/himself proposing to Hadass, and only afterward is able to rationalise the proposal as something that she (or he) is really doing for Avigdor.

After the wedding the bride's parents, according to custom, inspect the wedding sheets for signs that the marriage had been consummated, and discover traces of blood. As the narrative informs us, with an infuriating lack of specificity, 'Anshel had found a way to deflower the bride'. 'Hadass in her innocence was unaware that things weren't quite as they should have been.' This cool, almost detached tone is quite different from Streisand and Irving's highly eroticised scene of displaced instruction. Meanwhile 'Anshel' and Avigdor continue to be study partners, taking up – all too pertinently – the study of the Tractate on Menstruous Women (Singer, p. 179).

But all is not perfect. Anshel begins to feel pain at deceiving Hadass, and, besides, 'he' fears exposure: how long can he avoid going to the public baths? So Anshel stages a scene of self-revelation to Avigdor, proclaiming 'I'm not a man but a woman,' and then undressing in front of him. Avigdor, who at first doesn't believe a word of this story, and indeed begins to fear that the disrobing Anshel 'might want to practice pederasty' (Singer, p. 183), is swiftly convinced by what he sees, though when Yentl resumes her men's clothing Avigdor thinks for a moment he has been dreaming. 'I'm neither the one nor the other,' declares Yentl/Anshel. (Compare this to Théodore's declaration, 'In truth, neither sex is really mine'). 'Only now did [Avigdor] realize that Anshel's cheeks were too smooth for a man's, the hair too abundant, the hands too small' (Singer, p. 185). 'All Anshel's explanations seemed to point to one thing: she had the soul of a man and the body of a woman' (Singer, p. 187). 'What a strange power there is in clothing,' Avigdor thinks (Singer, p. 188). He, and later others, even suspects that Anshel is a demon.

In Singer's story, Anshel sends Hadass divorce papers by messenger, and disappears. Avigdor, who had been married to someone else (but that's another story) also obtains a divorce and, to the brief scandal of the town, he and Hadass are married. When their child is born, 'those assembled at the circumcision could scarcely believe their ears when they heard the father name his son Anshel' (Singer, p. 192).

One crucial difference, then, between the story and the film is that in the film 'Anshel' disappears and Yentl escapes, travels, traverses a boundary – in this case the ocean dividing Old World from New. In Singer's story, 'Anshel' is reborn as the child of Avigdor and Hadass. In both cases, however, 'Anshel' is an overdetermined site of desire. Both Amy Irving and Mandy Patinkin declare their love to Streisand; she is *not*, as was the original plan, merely a transferential object for Hadass, but is instead the chosen beloved. In Singer's account, both Avigdor and Hadass are full of sadness rather than joy on their wedding day. Speculation about why Anshel had left town and sent his wife divorce papers runs riot in the town. 'Truth itself', observes the narrator, in a Poe-like statement that reflects directly on cross-dressing in the text, 'is often concealed in such a way that the harder you look for it, the harder it is to find' (Singer, p. 192).

But what of the child, 'Anshel' – *this* Anshel demonstrably a boy, since his naming occurs at his circumcision? This boy, both addition and substitution, replaces and does not replace the absent Anshel who was brought into being by Yentl. Once again the transvestite escapes, and returns powerfully and uncannily as the 'loved boy'. What is the relation between this boy and the transvestite? Let us call him the changeling boy.

Why changeling? Not literally, in the sense in which the changeling is usually described: a child secretly exchanged for another by the fairies. Shakespeare's *Henry IV*, you may recall, wanted to believe that his son Harry and Harry Percy were changelings, the wrong one left in the Plantagenet cradle by mistake (*1 Henry IV*, I, i, 84–9). But the infant Anshel is a changeling in that he is substituted for (by being named for) a figure who herself/himself incarnated change, and was himself/herself exchanged. Yentl becomes 'Anshel' who becomes – in some quite complicated way – Anshel. A memory, a promise, a replacement, and a substitution.

The changeling boy. In *A Midsummer Night's Dream* he is all of those things. The locus of desire between, and for, Titania and Oberon. Omnipresent in his absence, not represented, beyond representation, even in a play in which there are fairies and monsters and amazons – and actors. The changeling boy is in one way a figure for the boy actor, for the anxieties which surround him, not only in Shakespeare's time, but, equally, in ours.

By now it should be clear that I regard appropriations of transvestism in the service of a humanist 'progress narrative' as both unconvincing and highly problematic. Unconvincing, because they ignore the complex and often unconscious eroticism of such self-transformations and masquerades (whether or not they are to be called versions of 'fetishism') and because in doing so they rewrite the story of the transvestite subject as a cultural symptom. Problematic, because the consequent reinscription of 'male' and 'female', even if tempered (or impelled) by feminist consciousness, reaffirms the patriarchal binary and ignores what is staring us in the face: the existence of the transvestite, the figure that disrupts. Such progress narrative readings, by their very nature, existentialise aesthetic questions, whereas, I want to suggest, the figure of the transvestite in fact opens up the whole question of the relationship of the aesthetic to the existential. This, indeed, is part of its considerable power to disturb, its transgressive force.

Rosalind and Théodore as 'Ganymede', Singer's 'Anshel' and the changeling boy of *A Midsummer Night's Dream* are versions of the same fantasy, the same mechanism of dream and desire. The transvestite, the changeling boy, and the boy actor point to the impossibility of realising that fantasy – and the necessity of the fantasy *as opposed to* any realisation. The fantasy child is the ultimate 'transvestite effect', the figure that comes between demand and desire, the signifier that plays its role only when veiled. The transvestite is a figure for something fundamental to human desire yet constitutively not there. For if it were there it would not be so indestructibly what is desired.

Notes

1. New York, Ballantine Books, 1981, p. 108.
2. In many readings of cross-dressing, the transvestite is said to embrace transvestism unwillingly, as an instrumental strategy rather than an erotic pleasure and play space; indeed, heterosexual desire is for a time apparently thwarted by the cross-dresser's assumed identity, so that it becomes necessary for him or her to unmask. This is what I call, in *Vested Interests*, the 'progress narrative'. The ideological implications of this pattern are clear: cross-dressing can be 'fun' or 'functional' so long as it occupies a liminal space and a

temporary time period: after this carnivalisation, however, whether it is called 'Halloween' (in Provincetown) or 'green world' (in Shakespeare) the cross-dresser is expected to resume life as he or she was, having, presumably, recognised the touch of 'femininity' or 'masculinity' in her or his otherwise 'male' or 'female' self.

3. Oscar Wilde, *The Picture of Dorian Gray*. (London: Penguin Books, 1985; orig. pub. 1891), p. 103.

4. Théophile Gautier, *Mademoiselle de Maupin*, trans. Joanna Richardson (Harmondsworth: Penguin Books, 1981), pp. 246-7. All further references are to this edition.

5. Lacan, 'The Signification of the Phallus,' in *Ecrits*, p. 287.

6. Greenblatt, 'Fiction and Friction,' *Shakespearean Negotiations* (Berkeley: University of California Press, 1988), pp. 90-1.

7. Otto Weininger, *Sex and Character*. (London: William Heinemann, 1906), p. 67.

8. Angela Carter, *The Passion of New Eve* (London: Victor Gallancz, 1977; rpt. Virago Press, 1987), p. 132.

9. Alan Bray, *Homosexuality in Renaissance England*. (London: Gay Men's Press, 1982; 2nd edn Boston: Gay Men's Press, 1988), p. 65.

10. Shaun Considine, *Barbra Streisand: The Woman, the Myth, the Music*. (London: Century, 1985), p. 345. All further references are to this edition.

11. Freud's note comes in the context of a discussion of the Wolf-Man's fears of castration and his association of it with 'the ritual circumcision of Christ and of the Jews in general':

> Among the most tormenting, though at the same time the most grotesque, symptoms of [the Wolf-Man's] later illness was his relation to every tailor from whom he ordered a suit of clothes: his deference and timidity in the presence of this high functionary, his attempts to get into his good books by giving him extravagant tips, and his despair over the results of the work however it might in fact have turned out. [The German word for 'tailor' is 'Schneider', from the verb 'schneiden', ('to cut'), a compound of which, 'beschneiden', means 'to circumcise.' It will be remembered, too, that it was a tailor who pulled off the wolf's tail.]

> Sigmund Freud, *From the History of an Infantile Neurosis*, (1918), *The Standard Edition of the Complete Psychological Works of Sigmund Freud*, general editor James Strachey (London: The Hogarth Press and The Institute for Psycho-Analysis, 1964), 17: 86, 87n.

12. James Brady, 'In Step with: Amy Irving.' *Parade Magazine*, October 30, 1988.

13. Rebecca Bell-Metereau, *Hollywood Androgyny* (New York: Columbia University Press, 1985), p. 231. See also Jack Kroll, 'Barbra, the Yeshiva Boy,' *Newsweek*, 28 November 1983, p. 109; David Denby, 'Educating Barbra,' *New York*, 28 November 1983, p. 111; Pauline Kael, 'The Perfectionalist,' *New Yorker*, 28 November 1983, p. 176.

14. Johnny Carson, *Tonight Show* 16 February 1984. Considine, *op. cit.*, 356-8.

15. Sigmund Freud, *New Introductory Lectures on Psycho-analysis*, 29, 'Revision of the Theory of Dreams' trans. James Strachey. SE vol. 22: p. 24.

16. Sigmund Freud, 'Medusa's Head,' trans. James Strachey. SE vol. 18: p. 273:

> To decapitate = to castrate. The terror of Medusa is thus a terror of castration that is linked to the sight of something. Numerous analyses

have made us familiar with the occasion for this: it occurs when a boy, who has hitherto been unwilling to believe the threat of castration, catches sight of the female genitals, probably those of an adult, surrounded by hair, and essentially those of his mother. . ..

Notice how close the quoted passage is to Dr Robert Stoller's account of the transvestite as phallic woman, with his 'reassuring' erection:

> The whole complex psychological system that we call transvestism is a rather efficient method of handling very strong feminine identification without the patient having to succumb to the feeling that his sense of masculinity is being submerged by feminine wishes. The transvestite fights this battle against being destroyed by his feminine desires, first by alternating his masculinity with the feminine behavior, and thus reassuring himself that it isn't permanent; and second, by being always aware even at the height of the feminine behavior – when he is fully dressed in women's clothes – that he has the absolute insignia of maleness, a penis. And there is no more acute awareness of its presence than when he is reassuringly experiencing it with an erection.

Robert J. Stoller, *Sex and Gender: On the Development of Masculinity and Femininity* (London: The Hogarth Press and the Institute of Psycho-Analysis, 1968), 1:186.
17. *The New York Times*, 29 January 1984.
18. Isaac Bashevis Singer, 'Yentl the Yeshiva Boy,' trans. Marion Magid and Elizabeth Pollet, in *Short Friday and Other Stories* (New York: Fawcett Crest, 1978), p. 160. All further references are to this edition.

10 Buzz Goodbody: Directing for Change

Dympna Callaghan

Pol.   The actors are come hither, my lord.
Ham.   Buzz, buzz.

(*Hamlet*, II, ii, 388-9)

'Buzz' (Mary Ann) Goodbody was born in 1947 into a relatively privileged family; her father was a lawyer and her mother a former actress. She demonstrated an early interest in theatre, writing a play, *The Knave of Hearts*, when she was only six years old, and by the time she was twelve she had seen the entire Shakespeare repertory at the Old Vic. She attended the prestigious South coast girls' public school, Roedean, where she ran the film society and was an active member of the drama club, directing its productions and often taking male parts in them. At the avant garde Sussex University she became a feminist, joined the Communist Party, and wrote a Master's dissertation on Shaw. Goodbody also directed notable student drama productions, including an adaptation of Dostoyevsky's *Notes From the Underground* which won a National Union of Student's Drama Festival Award, and brought her to the attention of directors at the Royal Shakespeare Company. She was also a founding member of the feminist Women's Street Theatre in London before joining the RSC in 1967 as assistant to John Barton, where she became the company's youngest director. She assisted on many of the company's productions, most notably in 1972 on Trevor Nunn's production of Shakespeare's four Roman plays, never before staged together. She worked solo as a director on the RSC's educational Theatregoround project and began directing for the main stage in 1973. Two years later, in 1975, she committed suicide.

*   *   *   *   *

Feminist theatre scholarship has developed increasing theoretical sophistication, particularly in its attention to the ideological implications of

163

drama. It has endeavoured to shift the emphasis of its analyses from a principally content-based examination of plays by female playwrights to the techniques and apparatus of theatrical representation itself.[1] Nonethess, there remains an emphasis on physical text as focus of analysis and an attendant residue of intransigent empiricism. One cannot however, take refuge in such strategies of interpretation when one's object of inquiry is the absent sub/super-text of a director. I do not wish, then, simply to look at the theme and content of the plays Goodbody directed but instead to offer an analysis of what is at once a less tangible and yet more comprehensive aspect of theatre productions, that of 'theatre praxis', including institutional as well as directoral practices, and more specifically, the complex relation between marxist/feminist politics and Shakespeare production. It becomes doubly necessary to invoke Barthes' slippery distinction between the work and the text, the physical object and 'a moment of demonstration' which only exists in 'the movement of a discourse'[2] because here not only does the director's production vanish with the performance, but the work of a woman director is likely to be excluded from the patriarchal record we accept as history.

There are, indeed, intractable problems inherent in addressing the work of a woman director – the very term curiously implies that the cultural activity described is qualified by the sex of the person engaging in it. Such a project involves the negotiation of piles of newspaper cuttings, scribbled prompt books, the critics' assessments (not always the mo t reliable source of information), brief mentions in books, personal inu:views,[3] production reviews, and obituaries, traces of an unconventional history already well under the process of erasure.[4] Despite the practical and methodological difficulties, my goal here is to use Buzz Goodbody's work as an instance of the problematic of feminist representation in Shakespearean theatre while remaining vigilant about the political purpose and the theoretical implications of doing so. Importantly, an analysis of the work of Buzz Goodbody is an instance where the business of appropriation itself, the central concern of this anthology, reaches a double crisis: first, that of defining and identifying the director's appropriation of the Shakespeare text; and second, my own appropriation of the director for feminism.[5] Appropriation, as Toril Moi defines it, is more than proprietal reclamation; it is the creative transformation of some patriarchal space, object or ideology: 'The point is not the origins of an idea (no provenance is pure), but the use to which it is put and the effects it can produce.'[6]

I make no attempt, then, to argue that Goodbody exemplifies a form of theatre practice which is fundamentally different from that of male directors; to do so would, as Jane Moore and Catherine Belsey put it, fall in the trap of misreading culture as nature: 'The danger here is that the emphasis on difference tends either to have the effect of leaving things exactly as they are, with women eternally confined to a separate sphere, or to lead to a politics of separatism, which despairs of changing patriarchy and settles instead for an alternative space on the edges of it.[7] Thus, while the subject position of women in theatre is clearly quite different from that of men, it is not possible to argue that specific theatre techniques can be isolated as 'feminist' in Buzz Goodbody's productions. Inevitably, her productions participate in many dominant theatre practices, and it could be argued that even her radical approach to theatre and education rely, in part, on certain humanist assumptions: culture and Shakespeare as sources of enlightenment for the masses, for instance. Her appropriation of Shakespeare, then, is complex and problematic since, like participants in the Women's Theatre Movement, she certainly did not set out to propagate any precise embodiment of feminism, but rather worked to render plausible an alternative political and social reality through cultural intervention.[8]

Goodbody was in a cultural space, which, however contradictory, did not, as Marcuse put it, leave 'the traditional culture, the illusionist art behind, unmastered'.[9] This was a trap Buzz Goodbody fastidiously avoided. Her strategy was to intervene in the dominant production of culture.[10] She said, 'Living in Glastonbury and growing turnips doesn't appeal to me. You might feel purer by doing it, but it is escaping nonetheless'.[11] The Royal Shakespeare Theatre Company, after all, 'stands today as the most influential single theatre enterprise in the English speaking world'.[12] Yet given the institutionally marginal status of enterprises such as Theatregoround and The Other Place within the RSC, cultural interventions there were not always already recuperated by the institutional site which produced them. As Alan Sinfield points out:

> . . . there is no absolute rule – no intrinsically radical organization or formal principle. If you can get some money from business sponsorship, the Arts Council, a university or the BBC, go right ahead. For a while key institutions may be allowed to pursue a positive cultural policy . . . But don't come to depend on the authority and resources of business, the state, or the arts. Subcultural work is validated, rather, by the vigour of its engagement with its constituency. It may even be witness to the possibility of a workable socialism whose fuller achievement is not at the moment in sight.[13]

One reporter observed, 'She [Goodbody] doesn't want to burn down the RSC, merely reform it.' [14] Goodbody worked simultaneously within and against dominant paradigms of theatre practice, a tension her work embodies: she can perhaps best be described as an exponent of what I will call 'the techniques of marginality' within the parameters of mainstream theatre practices – practices to which her gender and political perspective placed her in ambivalent relation.

Importantly, Goodbody's commitment to a profoundly political dimension of dramatic space was most manifest in her adherence to the (potential) radicalism of Shakespeare: 'I love Shakespeare because he is saying all the time that politics is people, and people politics.' [15] Her productions were characterised by an effort to demonstrate the political relevance of Shakespeare to popular audiences. Goodbody, in contrast, was dedicated to bringing Shakespeare to one of the theatres most despised constituencies: schoolchildren. Her *King John*, devised for the RSC's Theatregoround, described as 'the most revolutionary activity that the RSC has promoted,' [16] had to deal with the play's notorious staging difficulties compounded by the constraints of a touring production, playing in unglamorous provincial outposts: community centres, town halls, and school gymnasiums. The model for staging and performance in these circumstances was a Renaissance one with simple costumes, stage sets and doubling of parts. [17] It was part of Goodbody's vision of theatre as democratised arena of cheap and free seats, of the anti-capitalist drama she sought to bring to the cultural margins of society.

Tension between marginality and engagement with the dominant cultural institutions was apparent in the material conditions of the *King John* production and in the treatment of the play's thematics. Though devised for schools, Goodbody's production was later incorporated into the Stratford repertoire. Her interpretation was, in part, a response to the patriotic treatment the play received when it was popular in the nineteenth century. Actors in her production marched onto a stage set with only slotted blinds, lit red or gold according to the scene, in stylised, mechanical fashion, toy soldiers marching to the beat of a drum. The play became a drama about evil produced within power relations rather than about individuals' propensity for evil. In such a context, the possibility arose for a comic interpretation, which Goodbody exploited to the full. Patrick Stewart's King John had a permanent grin, matched by the grimaces of Peter Needham's Philip of France, as they played out their duplicity with one another and the Church. The protracted death of Count Melun was accompanied with knock-about farce as crown and throne cushion were pitched about the stage. The Citizen of Angiers stood on the battlements surveying the war like a spectator at a tennis match, with his head following the war game from left to right. John's death too, was played for laughs. He played a childish game of peek-a-boo before slithering drunkenly from the throne to his death. For Goodbody the death of a sovereign who ruthlessly pursued national ambition became the death of a despicable clown. This comic cynicism put a different emphasis on the few emotional conflicts of the play usually considered necessary for its success. Thus, Hubert's inability to put out young Arthur's eyes, and Constance's grief for her dead son are placed in a context which renders them moving and emotional rather than simply sentimental.

The Bastard, played by Norman Rodway, was rendered cool and

intelligent as the marginalised sibling who when crisis threatens must decide whether to engage with the affairs of the realm, or shun them entirely.[18] Goodbody observed: 'I see the play as a blistering attack on politicians' one in which only John's bastard brother dare speak the truth.

> If one goes through the play one finds that the single most common word is 'right' – I am Right. I Am Defending Right, I am Fighting for Right. The next most important word is blood. [*sic*] The implications are apparent.[19]

The poignancy of the attack was not lost on her audiences at a time when national attention was focused on a general election and world attention on conflict in South East Asia. One critic wrote enthusiastically: 'This is Shakespeare for the masses. This is the sort of adaptation that retains interest and perhaps develops interest in new fields.' [20]

Despite its share of accolades (in Southampton it was heralded at its preview for the Stratford season as 'one of the most original, refreshing and highly entertaining adaptations of Shakespeare put on stage in recent years,'[21]) Goodbody's insistence that because Shakespeare's plays had political relevance they should be presented to the widest possible audience brought some predictable criticism about the play's comic irreverence ('You can't fool *King John* all the time'[22]).

Buzz Goodbody's first production for the RSC main stage, *As You Like It*, retained a commitment to the popular, eschewing lyricism and 'coherence' in order to address comic discord and disarray, particularly that represented by Rosalind, portrayed as a woman who must situate herself in an unfamiliar world. Goodbody constructed the play not as a comprehensive totality but almost as if it were an opera, treating the songs, set scenes (such as the wrestling match between Orlando and Charles) and speeches like 'All the world's a stage' as arias, each one worthy of a round of applause.[23] This was the effect of Goodbody's view that *As You Like It* is a play not best approached via a strong, controlling theme. Rather, Goodbody aimed to place the characters in a convincing social context: 'I've tried to set up *worlds* for them to live in.'[24]

Buzz Goodbody's conception of the world of Arden was far from orthodox but conveyed a sense of the conventions of pastoral tradition: 'Hardly anyone seems to do any work: the shepherds and shepherdesses – Phoebe, Sylvius and so on – are not really country people. I see them as art college students, drop-outs who live in the country and have mummies and daddies in town with large incomes.'[25]

The programme for this modern dress production, explains that its aim is to explore the issue of a woman's place in society; it was dubbed a 'Women's Lib As You Like It.'[26] Poster advertisements juxtaposed a quotation from Luther about women's posteriors being divinely ordained as broad, sedentary, and better for motherhood with Eileen Atkin's slim, androgynous rear in denim hipsters. Anne Barton's programme notes argue that Shakespeare is the anti-patriarchal bard whose play shows the understanding carefully and slowly negotiated between a man and a woman in the process of courtship. Goodbody explored the impression that of all Shakespeare's heroines, Rosalind bears the closest parallel to the modern idea of a liberated woman in what was a challenging response to the all-male, and allegedly completely historicised production, at the National Theatre in the previous season. Goodbody's production, unlike the one at the National, sought to underscore rather than erase the historicity of its own enterprise.

At the beginning of the play raffish Duke Frederick (played by Clement McCallin) in velvet-lapelled black, presides over a soirée in evening dress. He sports a black monocle (to the good Duke's clear one) and a filthy cigarette. His guests watch indoor wrestling from the comfort of their gilt chairs. Brian Glover played Charles, a beefy, swaggering show-off oblivious of the grand company.[27] When the scene changed the young people tripped bare-foot through Christopher Morley's surreal forest of metallic stalactites suspended from 2,500 pulleys (variously described as resembling pipe organs, rope and spaghetti), guitars in hand. Forest explorations in such a striking set amid which the actors performed on a circular mat, had the effect of conveying an anguished sense of disorientation and displacement in the process of negotiating love relationships on a terrain where all prior assumptions about identity are reversed. The theatricality of 'nature' in semi-satirical pastoral was emphasised with discordant touches of realism; a log was brought in by very apparent stage hands for the first love match between Rosalind and David Suchet's stocky yet tender Orlando.

The rustic romances were played with considerable physical and slapstick humour. Janet Chappell played Phebe, and Annette Badland, described as physically analogous to a 'cute, heavy lorry' by one rather acerbic critic, played a 'gargantuan,'[28] but boisterously funny Audrey, 'whether in tight dungarees or mini-skirted summer frock'.[29] Derek Smith's balding Touchstone in modern motley – checked pants with braces and patent leather shoes – was a music-hall clown with a Cockney nasal whine. He goes to his wedding to the beat of the Funeral March wearing a top hat with a 'Just Married' placard around his neck, while Audrey sports bridal posy and dungarees. The priest officiating at the nuptials carries wedding cakes, and a swinging censer in a white pram. The festive denouement in which Hymen appears was staged to a rock'n'roll arrangement by Guy Woolfenden amid a shower of giant confetti, liberally dispensed upon the heads of cast and audience alike.

Richard Pasco's Jacques, a counterpoint to the lovers, was played as a

Scottish, Chekhovian figure, becloaked, bespectacled, with thinning hair and bookish stoop. According to Benedict Nightingale of *The New Statesman*[30] he blinked, twitched, hiccupped, screwed round his shoulders, and half loped across the stage, putting a sneering emphasis on his words and ending his speeches with a tiny cracked laugh, the gesture betokening some secret trauma at the root of his misanthropy: 'This is a man with one skin too few, for whom the death of a wild animal is painful, and the embrace of lovers a living torture.'[31] The Seven Ages of Man speech became not the usual philosophical treatise but 'the repugnant vision of a blinkered cynic: and when Jacques finally exits to the Duke's abandoned cave it is as if a cloud were passing over the sunlit world of Arden.'[32] His derisory panache was unanimously acclaimed by the critics.

Predictably, the production was attacked in some quarters for the disrespect it showed for the Bard: 'Shakespeare made into with-it fun'[33] owing 'as much to Biba [the fashionable sixties store] as the Bard',[34] with the air of 'a rustic pop festival'.[35] Critics were particularly concerned about the implications of modern dress for Rosalind's gender identity. Goodbody played up Rosalind's femininity in blue jeans unisex disguise which thwarted those who desired a traditional interpretation, i.e. a clearly female actor in Elizabethan male garb. Milton Shulman of the *Evening Standard* wrote: 'It is true that with her wearing blue jeans as her only means of disguise, one has to assume that Orlando is either extremely short-sighted or very naive about the facts of life to mistake the very feminine Miss Atkins as being anything remotely resembling a boy.'[36] For Michael Billington of *The Guardian*, Goodbody's approach destroyed any sexual ambiguity: 'Any hint of sexual equivocation is knocked on the head by Eileen Atkin's minimal attempt to disguise her femininity as Rosalind. Indeed, with her headband, fringed blouse and crotch hugging jeans, she seemed even more seductive as Ganymede than before.'[37] Jack Tinker of the *Daily Mail* similarly pointed out that 'Unisex is the misnomer of the decade. Nothing serves to point up the differences in the wearers' sex more eloquently.'[38] For one reviewer however, the gender issues of the play were obliterated by the association of hallowed Shakespeare with what he regarded as the epitome of contemporary degeneracy – jeans: 'By all means wear jeans for painting sets, manning switchboards or sweeping the stage, but – please – let our Rosalinds and Violas be togged out in natty suede, or ever-so-slightly tatty tweed and not looking as if they were en route for the latest student "demo". Let us, indeed, borrow current student cant and demand "Jeans . . . Out".'[39]

Similarly, the *Birmingham Post* critic claimed that Goodbody's approach would be inappropriate for a newcomer to Shakespeare. Paradoxically, in bemoaning the lack of respect for Shakespeare, another critic, this time for *The Spectator*, revealed that he regarded the play as containing one of

Shakespeare's own condescensions to vulgar tastes: 'Without putting it as high as a shrine, it [Stratford] is a place where more than ordinary regard for the Shakespeare canon might be justifiably expected . . . Perhaps Shakespeare's most repellent comic invention, Touchstone is a droll of a singularly childish and exasperating design who, in the costume of some remote period, might be tolerantly indulged as an example of low comedy style mercifully no longer with us.'[40] Audiences, however, as the critics reluctantly admitted, responded with great enthusiasm: 'All in all, this is pop Shakespeare and as such will be most enjoyed by the non-Shakespeareans in the audience to whom the highlights will be the music – attractive song and dance numbers by Guy Woolfenden and Jon Boome.'[41] To the critics 'pop' meant gimmicky – only a few recognised it as a welcome departure from 'hey nonny-nonsense' of traditional productions[42] – whereas to Goodbody, 'pop' meant popular. That non-Shakespeareans enjoyed the play was no doubt exactly what Goodbody had intended, and given that, perhaps the disparity between audience and critics' responses was to be expected.

In 1974, Goodbody was appointed Artistic Director of the RSC's Other Place. At this location, literally marginal to the main theatre building, Goodbody wove the techniques of marginality into the fabric of mainstream British theatre: 'Across the road from the prestigious Royal Shakespeare Company theatre at Stratford-upon-Avon is a small tin hut. On one side of the road the bard plays to US coach parties and wealthy southerners – on the other side to young people at school in the Midlands.' Here Buzz Goodbody directed the internationally successful *Lear*, a much abridged version of Shakespeare's play at a fraction of a regular RSC budget (£150 as opposed to the usual £10,000, with tickets at 30p rather than £4 or £5).[43] The Other Place provided the perfect parallel to her Theatregoround work; and the decision to opt for 'a filleted version' of Shakespeare's tragedy,[44] was taken in order to accommodate school audiences who, relying on public transport home from the performance, would miss the last bus if they attended a full-length production. Goodbody argued: 'The theatre has got to become much more of an education centre than it is at the moment. There should be talk-ins and teach-ins with the actors and producers for anyone who wants to come.'[45] The cast consisted of a mere nine actors, since France, Cornwall, Albany, Oswald and his subplot were all edited out. The production was planned for a small space where the audience would be thoroughly involved in the action: two acting areas – the main stage enclosed by seats on three sides with a blank wall on the fourth, and a narrow balcony on top of the central tier of seats. Soliloquies had their theatricality emphasised by being aimed directly at the audience and being lit by spotlights.

Goodbody's *Lear* showed 'how much the sisters had to put up with before turning against their father' in what was called 'the most dis-passionate re-examination of the play since Peter Brook's 1962 version.'[46] The central plot lost its fairy-tale nuances: Goneril and Regan were 'no longer the ugly sisters to Cordelia's Cinderella', rather they were strong women with reason to be angry at their peremptory father who is always playing the feudal patriarch[47]: 'Goneril comes into the room while he [Lear] is staying with her, to find the place in a mess; books, papers and hunting gear strewn all over the floor. While she is tidying up after him, her impatience cracks into anger.'[48]

In Goodbody's production it was Goneril (played by Sheila Allen) who gouged out Gloucester's eyes with a hairpin while iron-masked attendants held him down. All light was extinguished at his blinding which gave the effect of the audience experiencing a darkness to match Gloucester's.[49] In contrast, the Fool's prophecy speech, which predicts no respite for stricken Albion until 'usurers tell their gold in the field', was recited in rasping tones by David Suchet with the lights up 'hard and bright'.[50]

Goodbody's production emphasised what might be termed the plays's proto-Marxist qualities,[51] particularly by means of a prologue spoken by Tony Church's Lear and Mike Gwilyn's Edgar, which combined poverty statistics and newspaper accounts of the ignominious deaths of elderly people in Britain, police brutality and seventeenth-century legal remedies for dealing with the itinerant poor:

> . . . in 1972 a sixty-eight year old woman in Liverpool was found dead – she had choked to death while trying to eat a piece of cardboard. . . . Be it enacted that if any man or woman being whole in body and able to labour having no land, nor using any lawful craft be vagrant and can give no reckoning how he doth lawfully get his living, then it shall be lawful to all the king's officers and subjects to arrest the said vagabond and bring them to any of the Justices of the Peace. That vagrant then be taken to the next market town or other place where the said Justice shall think most convenient and there shall be tied to the end of a cart naked and be beaten with whips throughout the same market town till his body be bloody. (Promptbook)

The prologue emphasised the cultural specificity of the Renaissance alongside references to current social issues, but did so in order to critique present injustices rather than to shelter in the bourgeois comfort of the universal Shakespeare. Thus, Goodbody did not work simply to establish 'contemporary relevance', a form of appropriation which has long shored up the idea of universal pertinence of literature, but rather worked for cultural intervention which manifests an explicitly political challenge. As Alan Sinfield has put it 'literature is of contemporary relevance, not because it corroborates our own attitudes but because it affords a perspective from which they may be perceived afresh.'[52] In this, Goodbody's *Lear* was quite different from conservative versions of contemporaneity produced by Peter Brook, Peter Hall and Michael Bogdanov, which read the Shakespeare simply as an allegory for modern times in a fashion that was more aesthetic than political.[53] Goodbody's innovative strategy was, however, met with considerable scorn: 'Dear God I thought, is Shakespeare a sort of theatrical Shelter?'[54] The derisive reference to the British organisation for the homeless implied that Shakespeare was sullied by contact with current social issues and that Shakespeare properly belonged to a sphere above and beyond the mundane troubles of twentieth-century poverty. In fact, Goodbody's prologue insisted upon politically committed interpretation of Shakespeare as textually verifiable and historically legitimate.

In *Lear*, Goodbody offered a Bondian rather than a Bradleyan approach to tragedy. She emphasised the material over the metaphysical by means of an uncluttered production where wealth and poverty are figured as the startling difference between being clothed and going naked so that the play became something tangible with cause and effects. The grandeur and sweep of language normally associated with 'unstageable' *Lear* was distilled and presented as if in close-up. Music, and thunderclaps alike came from the one-man orchestra of Robin Weatherall. Jon Peter of the *Sunday Times* noted that the play came over as 'an intimate family tragedy (which it partly is); it may be short on cosmic grandeur but it gives harrowing force to moments of private anguish'.[55] Goodbody was praised for distilling the essential themes of the play: 'Shakespeare's thought is in a sense clearer, because instantly the audience realises it is not watching the fall of an emperor (in the way of Greek Tragedy) but men facing old age, betrayal.' Lear then becomes a 'role assembled by an accretion of poignancies rather than a few bold tragic strokes'.[56]

Negative criticism of the play invariably focused on lack of grandeur: 'You cannot boil down Shakespeare. You can only cut him. And the cuts put the tragedy out of its grand context . . . There is no constant focus from which the tragedy's power might spring, since actors keep springing up all around us.'[57] Another critic complained, it 'is a clinical, downbeat affair in which the peripheral observations of the abused Edgar and the percipient Fool are more emphasised than the central emotional morass of Lear's experience'.[58] Yet Goodbody had anticipated the criticism she received: 'Every area of the production was dictated by the reason for doing it. The most obvious way in which I was guided was by the purely practical' (Programme Notes). Buzz Goodbody had indeed intended to produce what Clive Barnes rather derisively referred to as a 'utilitarian Lear'.[59] She wrote:

The staging of the production [by Ann Steiner] was also determined by the nature of the audiences we expected. Most school parties sit in the back of large theatres. However good the acting or the production may be, the experience can often be remote simply because of distance. Without expecting the audience to participate in the play I wanted them to be inside it. We therefore played in a three-sided auditorium with various acting areas. Finally, after every performance, we also spent half-an-hour with the audience who were able to stay, discussing the play. Splitting up a company round the auditorium, we found, worked best and our aim was to allow them to talk rather than to say it ourselves. (Programme)

The production of *Lear* was a bold intervention given the fact that it was a response to a direct need – the fact that it was the 'A level' set text for that year, and had not been performed by the RSC since 1968. Goodbody's programme note acknowledged the fact:

Doing Shakespeare at school is hard. For many people it puts them off going to see the plays for life. What sense can be made of the Hovel scene in *King Lear* by reading it round the classroom? At 15 I saw Peter Brook's production at the Aldwych. I emerged dazed – realizing THAT was what it had been about all the time, simple but – revelatory. Anyone who has experienced the immense emotional impact of Shakespeare when young knows that the plays can work for an audience who maybe won't follow the complexity of certain thematic ideas or even understand the language. To do a production of *King Lear*, therefore, to play an entirely schools audience for three months was for all of us concerned a meeting point – for actors, most of whom had spent several years working on Shakespeare in a classical company – for an audience, for whom it was all new. (Programme)

This sensitivity to the fact that 'Culture' is made inaccessible to certain classes of people who are then blamed for their lack of interest in it was combined with a sense that that very Culture could be used against those who appropriated it in order to maintain their own social superiority. Thus Goodbody succeeded in putting into theatre practice a notion which has only recently been argued in Shakespeare criticism, namely that while the uses of Shakespeare have been conservative, the texts themselves, especially perhaps the species of 'great man' tragedy of which *King Lear* is a prime example, are intrinsically quite radical and only rendered reactionary by dint of energetic ideological manoeuvring and devious fast footwork on the part of the dominant class.[60]

Hamlet, the crowning achievement of Buzz Goodbody's life (she died after critics' night and before the first public performance), seems to exemplify some of the political principles of her theatre practice and enables a fuller understanding of her earlier work. Modern dress was integral to the minimalist approach to the play; it avoided the distraction of Renaissance attire which could detract from the intense, concentrated focus on character interaction that this directorial conception achieved in an auditorium seating fewer than two hundred people. What becomes apparent here is the consistency of Goodbody's political vision precisely in those aspects of production which appear to differ most from her previous endeavours. Thus, modern dress occurs in a context in which there is no particular contemporary detail to impose contemporary relevance. There was no attempt, in this virtually uncut production of the play, to domesticate the radical otherness of the Renaissance text, even while subduing the remoteness of aspects of the play usually interpreted as grand and metaphysical. However, throughout the play, its field of vision was not reduced; it did not shrink by becoming more concentrated.

The spartan stage was not an entirely new development given the black and white of Trevor Nunn's 1970 production of the play and of Terry Hands' concurrent work in the main Stratford theatre. But in Goodbody's *Hamlet* minimal means were used to achieve complex effects by underscoring the power of social relationships both personal and political, and by extending them to involve the audience in the sense of danger, confrontation, surveillance, and impossibility of escape. The stage was set with sliding, grooved white paper panels and a Kabuki bridge led to the rear exit of the auditorium, which was swathed in white cloth.

Physical proximity of actors and audience was crucial in order to convey Hamlet as something other than the transcendent tragic hero, but it also conveyed unexpected nuances of the play's other relationships. For example, Polonius dispenses warmly affectionate advice while Ophelia sits on her brother's knee. Their sibling affection borders, in minute and subtle gestures, on incestuous fascination. Laertes played by Stuart Wilson is frenetic: his 'Show of grief' again reveals the aberrant nature of his fraternal attachment to his sister. This underlying discordance culminates as he participates reluctantly, almost suicidally, in the rigged duel. The audience was constantly encircled by the action and surprised by its incidence in unexpected places:

> And close to, we can *feel*, as well as see how this Hamlet enwraps his friends
> . . . the experience is a total vindication of Miss Goodbody's belief that
> Shakespeare can and should be more exciting if the actors confront each
> other and their audience unhampered by a proscenium.[61]

Yet, Goodbody conveyed distance as keenly as proximity. When Hamlet sees Claudius praying and says, 'Now might I do it, pat' he immediately rushes to the furthest reaches of the main acting arena. Similarly, Hamlet's ghost, direct from the depths of the supernatural, appears and vanishes near the exit. Griffith Jones as the ghost walked imperiously, disturbingly among the spectators to metatheatrical effect. An actor in the auditorium has the effect of a preternatural spectre: he is not supposed to be there, and the audience cease to be passive spectators in their active desire to go unnoticed by him; but at the same time they are unable to avoid being transfixed by his spectacular presence.

Goodbody's microscopic approach to *Hamlet* also led to important changes in tone: for instance the First Player, Bob Peck, delivered the Hecuba tirade quietly while sitting in whispering proximity of Hamlet's ear. Michael Coveney commented:

> Bob Peck plays the First Player (well and truly 'valanced' with rough dignity), radiating an approach to his trade that is completely betrayed by the rubbish he has to perform. Hence the 'rogue and peasant slave' speech is given an original drive as Hamlet sees this for himself. Polonius's comments on the 'Hecuba' speech are the words of a cultural philistine.[62]

Goodbody's Hamlet, played by Ben Kingsley, was an interesting mix of the theatre's Princes. In concert with the contemporary reaction against wavering, feminine, romantic Hamlet in the tradition of Barrymore and Olivier, he was a swarthy, mature man of sturdy physique, balding, and semitic. He has enough life experience to predict the disastrously irrevocable course of events, and it is this rather than the conscience-driven dithering ambivalence of youth which produces his considerable nervous intensity.

In contrast to Kingsley's Hamlet, Yvonne Nicholson's depiction of Ophelia's disarranged femininity was epitomised by having her 'pert and sexy' qualities[63] transformed by her degeneration into madness. Her face was disfigured by the lipstick smeared all over her chin, giving a sense that she has literally misapplied the cultural accoutrements of femininity. The effects of her suicide were thus conveyed through details as much as through the hurtling narrative impetus of revenge tragedy towards denouement. For example, the bureaucratic Claudius carried a posy at Ophelia's funeral, not unlike the ones she distributed earlier in the play.

The tragic nature of events in the play emanated from an almost complete absence of political choice. The inability to make meaningful interventions rendered Hamlet's paralysis as a meditation on the terrifying spectacle of contemporary complacency. There was an emphasis on the festering power relations in the state of Denmark. Thus, Claudius was played as 'the pin-striped, administrative mogul of the modern commercial state' rather than as 'some historic usurper' while Polonius plays 'the senior civil servant who has compromised natural affection for a place in the corridors of power'. In contrast to both, 'the bejeaned actors are the creative outcasts of this smug establishment world.'[64]

The play received critical acclaim, and many commentators attributed the success and originality of the production to the fact that it was irredeemably bleak. Gordon Parsons writing for the *Morning Star* commented: 'There are, of course, many "Hamlets". Buzz Goodbody presents a great tragic statement of despair. Not the histrionic despair of the bourgeois theatre, but the despair that all sensitive people must at times feel when faced by the grotesque comedy of our contemporary society.'[65] Hamlet was borne aloft from the stage, and yet this did not produce any sense that he had transcended the forces at work in Denmark. The political order of the realm, which Hamlet had subjected to radical interrogation throughout the play, nonetheless faithfully and alarmingly reproduced itself, in what was clearly an unmitigated cycle of corruption. Claudius's sly smile of sardonic inscrutability, which in his death, the final encounter with Hamlet, became a staggering leer was chillingly reproduced in the derisory smile worn by Fortinbras, the representative of mindless militarism. Irving Wardle of *The Times* wrote that, 'However delicate the personal nuances, the overall view of the play is the bleakest I can recall; not only is society poisoned but neither Hamlet nor anyone else has any chance of setting it right.'[66]

I began my account of Buzz Goodbody's productions with a pun on Goodbody's nickname as a way of negotiating the disparate traces of her achievement:

> *Pol.*   The actors are come hither, my lord
> *Ham.*   Buzz, buzz.
>
> (*Hamlet*, II, ii, 388–9)

The quotation is from the scene where Polonius excitedly heralds the arrival of the players and receives Hamlet's contemptuous rebuke, 'Buzz, buzz'. Yet by the end of the scene, Hamlet decides that the players may hold the key to political and personal change that he most urgently seeks to effect: to 'catch the conscience of the King'. By Act III, Hamlet has become a director, one who must quit the stage before the audience notices the mechanics of theatricality which shape the disparate performances of the actors into a coherent production. As a politically orientated director, Hamlet, must focus on the effect of theatre on his audience; it is his only hope for intervention in a world so out of joint.

Hamlet played on, though Goodbody, only twenty-eight years old, had decided to meet the Prince's question, 'To be or not to be?' with Ophelia's tragic response. Suicide compels us to read another's death, because, as Margaret Higonnet has written, it is 'a symbolic gesture . . . doubly so for women who inscribe on their own bodies cultural reflections and projections, affirmation and negation.'[67] Five years after Buzz Goodbody's death, Colin Chambers wrote:

> The fight to transform the work of one of the world's leading theatre companies and bridge the 'culture gap' took its toll, in spite of her success. It was, and still is, a male world, used to women behind typewriters, in the wardrobe and wigroom, but not yet directing on the rehearsal floor.[68]

Her career had been a remarkable anomaly, often met with predictable reactions in the press: 'Buzz Goodbody: Beauty with Brains' and 'Miss Goodbody has a good head too,'[69] 'a leggy brunette in boots and a mini skirt that is fashionably brief by London standards.'[70] She once said:

> I suppose there are only five women directors in Britain, and there isn't one of my age. Actors simply aren't used to women directors. But all this will change as women come into the theatre from the universities. Meanwhile one just has to learn to be tactful. Directing is as much handling people as having significant ideas about the theatre. You have to be an all-round type – part psychiatrist, part favourite friend, part stool pigeon.[71]

While Buzz Goodbody does not offer us a template for counter-hegemonic Shakespeare, she does offer a theatre practice which is always most forcefully directed towards social change. What is perhaps most striking about her work is the deployment of the techniques of the margin at the centre of culture, and it is this model of engagement, radical rather than reformist, which is probably more feminist than any single instance of her treatment of gender as a theme in Shakespeare's plays. Theatre practices, from minimalism and contemporary dress to a mature Hamlet and a fresh interpretation of *King Lear*, could perhaps be located in the work of her contemporaries, but whereas there they were used as formal devices to enhance aesthetic effect, in Goodbody's theatre praxis they became instruments of a cultural politics which altered the representation of plays' power relations (including and especially those of gender) and were aimed at instigating oppositional consciousness and entertaining (rather than simply edifying) the audience. As Bea Campbell wrote in her obituary for Buzz Goodbody:

> Buzz Goodbody was . . . an extraordinary woman – extraordinary for her persistent, stringent and militant application of her intelligence to art and politics, the politics of social relationships and the politics of personal relationships of intimacy.[72]

Goodbody's feminism/marxism, then, is not simply something that can be enumerated in a list of themes or devices because her politics was not superficial; it imbued her theatre practice to the very core. Appropriating Goodbody to the ranks of feminist Shakespeareans, then, involves acknowledging that feminism is not limited to strictly defined 'gender issues' but that it has implications for the social order and its cultural apparatuses in their totality.

Notes

1. Sue Ellen Case's pioneering study *Feminism and Theatre* (New York: Methuen, 1988), while very theoretically sophisticated, confines itself to an analysis of

plays. This is also true of Lynda Hart's important anthology, *Making a Spectacle: Feminist Essays on Contemporary Women's Theatre* (Ann Arbor: University of Michigan Press, 1989), despite its claim that 'The Shift in feminist perspective from discovering and creating positive images of women in the content of the drama to analyzing and disrupting the ideological codes embedded in the inherited structures of dramatic representation is documented in the articles contained in this collection' (p. 4). Only Janelle Reinelt's chapter on Michelene Wandor makes any significant endeavour to discuss anything other than the content of the plays and its ideological significance. In film criticism, there is an analogous problem, yet there is always a text in which to anchor discussion of the way in which the director is author of the film's production as opposed to the film's script. See Theresa de Lauretis, *Technologies of Gender: Essays on Theory, Film, and Fiction* (Bloomington: Indiana University Press, 1987).

For the problems inherent in analysing specifically women's relation to theatre see Jill Dolan, *The Feminist Spectator as Critic* (Ann Arbor: UMI Research Press, 1988), pp. 83–117; Susanne Greenhalgh, 'Occupying the Empty Space: Feminism and Drama' in *Teaching Women: Feminism and English Studies*, ed. Ann Thompson and Helen Wilcox (Manchester: Manchester University Press, 1989), pp. 170–9; Susan Bassnett-McGuire, 'Towards a Theory of Women's Theatre' in *Semiotics of Drama and Theatre: New Perspectives on the Theory of Drama and Theatre* eds Herta Schmid and Aloysius Van Kersteren (Amsterdam: 1984), pp. 461–6.

2. Janet Bergstrom, 'Enunciation and Sexual Difference' in *Feminism and Film Theory*, ed. Constance Penley, (New York: Routledge, 1988), p. 160.
3. I am grateful to Cicely Berry, voice coach at the RSC, for addressing some of my queries about Goodbody. Thanks are also due to the staff of Royal Shakespeare Theatre Library in Stratford-upon-Avon and the New York Public Library, who provided assistance in locating and photocopying large amounts of newsprint materials. See Dale Spender, *For the Record: The Making and Meaning of Feminist Knowledge* (London: Women's Press, 1985), for a concise account of the problem of 'lost' knowledge, 'non-data' and 'the omissions' of the patriarchal record which plague feminist histories.
4. Numerous newsprint sources inform this essay; often, descriptions of productions are compiled from several of them. To avoid confusing citations, I have noted the source only when it has a single origin. Authors of newspaper articles are cited whenever their names are available.
5. The essays in *Women's Re-Visions of Shakespeare* ed. Marianne Novy, (Chicago: Univ. of Illinois Press, 1990) show that there is a well-established tradition of women who find in Shakespeare a playwright unusually 'sensitive' to their interests. Carol Neely comments that women have challenged the dominant version of Shakespeare in our culture, the Shakespeare who 'everywhere authorizes the hegemonic power of a universalized male liberal human subject. . . . Shakespeare can be appropriated on behalf of other subjects and other sorts of power' (p. 250).
6. Toril Moi, 'Feminist, Female, Feminine' in *The Feminist Reader: Essays in Gender and the Politics of Literary Criticism*, ed. Catherine Belsey and Jane Moore (New York: Basil Blackwell, 1989), p. 118.
7. C. Belsey and J. Moore, *op. cit.*, p. 10.
8. See Alan Sinfield, *Literature, Politics, and Culture in Postwar Britain* (Berkeley: University of California Press, 1989), p. 303.

9. *ibid*, p. 304.
10. Goodbody, like other exponents of radical Shakespeare at the RSC was caught in the contradiction of engaging in such an enterprise under royal aegis, a contradiction which, Alan Sinfield has shown, tends to promulgate the notion of Shakespeare as a vital, and vitally centralising force in British culture. See Sinfield, 'Royal Shakespeare: Theatre and the Making of Ideology' in *Political Shakespeare: New Essays in Cultural Materialism*, eds J. Dollimore and A. Sinfield, (Manchester: Manchester University Press, 1985), p. 174, and Don E. Wayne, 'Power, Politics, and the Shakespearean Text' in *Shakespeare Reproduced*, ed. Jean E. Howard and Marion F. O'Connor (New York: Methuen, 1987), p. 51.
11. *Daily Telegraph*, 13 July 1973.
12. Colby H. Kullman and William C. Young, *Theatre Companies of the World* (New York: Greenwood Press, 1986), p. 698.
13. A. Sinfield, *Literature, Politics, and Culture, op. cit.*, p. 304.
14. *Daily Telegraph*, 13 July 1973.
15. *ibid*.
16. Nicholas de Jongh, *The Guardian*, 1 August 1970.
17. *ibid*.
18. *Sunday Times*, 25 January 1970.
19. *ibid*.
20. *Southern Evening Echo*, 3 June 1970.
21. *ibid*.
22. Wendy Monk, *Southern Evening Echo*, 13 June 1970.
23. David Nathan, *Jewish Chronicle*, 15 June 1973.
24. *Birmingham Post*, 9 June 1973.
25. *ibid*.
26. Gordon Parsons, *Morning Star*, 14 June 1973. The production was beset with difficulties. Eileen Atkins, who played Rosalind severely strained a ligament in the preview performance and had to be replaced by an understudy; while Bernard Lloyd who was slated to play Orlando, slipped a disc, on account of which he was forced to leave the cast. One critic reported feeling that the production might be a case of 'as you limp it' with both Rosalind and Audrey limping due to rehearsal accidents.
27. *Daily Mail*, 13 June 1973.
28. Irving Wardle, *The Times*, 13 June 1973.
29. *Malvern Gazette*, 14 June 1973.
30. *The New Statesman*, 22 June 1973.
31. *Daily Telegraph*, 13 June 1973.
32. *The Guardian*, 13 June 1973.
33. *Daily Telegraph*, 13 June 1973.
34. Michael Billington, *The Guardian*, 13 June 1973.
35. Martin Shulman, *Evening Standard*, 13 June 1973.
36. *ibid*.
37. Michael Billington, *The Guardian*, 13 June 1973.
38. Jack Tinker, *Daily Mail*, 13 June 1973.
39. *Oxford Times*, 29 June 1973.
40. *The Spectator*, 23 June 1973.
41. *Nottingham Guardian Journal*, 14 June 1973.
42. *Daily Mail*, 13 June 1973.
43. Colin Chambers, *Morning Star*, 29 October 1974.

44. *New York Times*, 26 February 1975.
45. *Daily Telegraph*, 13 June 1974.
46. *The Times*, 15 April 1975.
47. Colin Chambers, *Morning Star*, 25 October 1974.
48. John Elsom, *The Listener*, 31 October 1974.
49. Clive Barnes, *New York Times*, 26 February 1975.
50. Michael Coveney, *Financial Times*, 24 August 1974.
51. See Jonathan Dollimore, *Radical Tragedy: Religion, Ideology and Power in the Drama of Shakespeare and His Contemporaries* (Brighton: Harvester Press, 1984), pp. 189–203.
52. A. Sinfield, *Literature, Power, and Culture, op. cit.*, p. 1. For the conservative reading of 'contemporary Shakespeare' see *Is Shakespeare Still Our Contemporary?*, ed. John Elsom (New York: Routledge, 1989).
53. J. Elsom, *op. cit.*, p. 3.
54. John Peter, *Sunday Times*, 21 October 1974.
55. *ibid.*
56. Clive Barnes, *New York Times*, 26 February 1975.
57. Eric Shorter, *Daily Telegraph*, 24 October 1974.
58. Michael Coveney, *Financial Times*, 24 August 1974.
59. *New York Times*, 26 February 1975.
60. See for example Kiernan Ryan, *Shakespeare* (Atlantic Highlands: Humanities Press, 1989); J. Dollimore, *Radical Tragedy, op. cit.*, Dympna Callaghan, *Women and Gender in Renaissance Tragedy* (Atlantic Highlands: Humanities Press, 1989) chapter 4.
61. Michael Coveney, *Financial Times*, 19 May 1975.
62. *ibid.*
63. *ibid.*
64. Gordon Parsons, *Morning Star*, 27 May 1975.
65. *ibid.*
66. Irving Wardle, *The Times*, 17 May 1975.
67. Margaret Higonnet, 'Speaking Silences: Women's Suicide' in *The Female Body in Western Culture*, ed. Susan Rubin Suleiman (Cambridge: Harvard University Press, 1986), p. 68.
68. *The Guardian*, 12 April 1980.
69. Ian Woodward, *the Sun*, 9 June 1970.
70. *Sunday Times*, 25 January 1970.
71. Goodbody was also aware of the power hierarchy of theatre: 'Actresses are in a paradoxical position because they are more independent than most women, but they are used to, if not sleeping with the director, at least flirting with him because he is a man and they are used to having him boss them around. I have to convince them that I have a different kind of strength' (*Daily Telegraph*, 13 June 1974).
    'There has been a precedent of young directors and young actors at RSC – after all the boss, Trevor Nunn, is only 30. In directing I'd try to engineer a situation where the actor is working well, and then he's on your side. Shouting and yelling is so old-fashioned – a last resort – and giving orders isn't what you're there for.
    With lots of actors it's no disadvantage to be a bird because one of the most important qualities you need is an ability to contact people, and you can get very good contact with a male actor which can be great fun, just on work terms, of course. And I think it helps with women too, especially since

women are in a very isolated position in the Shakespeare company, there are so few of them. But me being a bird, if they don't feel well, they can just ring up and say they've got a period or whatever. And I think looking like I do gives an illusion of being in touch, knowing what's going on' (*Sunday Times*, 22 March 1970).

72. Bea Campbell, *Morning Star*, 21 April 1975.

11 Shakespearean Features

Graham Holderness and Bryan Loughrey

O sweet Mr Shakespeare, Ile have his picture in my study[1]

I

Like many artists, W. B. Yeats conceived of the relation between life and art in terms of an aesthetic of Platonic idealism. The poet, he declared, is never the bundle of accidents and incoherences that sits down to breakfast; he has been reborn as an idea, something intended, complete.[2] This disembodied authorial presence inhabiting the text rather than the world is of course a commonplace of literary criticism. George Orwell, for example, concludes his essay 'Charles Dickens' with this extraordinary fantasia:

> When one reads any strongly individual piece of writing, one has the impression of seeing a face somewhere behind the page. I feel this very strongly with Swift, with Defoe, with Fielding, Stendhal, Thackeray, Flaubert, though in several cases I do not know what these people looked like and do not want to know. What one sees is the face the writer *ought* to have. Well, in the case of Dickens I see a face that is not quite the face of Dickens's photographs, although it resembles it. It is the face of a man about forty, with a small beard and a high colour. He is laughing, with a touch of anger in his laughter, but no triumph, no malignity. It is the face of a man who is *generously angry* – in other words, of a nineteenth-century liberal, a free intelligence, a type hated by all the smelly little orthodoxies which are now contending for our souls.[3]

Physiognomy and literary criticism here coalesce. Dickens's fiction is read in the light of a powerfully realised image of its author. This image is, however, perceived as an idealised construct, 'the face that the writer *ought* to have', dependent upon a particular interpretation of the literary evidence. The critic's X-ray vision penetrates the patina of the text to reveal the author's true presence 'behind the page'. Or so Orwell would have us believe.

But it can surely be no accident that the idealised portrait of the novelist (which, of course, is also an unconscious self-portrait) which the critic finds, turns out to resemble so closely the face to be seen in surviving photographs of Dickens. Orwell's disclaimers (his lack of interest in what authors *actually* looked like and the merely grudging acknowledgement of the fact that his idealised Dickens is modelled on an image ultimately derived from real flesh and blood) betray a nervous embarrassment with the intertextual procedure adopted – one can almost hear Jonson's injunction echoing down the centuries, 'Reader, looke/Not on his Picture, but his Booke'![4] But it is in fact two very real texts, one literary and one photographic, which are read in conjunction to construct Orwell's Dickens. Word and image prove mutually dependent, each validating a precarious critical judgement founded in part on both.

Orwell's embarrassment, however, is misplaced. For one thing, he is in good company. His procedure is one that has been often adopted, albeit in a more guarded fashion, by professional critics of the academic establishment. Here, for example, is Anne Barton on Ben Jonson: 'In the famous, and much copied, portrait of the mature Jonson attributed to Abraham van Blyenberch, the sitter almost seems to belong to a different race from Sidney, Spenser, Marlow, Raleigh and Donne – or even from Shakespeare who stares out from the woodenly inept Droeshout engraving. Jonson's broad, blunt, vigorously plain face dissociates itself oddly in any portrait gallery from the more elegant, attenuated faces of his Elizabethan contemporaries. His artistic detachment from them, during much of his life, was equally radical.'[5] Here a substantive critical evaluation is located, rhetorically if not in logic, in the physiognomic differences offered by contemporary portraiture. The intertextuality of word and image is harnessed to the purposes of a characterising and distinguishing literary judgement of the artist's work.

The critical practice of both Orwell and Barton points towards issues of considerable theoretical significance. Literary works are not, after all, Platonic ideas, but exist in material culture. They have no life outside of the contexts in which they are read. And the meanings which they generate in and for any given culture are determined cumulatively by a wide range of factors which include 'how they are edited, what kinds of commentary they generate, whether they are translated into other languages, how often they are quoted, how they (and their author's name) are spelled, *how they (and their author) are visually represented*' (our italics).[6] This chapter focuses on a few of those images of Shakespeare which have helped shape the way we read his works, and attempts to destabilise the traditional hierarchy of discourses in which hermeneutic appropriations of dramatic literature and poetic language rank far higher than the material processes through which poetry and drama circulate within a culture.

'The Droeshout engraving'

II

Shakespeare's face is one of the most insistently reproduced icons in the world. It adorns countless book covers, hotel and restaurant signs, beer mats, tea caddies, confectionery packets, cigarette and playing cards, ceramics, theatre and museum foyers, advertisements, and banknotes. Its currency is based in large measure on the cachet of high culture (Shakespeare metaphorically authorises those products he vicariously and posthumously endorses), combined with its instant recognisability. The high balding dome – 'what a forehead, what a brain!'[7] – has been parodied by Picasso and innumerable other artists and become an almost totemic guarantor of the author's unique genius. In that iconic image we can read a discourse both acculturated and commodified, constituted by the alien but strategically related languages of art and economics, bardolatry and business. From its accrued historical traces, and from the cultural and economic contexts in which it has been mobilised, we can decode from this image the embodiment of a symbol: a symbol, pre-eminently, of British national culture. It is this symbolic 'Shakespeare' we encounter as an image that permeates the fabric and texture of everyday common life. It is probable that every English-speaking citizen of the U.K. is acquainted with Shakespeare; not necessarily from plays or books, but from the visual images borne by the ubiquitous advertisements, tourist attractions, pub signs, biscuit-tins, credit-cards and calendars. An agency offering elocution lessons used to advertise itself through a cartoon drawing of a puzzled Shakespeare, bewildered by a voice from a telephone receiver: to be understood by 'Shakespeare' would be a guarantee of correct speech. In the television series of *Batman* the entrance to the 'Batcave' is controlled by a switch concealed within a bust of Shakespeare: the decorative property of a millionaire's house opens to activate an exotic world of drama and costume, fantasy and adventure. The *Radio Times* once carried a cover design, heralding a programme on language, the 'Story of English' ('the great adventure which transformed the island speech of Shakespeare into the world English of 1,000 million'), entitled 'From Will to the World' in which the imperial, brain-impacted forehead of the Bard, set amidst an English pastoral landscape, had swelled to encompass 'the great globe itself'.

III

But from where do we derive this familiar received image of the national poet? There are only two portraits of Shakespeare which have claims to

'Pale Dry Playwright'
reproduced by kind permission of Tesco.

'Authenticity', Gheerhart Janssen's bust in Holy Trinity Church, Stratford, and Martin Droeshout's title-page engraving to the 1623 First Folio. Both were commissioned some years after Shakespeare's death and probably both relied on some form of preliminary sketch supplied by friends or relatives. They seem to have been acceptable to those who commissioned them, although this in no way guarantees any certainty of realism on the part of the artists. Although they depict what is obviously the same man, there are striking differences between them in their modes of representation. The Janssen bust honours the well-to-do Stratford burgher, offering us a corpulent, older man with up-turned, trimmed moustaches, neatly bobbed side-locks, expensively tailored robes, who holds in his hands the stylised reminders of the source of his wealth in the foregrounded pen and sheet of paper. The image of the Droeshout Shakespeare, with its younger, more dishevelled appearance and encephalous forehead, has proved, despite the 17-year-old engraver's obvious technical incompetence in such matters as relating the proportion of the head to that of the torso, the more popular image of the artist. Some scholars have therefore felt free to hijack Shakespeare's features and mould them to something more approximating the Shakespeare of their own conception. Edmund Malone attempted the most extreme form of revisionism on record. In 1793, in search of a neo-classical paradigm, he persuaded the vicar of Holy Trinity to have the original gaudy paintwork of the Janssen bust whitewashed, earning the opprobrium of a contemporary pilgrim who, acutely noting the conjunction of aesthetic and editorial vandalism, adapted for his own anathematisation the curse engraved on Shakespeare's tombstone:

> Stranger, to whom this monument is shewn
> Invoke the Poet's curse upon Malone;
> Whose meddling zeal his barbarous taste betrays,
> And daubs his tombstones, as he mars his plays![8]

But generally critics have confined themselves to championing one or other of the various rival portraits.[9] Scholars have detected in the aesthetic and semiotic differences between portraits appropriate impressions of the Bard's personality: romantic bravura in the Chandos, sensitive aristocratic features in the Janssen, a gentle, pensive expression in the Felton, and a soulful gaze in the Grafton. All these are, predictably, the qualities these same scholars admire and want to find in their matchless Bard. Samuel Schoenbaum is surely right to suggest that, whatever else they are, these portraits are an index of the way our greatest poet has been imagined, functioning as Rorschach blots onto which the critic 'projects the image of his own conceit'.[10]

IV

Caroline Spurgeon, for example, wanted to use the so-called 'Chess Portrait'[11] of Shakespeare and Jonson as the cover illustration for her *Shakespeare's Imagery*:

> No other presentation I have yet seen of Shakespeare approaches it in

'The "Chandos" portrait',
reproduced by permission of the National Portrait Gallery.

satisfying quality. You will find in the face thought, imagination, great intellectual power, great sensitiveness and refinement, and altogether a feeling of strength and power behind sensitiveness which is remarkable.[12]

What is most remarkable, of course, is that these are precisely the qualities she detected in Shakespeare's imagery. Disarmingly, Spurgeon admits to the charge of wish-fulfilment: 'If there is one thing certain in a world of uncertainties, it is that Shakespeare did not look like the Droeshout portrait. On the other hand he might have looked like the man to the right in the 'chess portrait'; so, for my part, I prefer to look at that.'[13]

There were, of course, financial imperatives to many of the visual appropriations. The explosion of demand for Shakespeariana which began in the eighteenth century led to the 'discovery' of a host of 'Shakespeare' portraits. Some were perfectly genuine early paintings of individuals whose features happened to include a high forehead (and therefore 'must' be of Shakespeare).[14] But many were the productions of such enterprising forgers as the celebrated Paul Zincke, who carefully reworked old canvasses and then artificially aged the overpainting. Such counterfeits were so common in the nineteenth century that Lionel Cust, Director of the National Portrait Gallery, reckoned on being offered more than one a year, usually at an extravagant price. Some of the better counterfeits, such as the Folger Library's famous Ashbourne portrait have only recently been exposed as fakes.[15] More insidiously, the enormous sums of money which a genuine portrait could command tended to cloud scholarly judgement. The owner of the 'chess portrait', for example, sent it for verification to Paul Wislicenus, the author of several books on the so-called 'Kesselstadt Death Mask'. Perhaps it should not be particularly surprising to find that, on very flimsy evidence, Wislicenus came to a firm conviction of the portrait's authenticity, bearing in mind the fact that the contract Wislicenus negotiated with the painting's owner guaranteed him ten per cent of the eventual sale price of the portrait.[16]

Commercial considerations have, of course, always surrounded Shakespearean portraiture. The Droeshout engraving, for example, owes its origins to enterprising literary entrepreneurs and a new conception of the nature of authorship. It is probable that Shakespeare subscribed to the then common view which sharply distinguished between works of literature and play-texts. Plays were generally regarded as light entertainment, the property of the theatrical houses that commissioned them, often from a pool of anonymous hacks. Shakespeare went to his grave without ever having seen plays of the stature of *Macbeth*, *Antony and Cleopatra*, or *The Tempest* reach print. Those plays that had been published had appeared in cheap quarto format with few signs of authorial supervision. It is therefore tempting to agree with Terence Hawkes that

'The notion of a single "authoritative" text, immediately expressive of the plenitude of its author's mind and meaning, would have been unfamiliar to Shakespeare, involved as he was in the collaborative enterprise of dramatic productions and notoriously unconcerned to preserve in stable form the texts of most of his plays.'[17]

V

Hawkes's view, however, needs to be treated with care. It applies specifically to Shakespeare's dramatic output and it appears that he regarded his 'literary' output in a very different light. Both *Venus and Adonis* and *The Rape of Lucrece* were published in carefully prepared copy, complete with signed dedicatory epistles to the Earl of Southampton, with every sign of careful authorial supervision. Within Shakespeare's lifetime, moreover, Ben Jonson had already staked a claim for a far loftier status for the true playwright, who was a poet rather than the follower of the 'trade of the stage, in all their misc'line enterludes'.[18] In the year of Shakespeare's death he brought out the first-ever collected edition of English dramatic texts, *The Workes of Beniamin Jonson*, a carefully prepared and expensively produced folio volume, featuring an engraved title-page, Latin epigrams, epistles dedicatory and the Vaughan portrait of the poet (the only one which can be proved to have been executed during his lifetime).[19] It bore, in fact, the hallmark of a prestige publication, although its contents included not only his incidental poetry and court masques, but also a selection of those plays he had written for the public and private theatres, even going to the length of including the cast lists of the original productions. The text of *Sejanus*, a play originally written with an unknown collaborator, was carefully revised to preserve the purity of authorial input.

Jonson's 'presumption' did not go unnoticed and provoked derisive comment: 'Pray tell me, Ben,' a wit demanded,

> where doth the mystery lurk,
> What others call a play, you call a work.[20]

Jonson's *Works* were nonetheless commercially successful and probably inspired William Jaggard and Thomas Pavier to initiate the publication of Shakespeare's plays in a multi-volume edition. They were restrained from completing this venture by the Lord Chamberlain, probably after complaint from the King's Men. Jaggard and his son Isaac, however, went on to print the First Folio, MR. *WILLIAM SHAKESPEARES COMEDIES, HISTORIES, & TRAGEDIES.* Like Jonson's *Works* this was an expensively produced volume, which probably accounts for the fact that its publication was a risky venture undertaken by a consortium of stationers. The 1200 or so volumes printed sold at the premium price of £1 and came adorned with a full panoply of dedications and com- mendatory verses, as well as the Droeshout engraving. What it is important to recognise is that the general tendency of these introductory materials is to *personalise* the plays, to attach them firmly to the *author* rather than to the theatrical milieu in which they had been first produced. The early quartos of his plays had tended to stress theatrical rather than authorial provenance. The title-page of the popular *Titus Andronicus*, for example, merely records that it was 'Plaide by the Right Honourable the Earle of *Darbie*, Earle of *Pembrooke*, and Earle of *Sussex* their *Servants*', and not until 1598 was Shakespeare's name attached to a printed version of one of his plays, *Love's Labour's Lost*. Heminge and Condell instead emphasise Shakespeare's 'authorly' status and the 'readerly', literary nature of the texts, 'reade him, therefore; and againe and againe'[21] (they were well aware also of the commercial dimension of the project: 'read, and censure. Do so, but buy it first.'). Similarly, in their commendatory verses, Jonson focuses on 'my beloved, The Author', Hugh Holland on the 'Scenicke Poet', Leonard Digges, 'the deceased Author' and I. M. simply 'the memorie of M. W. Shakespeare'.

VI

The Droeshout engraving, strategically placed on the title-page, has to be viewed in this context, a personalising, validating presence, literally authorising the works that follow. Ben Jonson's accompanying epigram, 'To the Reader', is less obviously part of this strategy, but plays its role. At first glance it seems to direct attention away from the image of the author towards the works themselves, 'Reader, looke/Not on his Picture, but his Booke'. But, of course, it is impossible to obey this injunction. Jonson's lines appear on the verso, but Shakespeare's face dominates the recto; neither can be viewed without sight of the other. Engraving and epigram prove mutually dependent, constituting a unified design, the effect of which is to invite 'the Reader' to view the plays in the context of a formidable authorial presence. Early purchasers of the First Folio, that is, were at the beginning of a process all modern readers of Shakespeare must be familiar with, coming to the plays having first confronted a carefully constructed picture of a culture hero, transcendent genius and omniscient seer. In an important article on new bibliographical approaches, Roger Chartier provides a theoretical foundation for the point:

'Forms effect meaning' . . . To attend to the material, formal inscriptions of literary works goes against that spontaneous and misleading image which readers have of their relation to a text as being a transparent and purely intellectual one. It reminds us of the unsuspected power of signs whose supposed insignificance generally leads us to overlook them, such as (to speak only of the printed book) the format chosen, the division and layout of the text on the page, the place of illustrations, the organization of reference and notes, and so on.[22]

VII

One of the most familiar representations of Shakespeare derives from a key moment of historical transition in this strange eventful history, that point where the face of Shakespeare, shadowy and inscrutable in darkening canvases, was actualised into the relative fixity and permanence of statuary form, seeking and finding a marble or a bronze repose. The creation of a sculpted bust or statue is of course a different process of artistic production, implying different social relationships and different cultural purposes. The first sculpture of Shakespeare was the funereal effigy in Holy Trinity church at Stratford, where the formal properties of the representation are at one level a contribution to the surrounding ecclesiastical architecture. Despite the self-evident spirituality of the context, and the artistic bravura of the ostentatiously-flourished quill pen, this particular image has not provided Shakespeare's admirers with an acceptable effigy, a suitable objective correlative for the amazing monument of his artistic achievement. In his own funereal bust Shakespeare looked, to John Dover Wilson, like a 'self-satisfied pork-butcher'.[23] If one knew no better, the pen wielded by this portly Stratford bourgeois could just as well be recording a retailer's business transactions as forming the dramatic poetry of *King Lear*, penning (in Keats' words) 'red-lined accounts' rather than 'the songs of Grecian years'.

Shakespeare was not after all entitled to a burial space in the chancel of Stratford church on account of his poetic or theatrical achievement, but because he was a local landholder and lessee of tithes. If the image depicted by this bust forms the characteristic features of a complacent Stratford bourgeois, then there is no reason in principle why they should not have been assigned to Shakespeare, son of a local tradesman, successful professional and businessman, shrewd investor and property speculator. In Dover Wilson's complaint can be heard the accent of that aristocratic revulsion from the bourgeois origins of the national bard, which is the basis of so many claims, on Shakespeare's behalf, for an alternative and superior social identity.

The visual languages used to represent persons were in this period only partly concerned with accurate physical representation. The discourses of portraiture were also designed to represent, through the development of visual conventions, general categories of social type, historical contexts, ideas and values. The question of whether Shakespeare at the point of death actually *looked like* the bust in Holy Trinity church is perhaps more an anachronistic curiosity of the modern photographic imagination than a proper concern of the seventeenth-century plastic artist, who was probably more interested in the question of whether the image 'looked like' whatever the individual's family and friends, the commissioners of the portrait, the commercial and professional middle-class of Stratford and the governers of the church wanted to *signify* by means of the statue.

VIII

Sculpture from this period tends to *commemorate* rather than *imitate* the person, overtly using the person's physical attributes as a source for the direct communication of cultural meaning. The best-known sculpted representation of Shakespeare, source of many stone and metal imitations, is the marble statue commissioned by public subscription, executed by Peter Scheemakers and erected in Westminster Abbey as a memorial to the national poet in 1741. It functioned therefore both as a collective tribute, drawn on what was already a substantial fund of reverence and admiration; a memorialisation of a pre-eminent genius of English culture; and an official emblematisation of Shakespeare's reception into the structures of national authority and power, constituted by church, state and monarchy. Housed in Westminster Abbey, the image of a writer becomes expressive of the spirit of a nation. Here representation is at its most impersonal, a lapidary codification of the signs of cultural power. The features of Shakespeare scarcely resemble any of the earlier portraits, but are constituted by those conventions of idealised depiction which transformed the eighteenth-century English aristocracy into a pantheon of classical characters. Within an impersonal and idealising texture provided by the cold chastity of the medium, this figure etches the face into the sharp, clean lines of an 'English' countenance; and a clear, candid spirituality further hints (especially in the shaping of hair and beard) at a similarity to the religious icon of Christ.[24]

The semiotics of the statue also enact in microcosm a relation between the figure and its institutional space. The form of Shakespeare is shown leaning on a pedestal, embossed with the faces of a pantheon of English monarchs. The supportive pedestal expresses monumental authority, and links the image to its surrounding context of royal and state power. The figure by contrast expresses relaxed contemplation and nonchalant mastery; the pose is derived from the conventional Elizabethan image of the melancholy young man leaning against a tree (as in Nicholas Hillyard's miniature). Thus the artefact juxtaposes the weight and stability of the monumental context against an aristocratic insouciance, a relaxed grace and elegant langour appropriate to the eighteenth-century image of the man-of-letters. The pile of books surmounting the pedestal partakes of both dimensions: the solid, weighty, heavily-bound records of monumental achievement, they are merely a prop for the casual elbow of the leaning poet, rapt in an impassioned stillness of meditation.

IX

Like a Coronation mug, this particular icon offered the perfect form for reproduction and circulation, and as a miniature souvenir became a standard item in the old curiosity shops of Stratford-upon-Avon. The history of its reproduction actually began very early, and in a context that neatly illustrates the relationship between bardolatrous reverence for the symbol of cultural hegemony, and its reduction to tourist curiosity in the acquisition of commodified bardic mementos. In the form of a leaden copy executed in a mass-production factory at Hyde Park corner, Scheemakers' statue appeared as a centre-piece in David Garrick's Great Shakespeare Jubilee, held in Stratford in 1769. This event, which was at one level a genuine tribute to Shakespeare from a great man of the theatre, was also the ancestor of all the rituals of organised silliness that have since occurred, and are still occurring, around the name, fame and reputation of Shakespeare. Garrick's celebration, which really put the tiny West Midlands market town of Stratford on the map, was as much about Garrick as it was about Shakespeare: a contemporary illustration shows the actor-manager declaiming his great bardolatrous *Ode*, with the statue well in the background (the best place to be, considering some of the lines Garrick was delivering):

> Untouched and sacred be thy shrine
> Avonian Willy! Bard Divine!

Garrick's Jubilee can be regarded as the great formal inauguration of bardolatry as a national religion; the moment, in the words of one scholar, which 'marks the point at which Shakespeare stopped being regarded as an increasingly popular and admirable dramatist, and became a god'.[25] At the same time, it employed as a central symbolic icon an image of

Shakespeare which became, in a later age of mechanical reproduction, an instantly recognisable souvenir. The movement from fetished object of worship to festished token of commodity production is a graphic curve typical of the cultural distribution of the Shakespeare industry.

X

The contradictory apotheosis of this statuesque image is its incorporation into the design of the British £20 note, where the mystical aura of monumental magnificence and the millionfold multiplicity of mechanical reproduction occupy a single dimension. The device on the banknote transacts a complex exchange of values: the currency of Shakespeare as a cultural token, a symbol both of high art and national pride, enhances the material worth of the promissory note; while the high value of the note itself confers a corresponding richness on the symbol of national culture. A bank-note is both a sign of value and a legal contract, a 'bond' between citizen and state: the exchange of such symbolic tokens represents both a constitutive material activity and a process of bonding and socialisation. The fortunate holder of a Shakespeareanised banknote possesses both monetary wealth and aesthetic richness; and by virtue of that possession is integrated, both materially and culturally, into the dominant ideology of a monetarist society. Here the solid bulk of another major apparatus of British society, the Bank of England, is articulated with the marble gravity of Shakespeare and the immense solidity of Westminster Abbey, in an institutional configuration grouped to link the strength of a currency with the power of traditional authority.

This paper portrait of Shakespeare probably represents the culmination of eighteenth-century bardolatry; but it represents also its terminal point. Here all the contradictions of the bardic ideology are held in a paradoxical unity. That which is specific, unique, supremely individual, here appears in its most generalised, impersonal form. The incomparable, irreplaceable, unrepeatable genius of Shakespeare is fragmented by the process of mechanical reproduction into millions of identical simulacra. Those specialised public domains which are in reality the private spaces of our society's prominent individuals, are here offered for imaginative occupation by anyone possessed of that minimal financial qualification, as Buckingham Palace used to be occupied every morning by a million breakfast plates slapped onto a million cheap table-mats. But the over-riding premise of this ideological structure is that authority and power are vested in the material presence of a concrete substance, embodied in the solidity and weight of a positivistic 'reality'. The banknote may be merely fragile paper, but it bears the signature of authority, the images of reliability, the stamp of power. The mysterious potency symbolised by the financial token is by definition absent (even a banknote is really abstract 'credit', declares itself explicitly to be a 'promise'): but it is a god with a countenance of marble, with feet of lead, and with printing-presses of solid steel. What happens however when, as we see today, the identity of money as abstract value supersedes and obliterates the character of money as material substance?

XI

In the contemporary social economy money is debt and credit, profit, and investment, the cheque and the creditcard, figures scrolling across a computer screen or printed on a bank-statement, as much for the private citizen as for the industrialist or commercial entrepreneur. Wealth is no longer piled up in greasy banknotes, or accumulated amid the clashing cacophony of industrial production, but amassed through the techno-logical media of computers and carphones, realised in the vacuous non-existence of the futures market. Commercial exchange at even the simplest level is as likely to proceed via the paper or plastic authorisation of credit, as through an exchange of physical tokens like coins or notes. Clearly if the traditional resources of culture are to be mobilised in support of these developments, they will require new forms of representation. Enter the 'Bardcard'.

The traditional iconography of Shakespeare reproduction traded in effects of mass and solidity, gravity and substance. We now witness the evolution of a new 'post-modern' inconography, appropriate to a society where money can be referred to as 'plastic'. Like the £20 note, cheque guarantee cards issued by some banks carry a picture of Shakespeare. Where on the banknote the bardic image only symbolically authorised value, on the Bardcard it does so literally, since the image is depicted in the form of a high-technology visual 'hologram', designed to inhibit fraudulent use and reproduction. The hologram was developed from a photograph, which is not (as one might reasonably expect) a copy of one of the standard Shakespeare portraits, but a photo of a costumed actor pretending to look like Shakespeare.

The authenticity of the card is thus demonstrated not by a display of cultural power, but by a technological *coup d'oeil*. In terms of content, the image approaches grotesque self-parody, since the proof of individual ownership, by the cardholder, of certain resources of credit held by a bank, is attested by the most fraudulent and artificial means imaginable: a hologram of a photograph of an actor pretending to be . . . Shakespeare. Where the traditional imagery of the Scheemakers statue invoked cultural and economic solidity, the image on the Bardcard is pure post-modernist surface, yielding to the efforts of interpretation only a ludicrous self-reflexive playfulness. Where the £20 note points to the legitimate state ownership and control of both economic and cultural power, the Bardcard proves your title to credit by displaying the image of a major author whose responsibility for the cultural productions attributed to him has been consistently and systematically questioned. This quality is compounded by the reverse of the card, where the holder's signature authorises individual ownership of its power, irresistibly recalling the illegible scrawl of the six signatures attributed to Shakespeare, which some experts have described as apparently belonging to six different people, at least three of them illiterate or terminally ill. One wonders how the bank would react to a cardholder who signed his name with the flexible and cavalier approach to spelling also visible in those 'Shakespearean' autographs.

Has the wheel come full circle, or has the whirligig of time brought in its revenges? Our natural propensity, in contemplating relations between past and present, to imagine a chronological decline from reality to image, from substance to shadow, points us towards the latter explanation. On the other hand, as we have demonstrated, the intertextuality of verbal and visual signs from the earliest stages of 'Shakespeare' reconstruction might persuade us to consider continuity as the keynote of this historical process.

XII

We would not wish our argument to be understood as a crude materialism, a cynical assertion that this immense accumulated repository of cultural production is all nothing more than fraud, forgery and fabrication. Neither would we wish to be perceived as academic alternative comedians, facetiously playing in the marginal spaces of history and culture, demystifying a peripheral area that has never been more than tangentially related to the dominant concerns of literary and theatrical criticism. On the contrary, just as there are clear resemblances between the discourse of bardolatry employed in tourism and advertising, and the language of some twentieth-century Shakespeare criticism, we can observe striking parallels between the playful irresponsibility of deconstructionist criticism, the eclectic pastiche visible in contemporary theatrical production, and the depthless luminescent shimmer of the Bardcard's hologram.

'Best Bitter Bard',
reproduced by kind permission of Flower and Sons.

We would like to see both the methods advocated and the materials studied here installed closer to the centre of contemporary criticism. As far as 'Shakespeare' is concerned to reverse Ben Jonson's (in any case ambiguous exhortation) we recommend the reader to look with the same kind of attention here, 'on his Picture', as he or she has been accustomed to exercise in the scrutiny of 'his Booke'.

Notes

1. *The first part of the Return to Parnassus*, in J. B. Leishman (ed.), *The Three Parnassus Plays* (London: Nicholson and Watson, 1949), pp. 192–3.
2. W. B. Yeats, 'A General Introduction for my Work' (1937), *Essays and Introductions* (New York: Macmillan, 1961) p. 10.
3. George Orwell, 'Charles Dickens' in *Collected Essays, Journalism and Letters*

Vol. I: An Age Like This, 1920–1940 ed. Sonia Orwell and Ian Angus (London: Harcourt Brace Jovanovich, 1968), p. 460.

4. 'To the Reader' facing the Droeshout title-page engraving to the First Folio.

5. Anne Barton, *Ben Jonson, Dramatist* (Cambridge: Cambridge University Press, 1984), p. 3.

6. Gary Taylor, *Reinventing Shakespeare: A Cultural History from the Restoration to the Present* (New York: Weidenfeld and Nicolson, 1989), p. 6.

7. A. L. Rowse, *The English Spirit: Essays in History and Literature* (London: Macmillan, 1945, rpt. 1966), pp. 5–6.

8. Entry in the Stratford Visitors' Book, cited in Samuel Schoenbaum, *Shakespeare's Lives* (New York: Oxford University Press, 1970), p. 187.

9. The Chandos portrait is the only other serious contender. For details of it and other so-called primary portraits of Shakespeare see Oscar James Campbell and Edward G. Quinn, eds. *The Reader's Encyclopedia of Shakespeare* (New York: Cromwell, 1966), pp. 652–6; Samuel Schoenbaum, *William Shakespeare: Records and Images* (London: Scolar Press, 1981), chap. 5; and David Piper, *The Image of the Poet: British Poets and Their Portraits* (Oxford: Clarendon Press, 1982), passim.

10. Samuel Schoenbaum, *Shakespeare's Lives, op. cit.*, pp. 13–14.

11. For details of this portrait see Bryan Loughrey and Neil Taylor, 'Shakespeare and Jonson at Chess?', *Shakespeare Quarterly*, vol. 34, no. 4 (Winter) 1983, pp. 440–8.

12. Letter to M. H. Spielman, dated 10 September 1934 and now in the Folger Library.

13. Unpublished appendix IX of *Shakespeare's Imagery*, pp. 385–6, in the Folger Shakespeare Library. Spurgeon was eventually persuaded that to use the chess portrait as her cover illustration might distract from the force of her argument.

14. We are reminded of the fact that Charlie Chaplin is reputed to have entered a 'Charlie Chaplin look-alike' competition and to have been placed third. On 23 April 1988 the International Shakespeare Globe Trust organised a 'Shakespeare look-alike' competition in which foreheads featured prominently. The Trust celebrated the Bard's 1990 birthday with a huge banner of the Droeshout engraving held aloft for aerial photography by more than sixty people who share the Shakespeare surname.

15. Recent restoration has revealed it to be a genuine contemporary portrait of Sir Hugh Hammersley, Lord Mayor of London, strategically falsified.

16. Details of the contract are contained in the files of the portrait's current owner.

17. Terence Hawkes, *That Shakespeherian Rag: Essays on a Critical Process* (London: Methuen, 1986), p. 75.

18. Epistle prefixed to the 1607 quarto of *Volpone*.

19. See C. H. Hereford and Percy and Evelyn Simpson (eds) *Ben Jonson* (Oxford: Clarendon Press, 1952), vol. III, p. ix.

20. Cited in Samuel Schoenbaum, *Shakespeare: the Globe and the World* (New York: Oxford University Press, 1979) p. 174.

21. 'To the Great Variety of Readers', prefatory matter to the First Folio (1623).

22. Roger Chartier, 'Meaningful Forms,' *Liber*, no. 1, p. 8. Chartier's argument derives from D. F. McKenzie's pioneering *Bibliography and the Sociology of Texts* (London: British Library, 1986).

23. See Dover Wilson, *The Essential Shakespeare* (Cambridge: Cambridge University Press, 1932), p. 6.

24. The Folger Shakespeare Library has a Victorian 'Bible-Shakespeare Calendar,' the cover of which features a Shakespearean visage assimilated to the traditional iconographic conventions used for representing Christ. In contrast, most cartoon illustrations of Shakespeare resemble, if they are not derived from, Picasso's famous sketch. The bust used in *Batman* is derived ultimately from the Scheemakers statue.

25. Christian Deelman, *The Great Shakespeare Jubilee* (New York: Viking Press, 1964), pp. 69–70.

12 *Cymbeline's* Other Endings

Ann Thompson

I

It has become standard for critics to admire the ending of Shakespeare's
Cymbeline. Alexander Leggatt writes that 'The finale is an intricate,
beautiful machine in which an astonishing number of disguises are
removed, misunderstandings swept away and reunions accomplished.'[1]
Bertrand Evans, who finds that *Cymbeline* 'surpasses all other plays' in the
'fantastic complexity of its use of discrepant awareness and the consummate skill with which its intricacies are managed', remarks that at the
end 'the process of making everything known is extended and exploited as
nowhere else in Shakespeare.'[2] Judiana Lawrence praises the way in which
'Not only the oracles but every aspect of the conclusion become finely-
managed instances of *peripeteia*' in the 'particularly protracted juggling act'
of the last scene with its 'two dozen or more revelations'.[3]

But this admiration is a relatively recent phenomenon and is not
universally shared. A reviewer of the most recent Royal Shakespeare
Company production of the play (Stratford-upon-Avon, 1989) complained of the 'interminable tying up of loose ends' in the last scene,[4] and
another reviewer ten years earlier wrote: 'When a character rushed into
the welter of revelations crying "let me end the story", there was a sigh of
amused relief from all who were unaware that there was still some way to
go.'[5] George Bernard Shaw recalled Henry Irving's production of 1896 in
which Irving, as Jachimo,

> a statue of romantic melancholy, stood dumb on the stage for hours (as it
> seemed) whilst the others toiled through a series of *denouements* of crushing
> tedium, in which the characters lost all their vitality and individuality and had
> nothing to do but identify themselves by moles on their necks, or explain why
> they were not dead.[6]

Earlier, in the preface to Oxberry's acting edition of the play, we find
these disparaging remarks:

> The plot of *Cymbeline* is more intricate than interesting; and when the knot

is at last to be untied, the process is infinitely too tedious; explanation follows explanation, when all the excitement is over, and the impatient spectator feels himself in the painful state of a well-fed guest who is obliged to listen to a long grace after a long dinner. What is still worse, these explanations, however requisite to the characters of the play, are by no means requisite to the auditor, and he feels therefore, little pleasure in listening to the detail of that which he already understands. He knows that the page is Imogen; that the soldier is Posthumus; and that Polydore and Cadwal are the King's sons: with what pleasure then can he listen to the development of their relationship?[7]

Reviewers have traditionally spent their time counting the number of separate explanations or revelations: I have found totals of fourteen, twenty-four and just about every number in between. One exasperated journalist in 1957 gave up and wrote

Some more enterprising observer than myself once counted two dozen *denouements* in the final scene, which means that every twenty lines someone proves to be someone else, or else is revealed as responsible for some undetected crime or act of chivalry. The final piling up of complications is far too much for a modern audience, even at Stratford.[8]

It is frequently claimed, both by reviewers and by critics, that *Cymbeline* has the longest last scene in the Shakespearean canon, which is not in fact true: at 485 lines it is shorter than those of *Measure for Measure* (539) and *Love's Labour's Lost* (931) and not enormously longer than that of *A Midsummer Night's Dream* (438).[9] Clearly, however, it can *feel* long, and it has very often been abbreviated on stage; not just the last scene but the entire last act has been presented in an altered, cut, rearranged or rewritten version more often than it has been presented 'straight'. One of my purposes in this chapter is to trace and comment on this history, but I also want to look at the peculiar nature of the ending as it stands, and to consider the ways in which the play's most recent critics, especially psychoanalytic critics and new historicists, have in effect rehabilitated it. But before launching into alterations and critical readings I shall begin with a synopsis of Act V as it stands in the First Folio, the only authoritative text of the play:

V, i. Posthumus, in soliloquy, repents of having given the order for his wife's murder, even though he still thinks her guilty of adultery. Having come to Britain with the invading Roman army, he resolves to change sides and seek death dressed as a British peasant.

V, ii. Posthumus fights with and defeats (but does not kill) Jachimo, not recognising him as the man who convinced him of Imogen's infidelity. Jachimo, taking Posthumus for a peasant, assumes the very air of Britain is avenging itself on him for his betrayal of its Princess. In a further battle episode, the Britains are fleeing and King Cymbeline is captured by the Romans, but then rescued by Belarius, Guiderius and Arviragus assisted by Posthumus. This is the turning-point of the battle and the Romans now flee. Again, neither Posthumus nor Belarius is recognised by Cymbeline; he does not know that Guiderius and Arviragus are his sons, and they do not know him to be their father.

V, iii. Posthumus meets an unnamed British Lord and gives him a long and increasingly angry account of the battle we have just seen. After this, in soliloquy, he repeats his resolve to die, changes his dress again and is duly arrested as a Roman.

V, iv. Under arrest, Posthumus again expresses his penitence and then falls asleep. The ghosts of his dead family (father, mother and two brothers) appear and complain in fourteeners to Jupiter about Posthumus' sufferings. Jupiter, according to the stage direction, 'descends in thunder and lightning, sitting upon an eagle: he throws a thunderbolt'. He tells the ghosts to stop complaining: everything will work out all right. He leaves behind a tablet with a prophecy inscribed on it. Posthumus awakes and cannot make sense of the prophecy. Ready for execution, he is instead sent for by the King.

V, v. Cymbeline thanks his unknown rescuers, Belarius, Guiderius and Arviragus, and regrets the disappearance of the fourth man (i.e. Posthumus). Cornelius the doctor enters and reports the death of the Queen and her confession of her plots against both Imogen and Cymbeline. The Roman prisoners are brought on, including Posthumus, Jachimo and Imogen (in her disguised role as page to the Roman general, Caius Lucius). Cymbeline, not recognising his daughter, is nevertheless taken with the page and tells 'him' to 'ask what boon thou wilt.' (She is also half-recognised by Belarius and the two boys who thought her dead.) Imogen, recognising Jachimo; demands that he relate 'of whom he had this ring' (the one she gave Posthumus and which he wagered on her chastity). He, at some length and with expressions of remorse, recounts the story, but is finally interrupted by Posthumus who identifies himself as the murderer of Imogen. When she tries to intervene, he knocks her down, but eventually recognises her and they are reconciled. Her supposed death is explained by Pisanio as being caused by the Queen's drug. Pisanio also relates the story of Cloten's pursuit of Imogen to Wales dressed in Posthumus' clothes, and it is Guiderius' turn to interrupt and provide the climax: 'I slew him there.' Guiderius is arrested, but Belarius now intervenes to reveal his own identity and those of the boys. Posthumus is finally recognised as the unknown soldier who assisted in the rescue of the King. He forgives Jachimo. Cymbeline, following his example, frees the prisoners and says he will pay the tribute to Rome even though he has won the battle. The Roman soothsayer interprets the prophecy to have predicted all this and the play ends in general rejoicing.

It does seem that Shakespeare's procedure is unusual in the last act, and particularly in the last scene of *Cymbeline*, mainly in terms of the sheer quantity of recapitulatory narrative the audience experiences. Elsewhere he sets up opportunities for the characters to explain things to each other after the play is over. At the end of *The Merchant of Venice*, for example, Portia says:

> It is almost morning,
> And yet I am sure you are not satisfied
> Of these events at full. Let us go in
> And charge us there upon inter'gatories,
> And we will answer all things faithfully. (V. i, 295–9)

Similarly, at the end of *The Winter's Tale*, Leontes says:

> Good Paulina,
> Lead us from hence, where we may leisurely
> Each one demand, and answer to his part
> Perform'd in this wide gap of time, since first
> We were dissever'd. Hastily lead away. (V. iii, 151–5)

Ten other comedies end with some such request or promise whereby the audience is spared the narrative satisfaction granted to the characters. There is even such a moment in *Cymbeline* when the King – in the midst of what has the reputation of being the longest and most tedious scene in the canon – actually complains that things are happening too fast:

> When shall I hear all through? This fierce abridgement
> Hath to it circumstantial branches, which
> Distinction should be rich in. Where? How liv'd you?
> And when came you to serve our Roman captive?
> How parted with your [brothers]? How first met them?
> Why fled you from the court? And whither? These
> And your three motives to the battle, with
> I know not how much more, should be demanded,
> And all the other by-dependances,
> From chance to chance; but nor the time nor place
> Will serve our long interrogatories. (V. v. 382–92)

The same technique is found in a tragedy such as *Hamlet*, when Horatio promises to tell the full story to Fortinbras and the other survivors after the last scene has ended. The only plays that are comparable to *Cymbeline* in insisting on recapitulating what the audience already knows are the earliest tragedies, *Titus Andronicus* and *Romeo and Juliet*. In *Titus* parts of the story are told three times in the last act: by Aaron in his gloating confession in V, i, by Titus in his justification for killing Lavinia in V, iii, and by Lucius in his public speech to the Roman citizens, also in V, iii. In *Romeo and Juliet* it is Friar Lawrence who re-tells the whole story to the

Prince and the others in the last scene. Both plays use these narratives in quite formal ways: they are public speeches on civic occasions which stress the consequences of the tragedies for the societies in which they have taken place.

Shakespeare uses narrative to a different effect at the end of *King Lear* and sets up an interesting contrast between sub-plot and main plot. In the sub-plot Edgar insists on telling his story at some length, including (in the Quarto text) the inserted narrative of Kent telling *his* story, the very telling of which is almost fatal. Edgar says that Kent:

> Told the most piteous tale of Lear and him
> That ever ear receiv'd, which in recounting,
> His grief grew puissant and the strings of life
> Began to crack. (V, iii, 215–18)

Edgar has already described how Gloucester's heart 'burst' when he finally 'from first to last / Told him our pilgrimage' (V, iii, 196–7), and the audience may be feeling that this indulgence in recapitulating the story of the sub-plot could also prove fatal to Lear and Cordelia if it takes up much more time. If we accept that the Folio text represents Shakespeare's own revision of *King Lear*, he must have felt himself that there was too much story-telling here as he cut the inserted narrative of Kent in that version. But there is still something like *Cymbeline*'s self-consciousness of narrative prolixity in both texts when Edmund, some fifty lines after receiving his death-wound, encourages Edgar to continue:

> This speech of yours hath mov'd me,
> And shall perchance do good: but speak you on,
> You look as you had something more to say.   (V, iii, 200–2)

In the main plot, the time for narrative is past. Kent tries to reveal his disguise to Lear and to tell him about the deaths of Goneril and Regan, but, as even Edgar acknowledges, such explanations are by now 'very bootless'.

Cymbeline's dwelling on narrative repetition is of course very different in tone, but Shakespeare seems to want, as with the sub-plot in *King Lear*, to slow the play down at this point, to allow the audience to savour the recognitions and reversals at more than naturalistic length. A precedent could be found in *Twelfth Night* where the mutual recognition of Viola and Sebastian is spun out to a degree which is strictly unnecessary in view of the literal circumstances of their separation and the time they have been parted but which is required for the moment to have its proper weight – almost like an aria in an opera. The pleasure we take in the ending of *Cymbeline* has nothing to do with surprise – as usual in Shakespeare the audience already knows all the secrets – but depends on our anticipation of the characters' pleasure. Shakespeare manipulates the events of Act V in such a way that this anticipation is prolonged by a number of factors. He sets up for example a sequence of tantalising non-recognitions in the battle-scenes (between Posthumus and Jachimo, Posthumus and Cymbeline, Cymbeline and Belarius, Cymbeline and his sons) followed by the half-recognition of Imogen by both Cymbeline and Belarius. Then revelations are delayed by interruptions (as when Posthumus interrupts Jachimo and is in turn interrupted by Imogen) and by the need to sort out subsidiary misunderstandings (as when the reunion of Imogen and Posthumus is postponed by her accusation of Pisanio and his explanation about the drug).

Moreover, Shakespeare allows the audience to laugh. One of the traditional justifications for cuts, especially in the last scene, has always been that in *Cymbeline* Shakespeare's insistence on dramatising or rather narrating – and at length – things the audience already knows provokes unwelcome laughter. Modern theatre historians seem to accept the validity of this argument: Carol J. Carlisle for example remarks approvingly of Macready's cuts that 'The seemingly endless series of revelations in [the last] scene, so likely to provoke laughter after a while, was somewhat curtailed by leaving out reports of things the audience themselves had seen. Omissions relating to the Queen's confessions and the prophecy reduced the effect of improbability.'[10] And Alan Hughes says of Irving's production that 'The last scene was much abridged: the Soothsayer was entirely omitted, but none of the revelations except the Queen's death was left out. Guiderius' role was cut, together with numerous explanations of things the audience already knew, with the inevitable effect that laughter was avoided and illusion preserved.'[11] Reviewers of twentieth-century productions frequently allude to this potential problem, and some recent directors of the play, such as Peter Hall, who presented it with *The Winter's Tale* and *The Tempest* at London's National Theatre in 1988, have also tried to banish potential laughter, but it seems that the most successful of modern productions have allowed for laughter and even encouraged it. This was the case at Stratford-upon-Avon in 1962, 1974 and in 1987. The text itself offers some obvious cues for laughs, as when Cornelius, who has stood silent on stage for 200 lines after describing the Queen's death, suddenly responds to Imogen's accusation that Pisanio has poisoned her by saying 'O gods / I left out one thing which the Queen confess'd', (V, v, 243–4) and goes on to tell the story about the drug, or when Belarius, carefully following this account, makes the solemn aside 'My boys, / There was our error' (V, v, 259–60). And a skilful actor can make good comic capital out of the role of Cymbeline who is alone in knowing *nothing* about what has been going on and is totally baffled by everything.[12]

II

Turning to the play's stage-history, how did earlier producers cope with this extraordinary ending? What changes did they make and why? It is perhaps surprising to discover first how popular *Cymbeline* was in the eighteenth century. Reviewers even today still resort to quoting Samuel Johnson's adverse opinion of it:

> This play has many just sentiments, some natural dialogues, and some pleasing scenes, but they are obtained at the expense of much incongruity. To remark the folly of the fiction, the absurdity of the conduct, the confusion of the names and manners of different times, and the impossibility of the events in any system of life, were to waste criticism upon unresisting imbecility, upon faults too evident for detection, and too gross for aggravation.[13]

At the point when this was written (1756), *Cymbeline* had in fact recently been performed only in a much altered and adapted version by Thomas D'Urfey called *The Injured Princess: or The Fatal Wager* (first staged in 1682 but apparently written in 1673).[14] As can be guessed from his title, D'Urfey concentrates on the wager plot and makes it the focus of his heavily curtailed climax. The character who is the equivalent of Posthumus (D'Urfey changes most of the names) actually kills the Jachimo-figure in the battle, causing him to confess his slander in his dying speech. There is no dream of Posthumus' family, no descent of Jupiter and no oracle. The play's political theme is minimised; instead, D'Urfey adds a sub-plot in which Pisanio's daughter Clarina who is Imogen's servant becomes the focus of an attempted rape by the Cloten-figure. Pisanio is blinded acting in her defence and his role in the final scene is curiously similar to that of Gloster at the end of Nahum Tate's 1681 adaptation of *King Lear*.

In 1759 two rival adaptations of *Cymbeline* were written by Charles Marsh and William Hawkins for the Theatre Royal, although only that of Hawkins (a former professor of poetry at Oxford) was performed. These are interesting for attempting (perhaps in response to Johnson's strictures, or at least out of agreement with his disapproval) to impose the classical unities on the play. Marsh opts for unity of place, explaining in his Preface: 'I thought it a pleasing Task, to endeavor to amend the *Conduct* of the *Fable*, by confining the Scenes, at least, to this Island.'[15] Hawkins in his Preface calls *Cymbeline* 'one of the most irregular productions of Shakespeare' and continues 'I have accordingly endeavoured to new-construct this Tragedy, almost upon the plan of *Aristotle* himself, in respect of the *unity* of *Time*.'[16] As the New Arden editor J. M. Nosworthy comments, 'Hercules is remembered for lesser labours.'[17]

Both versions make considerable changes to the ending. In Marsh, the political content is played down and the revelations, as well as being abbreviated, are rearranged so that the rediscovery of the King's lost sons precedes rather than follows the reunion of Imogen and Posthumus, allowing that to become the ultimate climax. Posthumus is given the final speech – a warning to others against jealousy. His dream of his family, the descent of Jupiter, and the oracle are omitted. In Hawkins, the ending is stage-managed by Philario (confusingly, the equivalent of Shakespeare's Pisanio) who, in an attempt to test Imogen's forgiveness reminiscent of the Duke's manipulation of Isabella at the end of *Measure for Measure*, tells her that Posthumus is dead and that he died cursing her. Again there is no dream, no Jupiter, and no oracle, but the politics of the play become more important: Cymbeline celebrates victory over Rome rather than reconciliation and promises to demand ransom for his prisoners.

By 1760, London had seen about thirty performances of the D'Urfey and Hawkins versions. In 1761, David Garrick restored something more like the original to the stage. His *Cymbeline* was performed 163 times before 1800 and it established the pattern of cutting which was to last through the nineteenth century and well into the twentieth, especially as far as the ending was concerned.[18] On the first night, Garrick had cut 524 lines from the last act total of 824, explaining in the Advertisement to the printed text that 'It was impossible to retain more of the Play and bring it within the Compass of a Night's Entertainment.' Moreover, he reveals that a further passage, printed in italics, 'was omitted in the Representation after the first night'. This is the account of the Queen's confession and death, amounting to another 46 lines. Garrick played Posthumus, but only twenty-three times, giving his last performance in 1763 and resigning the role to William Powell and Samuel Reddish. He retained Posthumus' soliloquy which opens the last act and announces his repentance for the murder he thinks has been committed. After that, however, the part is much abbreviated: against his own histrionic interests, Garrick systematically undid most of Shakespeare's efforts to reinstate Posthumus as a sympathetic and important character at this late stage in the play. A shortened version of the description of the battle in the equivalent of V, iii is spoken by Pisanio (Posthumus does not appear in Garrick's text of this scene), and there is no dream, no Jupiter, and no oracle. Garrick also made significant cuts in the various recapitulatory narratives in the last scene, especially those of Jachimo and Belarius. The play ends on peace with Rome, the question of tribute tactfully forgotten.

Garrick's cuts were substantially retained by John Philip Kemble who played Posthumus between 1785 and 1817, but the pattern changed somewhat in the later nineteenth century when both William Charles Macready and Henry Irving chose to play Jachimo rather than Posthumus. *Cymbeline* always did represent something of a problem for actor-managers by not offering a really strong male lead: both Posthumus and Jachimo are absent from the stage for the whole of the third and fourth acts. (One possible solution, to double the part of Posthumus with that of Cloten, was not, I think, tried on stage until the production at the Royal Exchange Theatre in Manchester in 1984).[19] Samuel Phelps, who had played Posthumus at Sadler's Wells in 1847, was offended when he was asked to play Jachimo in the tercentenary Shakespeare festival production in 1864. He considered it a minor role and refused it, though he played Posthumus again that year at Drury Lane with William Creswick as Jachimo. (Creswick also played Iago to Phelps' Othello that season and had previously played Cassius to Phelps' Brutus, an arrangement suggesting a conscious repertory of hierarchically paired roles.[20]) The balance of the ending inevitably shifted with the increased importance of Jachimo: even in Garrick's version, Posthumus' part had been cut; under Macready and Irving it almost disappeared.

Macready did, in his production of 1843, restore an abbreviated account of the description of the battle to Posthumus, but he continued to cut the dream of Posthumus' family, the appearance of Jupiter, and the oracle, and he reduced the repentance speech to just three lines. His production apparently made up in spectacle what it lost in verbiage: the battle involved a large cast and elaborate machinery for creating smoke and dust. The last scene opened with Cymbeline in his tent on the battlefield surrounded by numerous attendants in symmetrical groups: there were twenty-four soldiers, eighteen lords, six pages and four banner carriers. The procession of Roman prisoners was headed by two British captains and twelve soldiers and included eighteen Romans in addition to the named characters. Altogether there were ninety-three people on stage for this scene, the dramatic focus of which was Jachimo as the repentant villain.[21] There was an even greater emphasis on Jachimo in Irving's production of 1896 (as seen by Shaw): his performance in the last scene was said to be based visually on paintings of the suffering Christ. On this occasion some reviewers actually complained that the focus on Jachimo and on *his* relationship with Imogen at the expense of Posthumus upset the balance of the play.[22]

Irving's production is perhaps now best remembered for Ellen Terry's performance as Imogen, partly because of her extensive correspondence with George Bernard Shaw about the role. Despite Shaw's instructions to Terry to try to 'leave the paragon out and the woman in',[23] most nineteenth-century critics and audiences seem to have idealised Imogen to the point of ideology: Swinburne summed it up by calling her 'the immortal godhead of womanhood'.[24] What they actually saw in her was the perfect *wife*, a model of domesticity, devotion and self-sacrifice. Specifically, they admired her total femininity which she cannot effectively conceal under her male disguise, the appropriateness of her figurative language (she refers to her needle twice), her womanly (if un-princessly) actions in cooking for Belarius and her brothers, her purity (unlike the problematic Isabella in *Measure for Measure* she calls for help as soon as she recognises the language of seduction), and her complete obedience to her husband even when he orders her death.[25] In the last scene, the Victorians especially emphasised the magnanimity with which she gives up her claim to the kingdom. When he is convinced that his lost sons have been found, Cymbeline says to his daughter, 'O Imogen, / Thou hast lost by this a kingdom.' To which she replies, 'No my lord; / I have got two worlds by't' (V, v, 372–4). These lines seem never to have been cut, whatever else was omitted, and they are quoted with approval by critics who make such comments as: 'This sweet soul knows no low ambitious promptings' and 'she loses without a pang the heirship to a kingdom'.[26]

Helen Faucit, who played Imogen in Macready's production in 1843 and again for Phelps in 1864, called the character 'Shakespeare's master-piece' and produced a sentimental fantasy of events after the final curtain, rather as Mary Cowden Clarke had imagined the pre-play events in *The Girlhood of Shakespeare's Heroines*. She sees Imogen helping her brothers to learn how to behave in the court and laughing at their mistakes, but the Princess never really recovers from her traumatic experiences:

> Happiness hides for a time injuries which are past healing. The blow which was inflicted by the first sentence in [Posthumus'] cruel letter went to the heart with a too fatal force. Then followed, on this crushing blow, the wandering, hopeless days and nights, without shelter, without food even up to the point of famine. Was this delicately nurtured creature one to go through her terrible ordeal unscathed? We see that when food and shelter came, they came too late. The heart-sickness was upon her: 'I am sick still – heart-sick.' Upon this follows the fearful sight of, as she supposes, her husband's headless body. Well may she say that she is 'nothing; or if not, nothing to be were better.' When happiness, even such as she had never known before, comes to her, it comes, like the food and shelter, – too late.
>
> Tremblingly, gradually, and oh, how reluctantly! the hearts to whom that life is so precious will see the sweet smile which greets them grow fainter, will hear the loved voice grow feebler! The wise physician Cornelius will tax his utmost skill, but he will find the hurt too deep for mortal leech-craft to heal. The 'piece of tender air' very gently, but very surely, will fade out like an exhalation of the dawn. Her loved ones will watch it with straining eyes, until it
>
> Melts from
>
> The smallness of a gnat to air, and then
> Will turn their eyes and weep.[27]

A very different interpretation of the ending is found in Shaw's rewriting of the last act ('*Cymbeline Refinished*') in 1937.[28] Starting with his exasperation with Irving's version, he surprised himself by developing a reluctant respect for Shakespeare's original ending. Nevertheless, he abbreviated it drastically and gave the characters more 'naturalistic' responses to the various revelations. Imogen's first response to Posthumus is hostile – 'You dare pretend you love me' – but ultimately one of grudging reconciliation: 'I must go home and make the best of it / As other women must.' The boys refuse to accept Cymbeline as their father, Guiderius saying, 'We three are fullgrown men and perfect strangers. / Can I change fathers as I'd change my shirt?' He also refuses to inherit the throne, having had a glimpse of courtly life and not finding it to his taste. Both boys choose to return to their cave, implicitly leaving Imogen reinstated as heiress, though Shaw does not emphasise this point. This version was commissioned for a production in Stratford-upon-Avon but was not actually performed there since it was feared it would be seen as a topical allusion to the abdication of King Edward VIII: Guiderius gives amongst his reasons for refusing the crown that he would be 'Not free to wed the woman of my choice' and he declares 'I abdicate, and pass the throne to Polydore.' [29] (In Shakespeare, Guiderius *is* Polydore; Shaw is not the only person to confuse these names.)

Shaw's version was subsequently performed in London, but the second half of the twentieth century has seen at least an intermittent restoration of the full Shakespearean ending to the stage. Michael Benthall's production in Stratford-upon-Avon in 1949 was praised by reviewers for the return of Jupiter, although he omitted Posthumus' family who do not seem to have reappeared until Peter Hall's production, also in Stratford-upon-Avon, in 1957. On that occasion they bleated and gabbled their lines – a techique Hall used again in his National Theatre production in London in 1988 and which has been adopted by other directors, for example Robin Phillips at Stratford, Ontario in 1986. John Barton's 1974 Stratford-upon-Avon production made radical cuts throughout the last act and omitted Posthumus' description of the battle, replacing it with a reading of the Folio stage directions by Cornelius (who had acted throughout as a sort of narrator). The battle itself and the appearance of Jupiter were both disappointing in Bill Alexander's studio production at The Other Place in Stratford-upon-Avon in 1987, but had been spectacular in the main theatre in William Gaskill's 1962 production and at Stratford, Ontario, in 1986 when the play was set in the late 1930s and early 1940s. This period setting also allowed for Jupiter to appear as a bomber pilot in the cockpit of his plane, and for the final scene to be set in a field hospital.[30] In general, however, *Cymbeline* has rarely been given a twentieth-century setting, though John Barton's use of large steel pipes for the Welsh set in 1974 made a jokey reference to the contemporary status of Milford Haven as a major oil terminal.

While some of the recapitulatory narratives have continued to be abbreviated (especially those of Jachimo and Belarius), some productions have even added material to the ending. A Romanian version in 1967 added a comic epilogue in which the Queen was brought back to life by Cornelius' medicines and Cloten retrieved his head. The Queen actually appeared to make her own confession and died onstage at Stratford, Ontario in 1970, and a production in Adelaide, Australia in 1979 made the most of a spectacular appearance of Jupiter by having him reappear whenever a prophecy was fulfilled, six times in all.[31]

III

It will be apparent that there has been something of a spate of productions of *Cymbeline* in recent years: Stratford, Ontario in 1986, Stratford-upon-Avon in 1987, London in 1988 and Stratford-upon-Avon again in 1989. In the Spring of 1988 theatregoers in London could even choose between (or compare) the one at the Barbican's Pit theatre (transferred from the previous year's season at The Other Place in Stratford-upon-Avon) and the one at the National. At the same time, the play has had more serious attention from literary critics than ever before and some of this has tended to rehabilitate or justify the peculiarities of the ending, although this has not been the explicit or conscious aim of the writers. The critics involved belong, as I have said above, to two identifiable groups: psychoanalytical critics and new historicists. I propose to look briefly at just two representative writers from each group.

The psychoanalytical approach can be exemplified by the work of Meredith Skura and Ruth Nevo. The very title of Skura's essay is 'Interpreting Posthumus' Dream from Above and Below: Families, Psychoanalysts and Literary Critics'.[32] She focuses on the dream as the climactic episode in the narrative in which Posthumus 'learns how to be a son' which he has to do before he can be a husband and father. The battle is also crucial: he fights alongside an unidentified father and two sons in a 'narrow lane'. For psychoanalytical critics conflict at a narrow entrance is inevitably Oedipal, but instead of killing the old man (Posthumus' father-in-law rather than his father) they save him, and Posthumus repeats his own father's heroic defence of Britain. The subsequent dream can be interpreted either as the intervention of the gods ('from above') or as the effect of family ('from below'): it does not change anything but allows Posthumus to recognise himself.

Ruth Nevo calls her chapter on *Cymbeline* in *Shakespeare's Other*

Language 'The Rescue of the King',[33] and she also reads that episode as Oedipal. She stresses the repetitions: the battle is elaborately staged and then *insistently* described. In her reading Cymbeline is in fact the central ego of the play although that ego is in abeyance or suspension during the earlier acts. In fact, Posthumus becomes his proxy in acting out his repressed desire for Imogen: like Skura, Nevo remarks on the thinly-veiled incest behind Cymbeline's determination to marry his daughter to his 'wife's sole son'. In the last scene he is properly the pivot and cynosure of all the revelations and recognitions as the complex family plot is resolved, but the severing of parent/child bonds is still causing pain, as when 'Fidele' abandons her surrogate father Caius Lucius ('your life, good master, / Must shuffle for itself'), and when Belarius loses 'Two of the sweet'st companions in the world'.

New historicist approaches can be represented by the work of Jonathan Goldberg and Leah S. Marcus, both of whom emphasise *Cymbeline* as a play which reflects contemporary Stuart politics and in particular James I's vision of the Union of the Kingdoms of England and Scotland. Goldberg briefly but suggestively compares *Cymbeline* to the ceilings of Inigo Jones' Banqueting House at Whitehall painted by Rubens: both summarise and celebrate Stuart ideology as a sort of paternalistic imperialism.[34] Marcus explores this theme in more detail; for her the insistence on the battle is because Posthumus most prove himself the equal of the sons of Cymbeline. Posthumus is here identified as a Scot (coincidentally he was played as one in Stratford-upon-Avon in 1989), and specifically as one of the 'Post Nati' – Scots born after James ascended the English throne but lacking equal rights to own property in England. The eagle / Jupiter is seen as James himself who had swooped down upon the English Parliament to champion his countrymen, and the twice-read prophecy links the personal narratives of the characters with the vision of the eagle of empire passing from Rome to a reunited Britain.[35]

Interestingly, both psychoanalytical and new historicist readings centre on Posthumus or even on Cymbeline. All four critics cited here barely mention Imogen. These readings would have seemed baffling to Victorian audiences who saw very little of Posthumus on stage and to Victorian commentators to whom he is an embarrassment, tolerated only because he is beloved of the divine Imogen. None of these critics has very much to say about staging, though it is apparent that their readings depend on a full text, complete with its apparently awkward repetitions and redundant narratives. In this they are in agreement with theatre directors today who seem also to have a general commitment to as full a text as possible – even the supposedly Folio-only production of *King Lear* at Stratford-upon-Avon in 1990 allowed passages from the Quarto to sneak in. Of course directors are limited by considerations of casting and budget: the battle and the descent of Jupiter in *Cymbeline* require resources as well as ingenuity. But do these readings bear any relation to modern stagings?

It actually seems unlikely to me that a new historicist 'Jacobean' reading could be staged in such a way as to make sense to a modern audience: *Cymbeline*'s stage history shows a very widespread consensus that the personal and familial aspects of the play are thought to be more attractive to audiences than its political theme which is, on the face of it, somewhat casually handled. Moreover, if Shakespeare was indeed celebrating the dawn of British imperialism at the end of *Cymbeline*, it is difficult for us, with hindsight, to share his enthusiasm. In the modern theatre (despite dutiful programme notes on 'Cymbeline's Britain' and 'Shakespeare's Britain'), the play's politics seem at times to have been reduced to an occasion for making jokes about the Common Market: in 1974 one reviewer remarked of John Barton's production at Stratford-upon-Avon, 'If the Prime Minister sees it, he will be glad to note that Cymbeline successfully renegotiated his terms of entry into the Roman Empire,'[36] and another developed at some length the fantasy that the play was not a Shakespeare text at all but 'a highly political spoof relating to the British membership of the European Community, probably by Roy Jenkins'.[37] Similarly in 1987, one reviewer referred to Cloten as 'an anti-marketeer of the day',[38] and another described the Queen 'tearing up the treaty of Rome like some frantic anti-marketeer.'[39]

Psychoanalytical readings have a better chance of succeeding on stage since they can build on our perennial fascination with Shakespeare's characters and on the relatively accessible notion that many narratives can be read as journeys of self-discovery. Although critics like Meredith Skura and Ruth Nevo necessarily back up their readings with Freudian and post-Freudian theory, their speculations about the characters' psyches are not completely remote from what we would now consider the naive and sentimental attitude of Helen Faucit – and indeed from the routine practice of performers past and present trying to discover the 'inner life' of a part.

The most thoroughgoing attempt to explore the issue of identity in the play that I have seen was in the doubling of Posthumus and Cloten at the Royal Exchange Theatre in Manchester in 1984, which was presumably intended to indicate that the villain is a sort of *alter ego* of the hero. Unfortunately, this device seems merely to have baffled people who did not know the play. Recent productions have demonstrated that the ending works best when a strong Posthumus balances a strong Jachimo, neither being allowed to dominate as the 'star' as used to happen in the past; and that Posthumus does need to keep most of his long speeches. At Stratford, Ontario in 1986 Robin Phillips initially divided up his description of the battle between other members of the cast but just before the first night restored it to the actor playing Posthumus who felt that it was essential to 'the arc the character has to complete in the second half of the play'.[40] The technique of splitting up and relocating Posthumus' longer speeches used by Elijah Moshinsky in his 1982 version for BBC television unhappily sacrificed continuity of both character and action.[41]

When Shaw published his 'Cymbeline Refinished' he wrote in a foreword:

> I shall not press my version on managers producing Cymbeline if they have the courage and good sense to present the original word-for-word as Shakespear left it, and the means to do justice to the masque. But if they are half-hearted about it, and inclined to compromise by leaving out the masque and the comic jailor and mutilating the rest, as their manner is, I unhesitatingly recommend my version. The audience will not know the difference; and the few critics who have read Cymbeline will be too grateful for my shortening of the last act to complain.[42]

A declining demand for total illusion or naturalism in the theatre together with a willingness on the part of audiences to laugh with the play rather than at it has made recent 'managers' more prepared to 'present the original word-for-word as Shakespear left it', but does this reduce any account of its 'other endings' to a mere catalogue of benighted error? I would argue that my study of the ways in which the ending has been rewritten, rearranged and reinterpreted over nearly 400 years is part of the larger story of our cultural history. It illustrates not only changing literary tastes and the specific requirements of different kinds of theatres, but also the extraordinary richness of the text and its openness to a wide range of meanings. The play of Shakespeare's own imagination in this text is astonishing to begin with, but he has also, as always, left room for the imaginations of others – performers, directors, critics – to contribute to the total effect. There is in a sense no such thing as 'Cymbeline', but a multitude of different Cymbelines available to audiences and readers. We may marvel today at the boldness of the alterations made by D'Urfey, Hawkins or Shaw, but we are still, like the eighteenth- and nineteenth-century actor-managers, refocusing the ending so as to concentrate on one character or one relationship rather than another, to play up the play's politics or to play them down, to enhance or to minimise elements such as as theatrical spectacle and narrative redundancy. In short, we are still participating in the appropriation of Shakespeare.

Notes

1. Alexander Leggatt, *Shakespeare's Comedy of Love* (London: Methuen, 1974), p. 260.

2. Bertrand Evans, *Shakespeare's Comedies* (Oxford: Clarendon Press, 1960), pp. 288; 248; 287.
3. Judiana Lawrence, 'Natural Bonds and Artistic Coherence in the Ending of *Cymbeline*,' *Shakespeare Quarterly* 35 (1984), pp. 455-6.
4. Martin Hoyle, *Financial Times*, 13 July 1989.
5. Anon., *Morning Star*, 20 April 1979.
6. *Shaw on Shakespeare* edited by Edwin Wilson (Harmondsworth: Penguin, 1961), p. 80.
7. W. Oxberry's Acting Edition, 1823, p. 5.
8. J. H. W., *Coventry Standard*, 5 July 1957.
9. Line numbers, references and quotations are from *The Riverside Shakespeare* edited by G. Blakemore Evans (Boston: Houghton Mifflin, 1974).
10. See Carol J. Carlisle, 'Macready's Production of *Cymbeline*,' in *Shakespeare and the Victorian Stage*, edited by Richard Foulkes (Cambridge: Cambridge University Press, 1986), p. 150.
11. See Alan Hughes, *Henry Irving, Shakespearean* (Cambridge: Cambridge University Press, 1981), p. 211.
12. For information about recent productions I have used the collections of reviews at the Shakespeare Centre Library, Stratford-upon-Avon, and Roger Warren, *Shakespeare in Performance: 'Cymbeline'* (Manchester: Manchester University Press, 1989). For a discussion of the deliberate humorousness of the last scene, see John Russell Brown, 'Laughter in the Last Plays,' in *Later Shakespeare*, edited by John Russell Brown and Bernard Harris (Stratford-upon-Avon Studies 8, London: Edward Arnold, 1966), pp. 102-25.
13. *General Observations on the Plays of Shakespeare*, as quoted in the New Arden *Cymbeline* edited by J. M. Nosworthy (London: Methuen, 1955), p. xl.
14. See the Cornmarket Press facsimile of D'Urfey's version (London, 1970). D'Urfey says in the Epilogue that 'this Play was writ nine years ago'.
15. Cornmarket Press facsimile of Marsh's version (London, 1969).
16. Cornmarket Press facsimile of Hawkins' version (London, 1969).
17. As cited in n.13, p. 211.
18. Cornmarket Press facsimile of Garrick's version (London, 1969). For a fuller account of this version, see George Winchester Stone, Jr., 'A Century of *Cymbeline*; or Garrick's Magic Touch,' *Philological Quarterly* 54 (1975), pp. 310-22. In my discussion of eighteenth- and nineteenth-century productions I have made use of the collection of promptbooks at the Folger Library.
19. It was however suggested in a critical article by Homer D. Swander, '*Cymbeline*: Religious Idea and Dramatic Design,' in *Pacific Coast Studies in Shakespeare*, edited by Waldo F. McNeir and Thelma N. Greenfield (Eugene, Oregon: University of Oregon Press, 1966), pp. 248-62. The idea was also taken up by Stephen Booth, 'Speculations on Doubling in Shakespeare's Plays,' in *Shakespeare: The Theatrical Dimension*, edited by Philip C. McGuire and David A. Samuelson (New York: A. M. S. Press, 1979), pp. 103-31.
20. See Shirley S. Allen, *Samuel Phelps and Sadler's Wells Theatre* (Middleton, Connecticut: Wesleyan University Press, 1971), pp. 296-7.
21. See Carol J. Carlisle, as cited in n.10, pp. 138-52.
22. See Alan Hughes, as cited in n.11, pp. 211-15.
23. *Shaw on Shakespeare*, as cited in n.6, p. 63.
24. A. C. Swinburne, *A Study of Shakespeare* (London: Chatto and Windus, 1880), p. 227.
25. For characteristic nineteenth-century views of Imogen, see M. L. Elliot,

Shakespeare's Garden of Girls (London: Remington, 1885); Helen Faucit, *On Some of Shakespeare's Female Characters* (London: Blackwood, 1885); Anna Jameson, *Shakespeare's Heroines* (London: George Bell, 1897); and Louis Lewes, *The Women of Shakespeare*, translated by Helen Zimmern (London: Hodder, 1895).

26. See Jameson, as cited in n.25; p. 199, Lewes, also cited in n. 25, p. 340; and William Winter, typescript of a commentary prepared for Viola Allen's acting version (1905) in the Folger Library (*Cymbeline*, Folio 1), p. ix. For further discussion of this aspect of Imogen's role, see my 'Person and Office: The Case of Imogen, Princess of Britain,' in *Literature and Nationalism*, edited by Vincent Newey and Ann Thompson (Liverpool: Liverpool University Press, 1991), pp. 76–87.

27. Helen Faucit, as cited in n.25, p. 222. Faucit also speculates about the post-play experience of other surviving heroines such as Portia and Rosalind.

28. *Shaw on Shakespeare*, as cited in n.6, pp. 85–95.

29. For discussion of the topical interpretation of '*Cymbeline* Refinished', see Alwin Thaler, *Shakespeare and Democracy* (Knoxville: University of Tennessee Press, 1941), pp. 3–44; and Ruby Cohn, 'Shaw *versus* Shakes,' *Modern Shakespeare Offshoots* (Princeton: Princeton University Press, 1976), pp. 321–39.

30. Again, I am relying on the collections of reviews at the Shakespeare Centre, Stratford-upon-Avon for these details, and on Roger Warren, as cited in n.12.

31. See Alexandru Dutu, 'Recent Shakespeare Performances in Romania,' *Shakespeare Survey* 20 (1967), pp. 125–31; Roger Warren, as cited in n.12, p. 85; and Alan Brissenden, 'Shakespeare in Adelaide,' *Shakespeare Quarterly* 30 (1979), pp. 267–70.

32. In *Representing Shakespeare* edited by Murray M. Schwartz and Coppélia Kahn (Baltimore: Johns Hopkins University Press, 1980), pp. 203–16.

33. Ruth Nevo, *Shakespeare's Other Language* (London: Methuen, 1987), pp. 62–94.

34. Jonathan Goldberg, *James I and the Politics of Literature* (Baltimore: Johns Hopkins University Press, 1983), pp. 240–1.

35. Leah S. Marcus, '*Cymbeline* and the Unease of Topicality,' in *The Historical Renaissance*, edited by Heather Dubrow and Richard Strier (Chicago: University of Chicago Press, 1988), pp. 134–68.

36. Anon., *Eastern Daily Press*, 23 December 1974.

37. The source of this anonymous review is illegible in the scrapbook at the Shakespeare Centre, but it is headed 'Cymbelism' and dated 23 December 1974. Roy Jenkins was at this time Foreign Secretary in Harold Wilson's Labour Government which was indeed trying to renegotiate Britain's terms of entry into the European Economic Community.

38. Michael Coveney, *Financial Times*, 14 November 1987.

39. Michael Billington, *The Guardian*, 24 March 1988. Billington is reviewing the first night of the London transfer of the 1987 Stratford production. There does not seem to have been a very specific reason for Common Market jokes to have been topical at this time but Margaret Thatcher's well-known hostility to Europe made them perennial.

40. See Roger Warren, as cited in n.12, p. 94.

41. *ibid.*, pp. 77–8. The text for this version is available in the BBC Shakespeare series (London: BBC, 1983), though it does not provide a full record of the

cuts and rearrangements. See also the reviews collected in *Shakespeare on Television* edited by J. C. Bulman and H. R. Coursen (Hanover, New Hampshire: University Press of New England, 1988), pp. 289–90.

42. *Shaw on Shakespeare*, as cited in n.6, p. 84.

Notes on Contributors

DYMPNA CALLAGHAN teaches Renaissance drama and feminist theory at Syracuse University. She is author of *Woman and Gender in Renaissance Drama* and is co-authoring *Feminist Shakespeare*.

MARGRETA DE GRAZIA is Associate Professor of English at the University of Pennsylvania. She has written numerous articles on Renaissance English drama and poetry and is the author of *Shakespeare Verbatim: The Reproduction of Authenticity and the 1790 Apparatus*.

MICHAEL DOBSON is Assistant Professor of English at Indiana University. His work on the reception of Shakespeare includes *Authorising Shakespeare: Adaptation and Canonisation, 1660–1769, Plays in Performance: Measure for Measure*, and a microfilm anthology of adaptations and acting versions of Shakespeare.

HOWARD FELPERIN is Professor of English at Macquarie University, Sydney Australia. He is the author of *Shakespeare Romance; Shakespearean Representation; Beyond Deconstruction*; and, most recently, *The Uses of the Canon: Elizabethan Literature and Contemporary Theory*.

MARJORIE GARBER is Professor of English at Harvard University and Director of the Center for Literary and Cultural Studies. The author of *Shakespeare's Ghost Writers*, has published extensively on Shakespeare; her most recent book is *Vested Interests: Cross-Dressing and Cultural Anxiety*.

JOHN GLAVIN is a playwright and Associate Professor of English at Georgetown University. He has published on Oscar Wilde, Anthony Trollope, Charles Dickens and Muriel Spark. He is currently writing a booklength study of Dickens, theatricality entitled *Stages of Shame*.

HUGH GRADY is Assistant Professor and Chair of the English Department at Beaver College, Glenside, Pennsylvania. He is author of *The Modernist Shakespeare: Critical Texts in a Material World*.

GRAHAM HOLDERNESS is Head of Drama at Roehampton Institute, London, and author of numerous critical studies in Renaissance and modern literature and theatre. Recent publications include *The

Shakespeare Myth; *Shakespeare in Performance: 'The Taming of the Shrew'*; Shakespeare: Out of Court (with John Turner and Nick Potter); and *The Politics of Theatre and Drama*.

BRYAN LOUGHREY is Director of Research at Roehampton Institute, London. He has published and edited widely in the field of Renaissance studies and in general literature and criticism. He is editor of *Critical Survey*; Editor of Penguin's *Critical Studies* series and the Longman's *Critical Essays* series. Recent publications include *Thomas Middleton: Five Plays* and *Shakespeare's Early Tragedies: a Casebook* (with Neil Taylor).

Graham Holderness and Bryan Loughrey are currently working on a joint study in the cultural production of Shakespearean iconography.

NANCY KLEIN MAGUIRE is Scholar-in-Residence at the Folger Shakespeare Library. She is editor of *Renaissance Tragicomedy: Explorations in Genre and Politics* and author of *Regicide and Restoration: Tragicomedy, 1660–1671*.

JEAN I. MARSDEN teaches English at the University of Connecticut. She is the author of the forthcoming *Plays in Performance: Cymbeline* and recently completed a book examining eighteenth-century adaptation of Shakespeare.

ANN THOMPSON is a Reader in English at the University of Liverpool. She has edited *The Taming of the Shrew* and is currently editing *Cymbeline*. She is author of *Shakespeare's Chaucer* and *'King Lear': The Critics Debate* and co-author with John O. Thompson of *Shakespeare, Meaning and Metaphor*.

NICOLA J. WATSON is Assistant Professor of English at Northwestern University. She has recently completed a book entitled *Purloined Letters: Revolution, Reaction, and the Form of the Novel 1790–1825* and is currently writing on ideas of history in the Romantic period.